Dickensian Laughter

Essays on Dickens and Humour

MALCOLM ANDREWS

OXFORD
UNIVERSITY PRESS

OXFORD

Great Clarendon Street, Oxford, OX2 6DP,
United Kingdom

Oxford University Press is a department of the University of Oxford.
It furthers the University's objective of excellence in research, scholarship,
and education by publishing worldwide. Oxford is a registered trade mark of
Oxford University Press in the UK and in certain other countries

First Edition published in 2013

Impression: 1

Published in the United States of America by Oxford University Press
198 Madison Avenue, New York, NY 10016, United States of America

British Library Cataloguing in Publication Data
Data available

ISBN 978-0-19-965159-7

Printed in Great Britain by
Clays Ltd, St Ives plc

For LIONEL WEST, my grandfather,
and his daughter
JOAN, my mother:
in loving memory

Preface and Acknowledgements

In his autobiographical *Father and Son* (1907) the poet and critic Edmund Gosse records how, as a mid-Victorian child, he became 'gloriously enslaved' to *Pickwick Papers*: 'My shouts of laughter at the richer passages were almost scandalous, and led to my being reproved for disturbing my Father while engaged, in an upper room, in the study of God's Word'. He felt himself to be in the company of a gentleman so extremely funny that he 'began to laugh before he began to speak'. *Father and Son* was written in the Edwardian period, and Gosse pondered the possibility that he might be the last of the generations 'who accepted Mr. Pickwick with unquestioning and hysterical abandonment'. But he wasn't. He would have been reassured to hear the experience of at least one child of the next generation, John Middleton Murry, who in turn had been reassured to read in *Father and Son* that his own particular affliction was shared. Up to that point, Murry records in *Pencillings* (1923), 'I was persuaded that the behaviour Mr Pickwick induced in me at the age of eight and nine was a clear proof of a peculiar madness'. Helpless laughter seemed to him to have a pathological significance:

> Even at that age I was half-ashamed of it. I used to begin to laugh before I had opened the book [...]. And I have never been able to read more than a few pages since then, because the helpless feeling of unquenchable Achaean laughter takes hold of me. I dare not let go my sanity; I am afraid of a second childhood.

That is how *Pickwick* affected generations of readers. A contemporary of Middleton Murray, Lionel West, used to return home from his office in an accounting firm, have supper with the family, retire to put on his slippers, light his pipe, settle in his armchair in the family living-room, and open his *Pickwick*. As he chuckled, pipe still clenched in his teeth, the incendiary *Pickwick* effect jiggled tobacco ash from the bowl down onto the pages. His daughter used to watch this slightly alarming routine, and years later often told the story to her children, still somewhat in awe of the power of *Pickwick*. Lionel's daughter was my mother. This book is dedicated to both of them.

'The qualities for which every body reads and admires him [Dickens] are his humour and wit', wrote one reviewer of Dickens's work at the start of his career, in 1837. After Dickens's death in 1870, his friend and biographer John Forster concluded his assessment of his subject: 'His leading quality was Humour'. Dickens was seen as the greatest English humorist since Shakespeare. And yet you might not know it from the vast accumulation of books and articles on Dickens over the last half century. As Philip Collins remarked in 1971, in introducing an anthology of contemporary reviews of Dickens, *The Critical Heritage*: 'from how many discussions of Dickens in the learned journals would one ever guess that (as Dickens himself thought) humour was his leading quality, his highest faculty?' Over forty years later has the situation changed much?

Perhaps we think Forster was wrong in identifying humour as Dickens's leading quality? Perhaps we think we now see more clearly than he could that it was the serious Dickens, the darker Dickens, where the real genius of the man showed itself? Or perhaps in order to take Dickens seriously attention always needs to be turned away from the comedy, from the farce, the irony and the facetiousness which were part of his identity? Whatever the verdict, there is relatively little in the way of sustained critical attention to Dickens's humour. There have been distinguished exceptions, of course, notably James Kincaid's *Dickens and the Rhetoric of Laughter* (1970) and John Carey's chapter on 'Dickens' Humour' in *The Violent Effigy* (1973). But search the indexes in any of the recent proliferating 'companions', 'guides' etc. to Dickens for 'humour', 'comedy' or 'laughter' and you would be hard put to find much. This gap is evident also in much of the modern popular conception of Dickens. Classical Comics brought out a glossy and handsome 'Graphic' version of *A Christmas Carol* in 2008. At the end of the book the editors added some historical and biographical information, including this 'Dickens Fact'; ' "Dickensian" = denoting poverty, distress, and exploitation, as depicted in the novels of Charles Dickens'. Who would have thought that Dickens, more than any other Victorian novelist, was famous for making people laugh, loud and long?

There is of course, and always has been, wider recognition of Dickens the humorist than the record of published criticism suggests. The shortage of critical studies may be due to intellectual market forces, as suggested above, but may also owe something to another kind of problem. One hears quite often that humour is very hard to write about in any intensively analytical way (trying to define humour is one of the definitions of humour, according to the cartoonist Saul Steinberg). Even professional comedians can be silenced when asked about, for instance, their gift of comic timing. The popular view is that under the anatomist's knife the vital essence of humour seeps away, elusive as ever, leaving a pile of mangled remains. 'Analysing humour is like dissecting a frog', according to a remark attributed to E. B. White, the American essayist: 'few people are interested, and the frog dies of it'. (Mrs Leo Hunter's batrachian sympathies might be called into play here). The reader of this book will have to judge whether or not this particular analytical endeavour has been worthwhile; and also whether or not I have inadvertently killed off Dickens's humour.

How does Dickens make us laugh?—that is what interests me here in this sequence of essays. How can words on a page fire off into the reader's consciousness and jolt him or her into a smile, a giggle, or a hearty laugh? The book's method of composition has been essentially reactive. By and large I have picked out extracts from Dickens's novels, stories, journalism and letters that make me laugh, and then explored (not necessarily discovered) how he has done it. That route, rather than through any prefabricated theoretical framework, is how I have preferred to approach the topic; at the same time, this reactive exploration has found useful navigational impetus from some of the stimulating laughter theorists of the last two centuries. At all events, if the analysis is not to the reader's taste, then the book can bid fair to be a tempting anthology of hilarious passages from a master humorist. My hope all along has been to make the reader laugh and also reflect on his or her laughter.

I must here acknowledge the help and encouragement from many people known and unknown. In the latter category I include and thank the two anonymous readers for Oxford University Press who commented most constructively on some draft essays. My wife Kristin has been unfailingly good-humoured and encouraging throughout this book's sometimes taxing gestation and writing. Andrea Samson of Stanford University and Sophie Scott of University College, London, have both been generous with information about current developments in cognitive neuroscience where it applies to humour studies. Nick Hiley of the British Cartoon Archive at the University of Kent has been hugely helpful with research and reproduction of many of the illustrations. I am also grateful to my fellow-Dickensian, Michael Rogers, for his proofreading.

I owe a great deal to the following for reading and commenting on early drafts, or otherwise stimulating ideas for the book: Jacqueline Baker, Simon Callow, Oliver Double, Anthony Hozier and Michael Slater. This book began life some years ago in an MA course at the University of Kent, 'Dickens and Comedy', and I cherish the memories of those hours of instructive enjoyment (and laughter) with students who contributed so much to the enriching of my ideas about the art of humour. Finally, I thank and heartily congratulate Sue Shields for her zestful cover drawing. No known Victorian portrait, in paint or photograph, shows Dickens laughing; solemnity was inflicted on the eminent by the protocol of portraiture and also by the paralysingly long exposure time required by early cameras. We have waited a long time to capture one of our greatest humorists in a fit of laughter.

Parts of some essays of this book have been published elsewhere in modified form: 'Dickens, Comedy and Disintegration' in *Dickens: The Craft of Fiction and the Challenges of Reading*, eds R. Bonadei, C. de Stasio, C. Pagetti and A. Vescovi (Edizioni Unicopli, 2000); 'Dickens, Comedy and "Bisociation"' in *Dickens Quarterly* vol. 28 (September 2011).

Malcolm Andrews
Canterbury, 2012

Contents

List of Illustrations

1

Opening a Fresh Vein of Humour

Dickens's genius as a humorist was the result of his skilful and strenuous cultivation of a community of readers who would laugh with him, and who would come to relish his particular idiosyncratic humour. He wasn't just a funny writer waiting for people to discover him. His principal mission in the mid 1830s was to convert his audience to 'Dickensian' humour. As William Wordsworth put it a generation earlier (conscious of his own pioneering status): 'Every author, as far as he is great and at the same time *original*, has the task of *creating* the taste by which he is to be enjoyed'. That formidable task, and how Dickens set about creating the taste for his distinctive humour, is the subject of the present essay, which concentrates on *Pickwick Papers*.

Regions of Exhausted Comicality

At the start of his career Dickens inherited and redeployed certain routines and techniques in contemporary comedy—the stock characterizations, farcical situations, linguistic tricks and so on—all associated with popular writers, performers and caricaturists such as John Poole, Pierce Egan, Charles Mathews the Elder, Robert Seymour and George Cruikshank. The derivative nature of his earliest substantial work, *Pickwick Papers*, was picked up immediately by those reviewing its first monthly number, sometimes with groans of boredom at the staleness of such material: 'the wit of the writer has no wider range than through that melancholy region of exhausted comicality, which Hood and Poole and Smith and Cruikshank have reaped, until they have not left a single laugh behind'. Ironically, according to one of Chapman and Hall's later chairmen, Thomas Hood and John Poole, as well as Theodore

Hook, may themselves have been suggested by the publishers as candidate authors for the *Pickwick* project before the firm approached Dickens. Hood confessed to Dickens later that on his first acquaintance with *Pickwick* he had thought it 'only a new strain of [Pierce Egan's] Tom-and-Jerryism, which is my aversion'; but then, on further readings, he had changed his mind and read it several times 'with increased delight'. This changing attitude typified the broader critical response to *Pickwick* as it trundled on towards triumph over a year and a half.

The notices of Number I in the spring of 1836 frequently stressed its comic provenance: the Pickwickians' 'whims and oddities he [Boz] has Hook-ed in with facetious felicity and Hood-ed over with most risible ridicule'; 'the idea of the work [...] was doubtless suggested by Poole's memorable researches into the marvels of Little Pedlington'; 'The *Pickwick Papers* [...] are made up of two pounds of Smollett, three ounces of Sterne, a handful of Hook, a dash of grammatical Pierce Egan'. There were dissenting voices to this chorus. The likening of Boz to Theodore Hook was particularly controversial. Percy Fitzgerald, the most assiduous historian of *Pickwick Papers*, cited the *Westminster Review*'s praise of Dickens's superiority in his 'truth to nature [...] abundance of wit [...] and a constant indication of a kindly and refined feeling', compared with Hook's 'broad farce' and 'constant straining after the ludicrous'. Fitzgerald, writing in the 1890s, recalled that at the time of *Pickwick* two kinds of story were in particular favour, the 'novel of fashionable life' (so-called Silver Fork fiction) and 'a sort of rollicking, boisterous narration, in which Theodore Hook revelled'. Hook, he felt, 'could only see the vulgarities of the *couche sociale*, whether bodily or mental, but Dickens may be really said to have created a new style by supplying the refinements and graces of humanity to "low life", and making interesting what would otherwise be repulsive'. That 'new style' was to be part of the taste Dickens created for his distinctive humour.

Another contemporary reviewer of *Pickwick*, G. H. Lewes (if indeed he was the author of a challenging review in *The National Magazine and Monthly Critic* in December 1837), also vigorously rejected the charge that Dickens was too derivative in his humour, and claimed that to compare him with Hook was absurd. On the basis of *Pickwick* and *Oliver Twist*, he thought, ' "Boz" should be compared to no one since no one has ever written like him—no one has ever combined the nicety of observation, the fineness of tact, the exquisite humour, the wit, heartiness, sympathy with all things good and beautiful in human nature, the perception of character, the pathos, and accuracy of description, with the same force that he has done'.

That humane feeling and precision of social observation marked Dickens off from his contemporary humorists, and indeed sometimes elevated him to the pantheon of great writers, according to some reviewers. Dickens would have been particularly pleased to find himself compared with his favourite eighteenth-century novelists, as the *Sunday Times* did in reviewing *Pickwick* Number 3: 'The style is that of Fielding and Smollett, and we can truly affirm that no modern writer has approached so nearly those great originals'.

Dickens's *Pickwick* publishers aimed to capitalize on just these developing humorous tastes when they engaged Robert Seymour and devised an illustrated periodical that would play on the 'innocents abroad' theme, featuring a group of pretentious incompetents, a 'NIMROD CLUB' who 'were to go out shooting, fishing, and so forth, and getting themselves into difficulties through their want of dexterity'. Dickens tells us that he raised objections from the start, among them his conviction that 'the idea [...] had been already much used', as indeed it had, and as the reviewers were to echo. One such precursor, about a quarter of a century earlier, and a very successful one, was *Dr Syntax in Search of the Picturesque* (1809). Like *Pickwick* this was a publishing enterprise that began with engaging a famous illustrator, Thomas Rowlandson, for a planned serial issue of comical prints, to be accompanied by some text, for which the publishers recruited the hack writer William Combe. It was hugely popular. Sequels by Combe and Rowlandson followed in the Regency years and *Syntax* spawned many imitations. *Pickwick* carried echoes of it, as I will be mentioning later.

Dickens, then, was initially stuck with the format devised by Chapman and Hall in deference to their famous illustrator, and had to make the best of it. It was at least the kind of comic material he had been brought up on, and when it was in the hands of some veteran practitioners he positively revelled in it. Charles Mathews's shows, for example, frequently drew their laughs from the spectacle of pretensions abruptly exposed, and naivety upset by confrontation with the wily world. Dickens, having learned Mathews's art so thoroughly, took the project on, confident that he could work this material to his own benefit. He had, after all, always been a gifted mimic: in his own words 'I believed I had a strong perception of character and oddity, and a natural power of reproducing in my own person what I observed in others'. Just so with *Pickwick*; Dickens was 'reproducing' a range of idiosyncratic speech-styles, stock routines and comic techniques he knew well and had been rehearsing for years. His early material might be old-fashioned, cobwebby even, but he dusted it off, polished it up, reanimated it with his own energies and enriched its colours. And all the time, month by month as he pushed *Pickwick* or the *Sketches* tales forward, he kept his ear close to the ground of public opinion, manoeuvring different comic routines in and out of the limelight, heightening hyperbole here and there, intensifying or muffling the mock-heroic mode, and chatting archly to the reader.

Pedlington and *Pickwick*

Thus the material became something distinctively his own: it was fresh even though it was familiar. Years later, among the fond retrospections that poured out in the weeks after Dickens's death, one writer for the *Graphic* recalled: 'Being from my earliest childhood a lover of humorous literature, I had already read Mr Poole's *Little Pedlington*, which may be regarded as a humble precursor of Boz's creations; but as soon as I got possession of *Pickwick*, I laid *Little Pedlington* aside'. What exactly was this *Little Pedlington*?

Dickens, like thousands of others in Britain and America in the 1820s and 1830s, was very fond of John Poole's plays and sketches, and in later life he campaigned vigorously to provide financial support for Poole in his frail old age. It was an affectionate homage: Dickens's own sense of humour had been nourished by Poole's high-spirited and good-natured facetiousness. Poole's chronicle of an imaginary English town, Little Pedlington and its eccentric characters, first appeared in 1835 and was undoubtedly one of the germs of *Pickwick*. The introductory passages are an exercise in bathos, playing on Grand Tour expectations:

> I had visited, as I believed, every spot in Europe which celebrity, from some cause or other, had rendered attractive. I had climbed many thousands of feet up Mont Blanc, and stood on the very summit of Greenwich Hill; [...] had found my way through the dark and tangled forests of Germany, and lost it in the Maze at Hampton Court [...] beheld the fading glories of old Rome, and the rising splendours of New Kemp Town [...] I had seen the Raphaels at Florence, the Corregios at Dresden, the Rembrandts at Rotterdam, and the camera-obscura at Margate.

Compare this with the sprightly *Pickwick* advertisement (surely at least partly by Dickens) that appeared in *The Athenaeum* (26 March 1836) just before the publication of the first monthly number. Dickens highlights the Pickwick Club's 'insatiable thirst for Travel':

> The whole surface of Middlesex, a part of Surrey, a portion of Essex, and several square miles of Kent, were in their turns examined, and reported on. In a rapid Steamer, they smoothly navigated the placid Thames; and in an open boat, they fearlessly crossed the turbid Medway. High-roads and bye-roads, towns and villages, public conveyances and their passengers, first-rate inns and road-side public houses [...] were alike visited and beheld, by the ardent Pickwick, and his enthusiastic followers.

In other words, this mighty Odyssey is to take its intrepid travellers to a few spots within a thirty-mile radius of London. This, the earliest taste of the *Pickwick* mode, was not well received by the *News and Sunday Herald*: 'a wretched attempt at tawdry smartness', thought its reviewer. The same mock-epic mode characterizes the first paragraphs of Poole's 'The Stranger's Guide through Little Pedlington' and *Pickwick*'s opening. First Poole:

> The Universal deluge, which transformed the variegated and smiling face of our terrestrial globe into one unvaried and monotonous mass of the aqueous element, and which in its ruthless and unpitying course, overwhelmned [sic] and swallowed up cities, empires, and nations, sparing neither the monarchs [sic] palace nor the peasant's hut [...] like the raging cataract, converted our rolling planet into a wide, vast, waste of waters, disfigured also the fair spot on which now stands the town of Little Pedlington.

> The first ray of light which illumines the gloom, and converts into a dazzling brilliancy that obscurity in which the earlier history of the

public career of the immortal Pickwick would appear to be involved, is derived from the perusal of the following entry in the Transactions of the Pickwick Club, which the editor of these papers feels the highest pleasure in laying before his readers, as a proof of the careful attention, indefatigable assiduity, and nice discrimination, with which his search among the multifarious documents confided to him has been conducted.

Both use the grand style, with ironic hyperbole and redundant descriptors, but Dickens is just a bit more orotund, and also more humorously self-conscious as cicerone-editor. It is that extra comic pressure and the heightened sense of the playful presence of the author—'full of sly and racy fun'—that mark out Dickens's humour from Poole's. That was particularly conspicuous in the opening numbers of *Pickwick*, and one early notice, though warming to its 'genuine humour', cautioned Dickens against 'extravagance' ('yet even extravagance may be pardoned in him, when he makes it so laugh-provoking'). However, by Number 4, the reviewer had modified his criticism: 'The wit of these papers is subtle and beneath the surface; their humour is not that of extravagance, but of nature'. Perhaps this is an instance of Dickens himself having caught the early criticism and subsequently re-adjusted his comic sights.

Dickens must have won over thousands of such readers who had been brought up on the comic traditions dominated by Poole, Mathews and others—and of course, he was one of those readers. It was 'the way he told it'. He had the advantage of serializing his work and thereby recognizing as soon as his readership tired of one mode; whereupon he could seize opportunities to capitalize on accidental humorous breakthroughs, as in the famous case of Sam Weller's promotion from a cameo role to a leading player. In July 1836 *The Literary Gazette* briefly noticed *Pickwick* Number 4, praising 'the humour and talent of the clever writer', and instancing, in a long quotation, 'the following droll description of Boots, at an ancient inn in the borough'. The following month Mr Pickwick adopted this entertaining 'Boots' as his manservant. In August the *Gazette* reviewed Number 5 (featuring the Eatanswill elections) and gave a generous sample, again from Sam, who was now prominent in the story: it was his anecdote about his father being bribed to cause a road accident to a coach-load of voters (which I will return to later). In September the *Gazette* again thanked Dickens for 'a monthly laugh, most refreshing to us in dull times', and hoped that 'Boz will stick to Mr Weller, "Boots", whose facetious character he is working out very humorously'. It then quoted yet more speeches from Sam. Dickens responded quickly to such selective promotion: it was, as I have mentioned, one of the great advantages of serialization, especially when, as in *Pickwick*, the author was moving from month to month with no long-term plot in mind. Dickens was improvising opportunistically before a live audience, and was as ravenous for shared laughter as any stand-up comic playing to a new venue. In its early stages, each monthly part of *Pickwick* was a pilot show, a performance by an apprentice comedian, and Dickens worked his audience every bit as much as he reworked his staple material.

While contemporary traditions in popular humour helped to fuel the rocket-like ascent of Dickens in 1836–37, his own phenomenal comic energy and inventiveness established him, in some eyes, as the pioneer of a new vogue for the comic. 'A fresh vein of humour had been opened' according to the *Quarterly Review* in October 1837; and among all England's comic writers, 'Mr Dickens is not simply the most distinguished, but the first'. Here is a writer for the *Court Magazine* reflecting (in April 1837) on the new phenomenon, suggesting that Dickens erupted on the scene and single-handedly generated a tsunami of humorous writing in mid-1830s England:

> Our readers cannot fail to have observed the sudden turn for the comic, which has recently discovered itself in the literary public. Formerly, the maxim was—'You are nothing if not critical;' now it is 'You are nothing if not comical.' The appetite for the jocose, the farcical, the extravagant, is immoderate. [...] Accordingly, the magazines have become as funny as it was in their power to become [...]. There is no doubt that this sudden taste for crowding upon the sunny side of the road, was originally generated by a facetious gentleman who, for some months, escaped detection under the name of 'Boz'.

For some, *Pickwick* acted as a mighty transfusion of humour into English literary culture, with its anaemic devotion to sensibility and its growing Evangelical puritanism. Twenty years after its publication here is how one enthusiast, in a 'Remonstrance with Dickens', recalled life before and life after the novel:

Before *Pickwick* there seems to us to have been but a serious world of
it, with plenty of pathos, poetry, romance, and character, but (except
here and there occasional glimpses of humour exciting a smile or a
chuckle, seldom a laugh) a decided drought of this last-mentioned
element, till it then burst forth in a genial flood, sweeping down all
restraints of primness and puritanism, drowning whole herds of jok-
ers, facetious diners-out and provincial wags, and causing dullards
and drivellers, hitherto priding themselves on the thickness of the
hide which rendered them impervious to fun, to laugh till their faces,
like Prince Hal's, resembled 'a wet cloak ill laid-up'—no matter
whether they had or had not the ache in their shoulders.

This sounds hyperbolic, but the writer goes on to tell of his own
excruciating experience on one occasion when he was attending a
church service. He had been reading *Pickwick* the night before and
suddenly in the middle of the service he recalled a ludicrous
episode involving old Tony Weller, and this set him off into fits of
smothered laughter: 'The choral symphonies of the anthem
invested Mr Weller's image with fifty-fold absurdity, blending
him, as they did, in his top-boots and shawls with angels ever
bright and fair'.

He was forced to hide his head under the pew's prayer-book shelf.
His quakings and stifled explosions drew the attention of the authori-
ties, and eventually the verger and two churchwardens marched him
away down the aisle, past faces staring in devout horror, with his
handkerchief crammed into his mouth. The next day, he went to
apologize to the dean, 'who, being himself a Pickwickian, gave us
absolution in the most kindly way'.

'Boz'

'Boz': let us get a close-up of this sensational new presence. Dickens's
Boz persona established itself in the Sketches of 1834–36 as an
ingratiating young fellow with a spirited and sophisticated line in
satirical 'cuts'. He was dry, sardonic, sometimes a little too facetiously
grandiloquent. He was also a prodigiously gifted mimic, especially
of London's low-life characters; and one of his signature comic turns
involved playing his high formal style off against his ventriloquized
vernacular speech styles. As we shall see later, this friction generated

many if not most of his laughs. These attributes combined to make the Boz Show increasingly distinctive.

Henri Bergson, one of the shrewdest theoreticians of laughter, wrote 'Laughter always implies a kind of secret freemasonry, or even complicity, with other laughers, real or imaginary'. Such a 'freemasonry' of laughers was encouraged in Boz's 'we'. Many, if not most of his Sketches of 'Scenes' and 'Characters' opened with 'We...' in the first or second sentences: e.g. 'We have always entertained a particular attachment towards Monmouth-street' ('Meditations in Monmouth Street'); 'We hope our readers will not be alarmed...' ('A Parliamentary Sketch'); 'We shall never forget the mingled feelings...' ('Criminal Courts'). True, the so-called editorial 'we' was a journalistic convention, but Boz's usage also gave a distinctly inclusive nuance to the pronoun, as Robert Douglas-Fairhurst has noted in his shrewdly analytical take on Boz. It implied companionship and it courted complicity, as if he were conducting a crowd of like-minded equals on a light-hearted sociological field-trip into remote parts of London. 'We' were all assumed to be pretty sophisticated folk, from middle-class backgrounds, out to be amused by the eccentricities of our picturesquely less decorous fellow-citizens. 'We' were all on Boz's wavelength and, though not perhaps quite as sharp and funny as he could be, content to be part of his coterie. 'Boz is really an agreeable fellow,' wrote *The Satirist* reviewing the first number of *Pickwick* in April 1836: 'and whether he travels by himself or in association, enough is seen of him to give us a high relish for his company'.

Boz was out to create the taste by which he was to be enjoyed. Not to be in on Boz's jokes implied exclusion from the circle he was so successfully drawing around him—and risked the reputation perhaps of a slight lack of sophistication. Thus some degree of peer pressure could come into play. 'So you have never heard of the *Pickwick Papers*!' chided Mary Russell Mitford in April 1837; 'It seems like not having heard of Hogarth'. Those who could somehow withstand the humorous onslaught were to be pitied: indeed, as the years rolled on and Dickens changed the culture of humour, were such people desirable as one's companions? 'It is conceivable that human souls exist who do not laugh at Dick Swiveller or Mrs Gamp. We should not, some of us, perhaps care greatly for travelling in far countries with such, or for passing many hours in commune with them anywhere'. The *Quarterly Review* remarked that 'in less than six months from the appearance of the first number of the *Pickwick Papers*, the whole reading public were talking about them—the names of Winkle, Wardell [sic], Weller, Snodgrass, Dodson and Fogg, had become familiar in our mouths as household terms'.

Pickwick's popularity was quite extraordinary, cutting right across class boundaries, as G. H. Lewes remarked: 'from the peer and judge to the merchant's clerk [...] even the common people, both in town and country, are equally intense in their admiration. Frequently have we seen the butcher-boy, with his tray on his shoulder, reading with the greatest avidity the last *Pickwick*; the footman, (whose fopperies are so inimitably laid bare), the maidservant, the chimney-sweep, all classes, in fact, read "*Boz*"'. The 'freemasonry' with other laughers was no longer 'secret' at all. Dickens's coterie of fellow-laughers was nationwide.

A New Style of Humour

Clearly many readers recognized traits of older, more established comic writers in the early numbers of *Pickwick*, but many more saw something very new in the type of humour Dickens developed. I shall be examining Dickens's comic techniques more closely later in the book, and suggesting what seems to be distinctive about them. At this point I want to explore a little more the contemporary reception of Boz's humour as he made his debut. I quoted above from the *Court Magazine*'s essay on 'Arch-Waggery' and the 'Genius of "Boz"'. The writer was investigating the new vogue for humour, and was particularly struck by the 'verisimilitude' of Boz's fiction, his 'exact representations of trivial things'. 'His dialogues, without straining for puns or mere surface effects, are excerpta from veritable life [...] heightened of course, to make their full impression'. The acclaim for Dickens's realism in *Pickwick* may surprise us, but it had the result, it seems, of reinforcing the comical effects, by giving a robust everyday authenticity to action, character and speech. Dickens's humour, with this distinctive asset, became an altogether more invasive species in national cultural life. By comparison with him, his humorous precursors were jesters performing on the margins of real everyday life, with an array of preposterous farcical situations or shallow caricatures. But, as the launching Nimrod Club motif faded away once *Pickwick* had really got going, Dickens increasingly grounded his characterization, dialogue, settings, and the detailed paraphernalia of life in the actual experience of the contemporary world, and the consequence was that the humour, for all its hyperbole, engaged with a firmer grip. His acute eye for idiosyncrasy raised popular awareness of the comedy inherent in everyday life: it was a kind of education in comic sensibility. 'He has much comic power,' wrote *Chambers's Edinburgh Journal* reviewing *Sketches by Boz*, '[he] perceives traits which are not consciously noted by ordinary observers, and yet, when mentioned, remind everybody of the things described'. The reader was invited to see the world through Boz's eyes; that Dickensian perspective became contagious, and thereby Dickens secured his 'freemasonry of laughers'.

Other reviewers over Dickens's career credited him with quite specific humorous innovations. His use of language is one instance. In 1861 the *National Review* remarked: 'There is a peculiar style which he has introduced into English composition, and which consists in giving what is conventionally accepted as a funny turn to language, without there being any fun whatever in the thought'. The reviewer's example comes from the first chapter of *Martin Chuzzlewit*, Dickens's mock-solemn account of the Chuzzlewit family pedigree, modelled on Fielding's opening to *Jonathan Wild*. G. H. Lewes also drew attention to the comical effects in the language, making the interesting point that those effects are lost when read aloud: 'his language, even on the most trivial points, has, from a peculiar collocation of the words, or some happy expression, a drollery which is spoiled by repeating or reading aloud, because this drollery arises from so fine an association of ideas that the sound of the voice destroys it'. This flair for comical stylistic gymnastics was picked up early on. The *Court Magazine* in 1837 asserted that Boz's genius was not 'dramatic', meaning that he could not write successful play-scripts in terms of letting dialogue alone carry the drama, so busy was he with the 'stage directions', and with giving comical illumination to fleeting gestures. It was not 'dramatic'; rather, 'It is in the intermixture of description and dialogue—of the language and tournure—the modes and costumes of his characters—that his merits and triumphs consist'. This characteristic was highlighted by Edgar Allan Poe, in reviewing *Barnaby Rudge* in 1842: 'The leading idiosyncrasy of Mr Dickens's remarkable humour, is to be found in his *translating the language of gesture, or action, or tone*'. He gave as an example a short passage from the opening of *Rudge* (with Poe's italics):

> The cronies nodded to each other, and Mr Parkes remarked in an undertone, shaking his head meanwhile, *as who should say 'let no man contradict me, for I won't believe him,'* that Willet was in amazing force to-night.

Yet another humorous trademark was detected in Dickens's reductive sketching of minor characters by giving them a signature eccentricity of speech or appearance, and not much more. 'A little point is taken in the outward look or ordinary talk of a person, and is magnified into absurdity', according to the *National Review* critic, who then instances a character from *Martin Chuzzlewit*: 'Mr Spottletoe, who was so bald and had such big whiskers that he seemed to have stopped his hair, by the sudden application of some powerful remedy, in the very act of falling off his head, and to have fixed it irrevocably on his face'. There Spottletoe remains for the rest of the novel. Many reviewers saw this reductive device as Dickens's leading one. Walter Bagehot took the issue a subtle stage further, arguing that the humour lay not so much in the caricature per se, funny though that may be, but in the paradoxical 'treating as a moral agent a being who is not a moral agent [because he is barely even human]. We treat a vivified accident as a man, and we are surprised at the absurd results [...] we have exaggerations pretending to comport themselves as ordinary beings, caricatures acting as if they were characters'.

From Regency to Victorian

I mentioned earlier Dickens's changing the culture of humour. A critic of the modern age, George Ford, suggested that *Pickwick*'s huge success in the 1830s was related to Dickens's skilful acclimatization of Regency humour to early Victorian tastes. In making his case Ford cites a passage that was 'approvingly reprinted in some of the early reviews'. It is the episode I mentioned earlier as reproduced in the *Literary Gazette*, July 1836, concerning Old Weller's story of having been persuaded, with a bribe, to tip some opposition voters off his coach, seemingly by accident (Chapter 13):

"'It's a werry bad road between this and London," says the gen'l'm'n.— "Here and there it *is* a heavy road," says my father—"Specially near the canal, I think," says the gen'l'm'n—"Nasty bit that 'ere," says my father—"Well, Mr. Weller," says the gen'l'm'n, "you're a werry good whip, and can do what you like with your horses, we know. We're all werry fond o' you, Mr. Weller, so in case you *should* have an accident when you're a bringing these here woters down, and *should* tip 'em into the canal vithout hurtin' any of 'em, this is for yourself," says he.'

Ford concedes that part of the humour comes from the robust cockney speech style, but he argues that the distinctive Dickensian touch comes from the way Boz rehabilitates a stock comic scenario:

The *situation* here is comparable to endless numbers of situations in Combe, Egan, Hook, and Lever. Thomas Rowlandson could have illustrated it [...] by one of his magnificently savage caricatures showing great fat men, with brutal and tremendous faces, tumbling headlong into the canal. The amusement provided would be the same as that of any pie-throwing scene in a farce. What Dickens has done to this traditional scene by means of his style and tone is to raise it from the level of savage laughter onto a more genial plane [...]. We do not feel that the canal-water actually penetrated the clothes of Tony Weller's passengers; they must have somehow emerged miraculously dry.

This is well observed. One of Rowlandson's comic productions would have been well known to Dickens, and that is the Regency satire mentioned earlier, *Dr Syntax in Search of the Picturesque* (1809). There is a good case for seeing *Pickwick* as a successor to that publication. Dr Syntax is a naive pedant tourist, just like Mr Pickwick, and like Pickwick his encounters with the real world are comically disastrous.

Certain misadventures of Syntax seem very similar to Pickwick's (see Illustrations 1 and 2), such as when, in the company of Squire Hearty (a genial host like Mr Wardle), Syntax attends a military parade, rhapsodizes about his country's valiant warriors (like Pickwick and his friends on the Chatham Lines), and then suffers the

Illustration 1: Thomas Rowlandson, 'Doctor Syntax at a Review', in [William Combe] *The Tour of Doctor Syntax in Search of the Picturesque: A Poem.* (5th Edition: London, 1813). British Cartoon Archive, University of Kent.

indignity of his horse bolting and his wig flying off (like Pickwick chasing after his hat). However, as Ford suggested, there is a greater geniality in the presentation of Pickwick's mishaps. He loses his hat and his dignity on the Lines, but both losses are temporary before he is restored to the affectionate company of the Wardles and the affections of the reader. The laughter is not as heartless as that prompted by Syntax's catastrophes.

Ford might have added Dickens's beloved Hogarth to the list of more 'savage' comic precursors. That would reinforce his point that Dickens's satire and caricature in *Pickwick* develop a gentler and more genial nature, and that Dickens judged his new readership shrewdly in this respect. The comparison with Hogarth also bears out James Kincaid's point that Pickwickian laughter 'rejects all that is predatory and possessive [...it] makes for the almost complete elimination of sex from the centre of the new society'. Sex and violence of the kind that so energize Hogarth's humour (and indeed Rowlandson's) are drastically modified in *Pickwick*. As Kincaid argues, laughter in *Pickwick* is against sex: desire is more often comical than

Mr. Pickwick in Chase of his Hat
(p. 50)

Illustration 2: Hablot Knight Browne ('Phiz'), 'Mr Pickwick in Chase of his Hat', in *The Pickwick Papers* (1836–37).

not—Tupman's wooing, Mrs Bardell's pursuit of Pickwick, Weller Senior's attitudes to Sam's amorous Valentine. So by these means too, Dickens senses changes in the moral climate of the mid-1830s, fashions his humour accordingly and thereby enlists constituencies of readership that might have been alienated by the older tastes in robust physical knockabout and comical sexual antics. In his 1837 Preface to *Pickwick* Dickens trusted that 'Throughout this book, no incident or expression occurs which could call a blush into the most delicate cheek, or wound the feelings of the most sensitive person'. (Perhaps he forgot this solemn pledge when, thirty years later in *Our Mutual Friend*, he pilloried Mr Podsnap's jingoistic boast of the English character's displaying an 'absence of everything calculated to call a blush into the cheek of a young person which one would seek in vain among the nations of the earth').

Thackeray in 1854 made a sharp distinction between the older, earthier humour and the newer kind that had become more nervous about upsetting delicate constitutions:

> [In the old days, during social gatherings at home] if our sisters wanted to look at the portfolios, the good old grandfather used to hesitate. There were some prints among them very odd indeed; some that girls could not understand; some that boys, indeed, had best not see. We swiftly turn over those prohibited pages. How many of them there were in the wild, coarse, reckless, ribald, generous book of old English humor!
>
> How savage the satire was—how fierce the assault—what garbage hurled at opponents—what foul blows were hit—what language of Billingsgate flung! Fancy a party in a country-house now looking over Woodward's facetiae or some of the Gilray [sic] comicalities, or the slatternly Saturnalia of Rowlandson! Whilst we live we must laugh, and have folks to make us laugh. We cannot afford to lose Satyr with his pipe and dances and gambols. But we have washed, combed, clothed, and taught the rogue good manners: or rather, let us say, he has learned them himself; for he is of nature soft and kindly, and he has put aside his mad pranks and tipsy habits; and [...] has become gentle and harmless, smitten into shame by the pure presence of our women and the sweet confiding smiles of our children.

Thackeray's mild nostalgia for the old fashion of graphic satire had been expressed in an earlier essay on one of his great contemporaries, 'On the Genius of George Cruikshank' (1840). He recalled in his youth going out of his way to find the old London print shops where Cruikshank and Rowlandson and other cartoonists were displayed:

> There used to be a crowd round the windows in those days of grinning, good-natured mechanics, who spelt the songs [...] and who received the points of honour with a general sympathizing roar. Where are these people now? You never hear any laughing at H.B.

Illustration 3: Thomas Rowlandson, 'More Miseries or the Bottom of Mr. Figg's Old Whiskey Broke Through' (detail). Print (1807). British Cartoon Archive, University of Kent.

[presumably Hablot Knight Browne]; his pictures are a great deal too genteel for that—polite points of wit, which strike one as exceedingly clever and pretty, and cause one to smile in a quiet, gentlemanlike kind of way.

George Meredith, in 'The Comic Spirit' (1877), recorded much the same change of spirit in the nation's humour, from the 'big round Satyr's laugh, that flung up the brows like a fortress lifted by gunpowder'. He forecast the eventual return of the laugh: 'but it will be of the order of the smile, finely tempered, showing sunlight of the mind, mental richness rather than noisy enormity'.

Thackeray's 1854 comments came from his review of John Leech's *Pictures of Life and Character*—Leech being a familiar *Punch* cartoonist as well as book illustrator (he had illustrated *A Christmas Carol*, 1843). Like Thackeray, Dickens was sharply sensitive to such changing tastes in humour; and, again like Thackeray, he was

Illustration 4: James Gillray, 'Farmer Giles and his Wife shewing off their daughter Betty to their Neighbours, on her return from School'. Print (1809).

explicit about such changes while reviewing some drawings by Leech (*The Examiner*, 30 December 1848):

> If we turn back to a collection of the works of Rowlandson or Gillray, we shall find, in spite of the great humour displayed in many of them, that they are rendered wearisome and unpleasant by a vast amount of personal ugliness. Now, besides that it is a poor device to represent what is satirised as being necessarily ugly—which is but the resource of an angry child or a jealous woman—it serves no purpose but to produce a disagreeable result. There is no reason why the farmer's daughter in the old caricature who is squalling at the harpsichord (to the intense delight, by-the-by, of her worthy father, the farmer, whom it is her duty to please) should be squab and hideous. The satire on the manner of her education, if there be any in the thing at all, would be just as good if she were pretty. Mr Leech would have made her so.

Pickwick Papers positioned Dickens midway between older and younger comic traditions; or perhaps one might say that *Pickwick* began in the older tradition and ended a year and a half later in the newer. He seemed to reconcile a version of the crude, robust comic picaresque with a more sentimental style of comedy. 'Within a very short time,' wrote Percy Fitzgerald, *Pickwick*'s historian, 'the better spirit of comedy overpowered the Seymour style of burlesque; and Mr Pickwick gradually crystallized into his most amiable shape'. The process of gradual crystallization came in for some criticism. The transformation of Mr Pickwick himself, from an arrogant and naive pedant into a more reflective and humble old gentleman, was seen by some as having been poorly managed and unconvincing, so much so that Dickens took occasion, in his Preface for the Cheap Edition of the novel (1847), to defend his handling of these changes in one of his most famous characters.

Wit or Humour?

Dickens also achieved another major success. For numbers of readers he had managed to reconcile different styles of comic writing: 'he was both witty and humorous, a combination rarely met with'. Victorians were fond of distinguishing between humour and wit, and generally felt more comfortable with humour; wit was likely to be abrasive and contemptuous. The spirit of liberal humanism was inconsistent with the Hobbesian belief that laughter is stimulated by our sudden perception of our superiority to the misfortunes of others and with forms of satirical comedy or caustic wit that humiliated the infirmity of others. Humour needed to adapt itself to an age that ushered in a number of humane reforms and purported to soften sharp social divisions and encourage inclusivity (as evidenced in the slave trade abolition and Catholic emancipation). Wit segregates; humour harmonizes. Wit is elitist; humour is inclusive, and furthermore was held to be 'natural'. Thus Hazlitt made the distinction: 'Humour is [...] the growth of nature and accident; wit is the product of art and fancy'; and Gerald Massey, writing on 'American Humour' in 1860, declared 'Wit is more artificial and a thing of culture; humour lies nearer to nature'. R. H. Horne, in his essay on Dickens in *A New Spirit of the Age* (1844), claimed Dickens's works 'furnish a constant commentary on the distinction between wit and humour; for of sheer wit, either in remark or repartee, there is scarcely an instance in any of his volumes, while of humour there is a fullness and *gusto* in every page, which would be searched for in vain to such an extent, among other authors'. However, Horne's famous *Spirit of the Age* precursor, William Hazlitt, had in 1819 defined wit in terms that could well include Dickens's distinctive comic gifts: 'the favourite employment of wit is to add littleness to littleness, and heap contempt on insignificance [...] or if it ever affects to aggrandise, and use the language of hyperbole, it is only to betray into derision by a fatal comparison'. Hazlitt instances the use of mock-heroics as a means of making this 'fatal comparison', and of course Dickens exploits that mode to the full in *Pickwick*. Horne, a generation later (and it is a sign of changing times and tastes), seems to be narrowing the definition of 'sheer wit' to something like abrasive repartee, and he correspondingly enlarges humour's scope. In effect, by most contemporary definitions of wit and humour, Dickens is equally adept at both.

Horne's point is that just as Dickens's humour seemed to introduce a new kind of geniality in contrast to older and more savage traditions, so it drew away from caustic wit. This distinction is made in a *Dublin Review* comparison of Dickens with Thackeray:

> He [Dickens] will make a few generations to come laugh. Not as the great and terrible wits make the men and women of the ages which come after them laugh,—by the sparkling results of their deep proficiency in the 'noblest study', whose subject, 'man,' is ever the same;—but because his humour is so rich, so thorough, so varied, and so original that it must always appeal to the liking for oddities and eccentricities inherent in human nature, which increases with the pace of life, and is felt more and more as a relief to its growing weariness. There is humour which does not exactly amuse, though it receive the utmost recognition. There is humour which simply amuses, which is merely quite delightful. Mr Dickens had extraordinary humour of the latter sort. He may have intended sometimes to be savagely satirical, but could not keep from caricature, and with exaggeration savageness, even severity, is done away. He was infinitely droll and various in his mirthful moods, and the animal spirits which overflow through all his earlier writings abounded up to the latest of them.

The remarks about humour adjusting itself to the changing pace of life are interesting. If I have understood it right, what the writer sees as Dickens's distinctive sense of humour is his eye for human eccentricities. As the pace of modern life quickened and pressures increased, Boz's loitering gaze on local oddities of behaviour and appearance, and his ear for quirky speech styles, constitute new material for richly comical treatment. That would find an echo in the opening to *Pickwick* Chapter 10, where the reader is tempted into a search for the obsolescent coaching inns of old London 'in the obscurer quarters of the town', where some have escaped the 'rage' for public improvement. 'Great, rambling, queer old places they are', rich in local colour and legends. This is an analogy to that 'liking for oddities and eccentricities inherent in human nature' which the reviewer identified as so distinctive in Dickens's humour. It was in one of those eccentric, rambling old places that the highly idiosyncratic Sam Weller, the source of so much of *Pickwick*'s humour, was first discovered. Sam embodies the spirit of Dickens's new humour: genial, sparky, irreverent, imaginative, playful with bizarre metaphors, and yet candidly affectionate—a true original.

The somewhat condescending tone of the *Dublin Review*'s verdict was echoed by many who tried to assess the nature and value of Dickens's humour. G. H. Lewes paid tribute later to the sheer force of Dickens's power to make people laugh. However unsophisticated his humour was, it was overwhelming. His opponents 'may be ashamed of their laughter, but they laugh. A revulsion of feeling at the preposterousness or extravagance of the image, may follow the burst of laughter, but the laughter is irresistible, whether rational or not, and there is no arguing away such a fact'. In his view, humour that simply amused people in an unreflective way and that revelled in preposterous exaggeration was inferior not only to 'wit', but perhaps also to more sophisticated kinds of 'humour'.

Lewes also was one of the first to reflect more fully on Dickens as a humorous satirist, and to suggest that Dickens practised a 'satire by *implication*, not personality'. Unlike Voltaire, Swift or Hobbes, he did not severely cut or crush his victims, as lampooning wit might do. It was done in a playful way, such that 'one might easily suppose an individual under the lash laughing at it himself, and feeling its deep truth at the same time'. Lewes was writing this in late 1837, with just the *Sketches*, *Pickwick* and the early part of *Oliver Twist* to work from; he may well have changed his views on the injurious (or otherwise) nature of Dickens's later more ambitious satires on the condition of English government and the law. However, even by the end of his career, some of those institutions and their representatives who had felt the force of his caricaturing satire acknowledged their enjoyment of it. The medical profession, for example, whom he had ridiculed since the appearance of Bob Sawyer in 1836, found itself able to reflect, in the *British Medical Journal:* 'we ourselves could well afford to laugh with the man who sometimes laughed at us, but laughed only as one who loved us'.

It was Thomas Carlyle who elevated the status of humour as part of a humane sensibility. 'True humour', he wrote in his essay on Jean Paul Richter, 'springs not more from the head than from the heart; it is not contempt, its essence is love; it issues not in laughter, but in still smiles, which lie far deeper'. He invoked the term 'inverse sublimity', used by Richter, to argue that true humour exalts 'into our affections what is below us, while sublimity draws down into our affections what is above us'. This benign faculty is marked by 'warm, tender fellow-feeling with all forms of existence', and the 'purest of all humorists' was Cervantes, 'so gentle and genial, so full, yet so ethereal'. Carlyle's notion of humour is markedly different from the savage, masculine humour of Hogarth and the Regency caricaturists: it is gentle, genial and humane, more fitted to the changing culture and developing domestic ideology of early Victorian England. Again, *Pickwick* arrived as the perfect expression of these transitional processes, as suggested earlier. Its humour in the opening, in its high ironic manner, its characterizations and its stock comic antics, belonged to the older traditions which inspired the Chapman, Hall and Seymour project. But as it developed it became something else. Instead of our laughing at Pickwick's idiocies, he becomes 'exalted into our affections'; and Boz's manner of treating him becomes more 'gentle and genial', matching the spirit of Carlyle's Cervantes. At the same time, Pickwick and Sam increasingly reminded readers of Don Quixote and Sancho Panza. The *Metropolitan Magazine* was one of the first (in January 1837) of the journals to make the point:

The world never saw drollery and wit offered to them before in a form so singular. The renowned Mr Pickwick is, himself, the legitimate successor to Don Quixote; indeed, he is the cockney Quixote of the nineteenth century, and instead of armour of iron, he is encased in a good coating of aldemanic fur, and instead of spear and sword, has his own powers of declamation with which to go forth to do fearful battle upon the swindler, the wrong-doer, and the oppressor of the innocent.

This would have pleased Dickens mightily, since as a child he had been such an avid reader of *Don Quixote,* as Forster tells us. This comparison was echoed in the following year in T. H. Lister's comments in the *Edinburgh Review,* seeing in Pickwick and Sam 'the modern Quixote and Sancho of Cockaigne'. And in 1841, another of Dickens's favourite writers, Washington Irving (whose own writings palpably influenced scenes in *Pickwick*), told Dickens in a letter that he had been re-reading *Pickwick* and commented that 'Old Pickwick is the Quixote of commonplace life, and as with the Don, we begin by laughing at him and end by loving him'.

Twelve years after completing *Pickwick* Dickens wrote to a friend, 'The world would not take another Pickwick from me, now'. He rightly judged *Pickwick*'s time was past, just as in 1836–37 he had acutely recognized what veins of humour to work for a contemporary readership brought up on Regency comedy and yet sensing the change of cultural climate. In one odd lapse of judgement, he tried, rather lamely, to revive Mr Pickwick and Sam in the pages of *Master Humphrey's Clock* in 1840. By this time they were already heritage waxworks, and Dickens has a hard time reanimating them while at the same time preserving their identities.

The truth is that the *Pickwick* moment was passing even as he was writing the *Papers* from month to month in the mid-1830s. He relinquished the prototype 'NIMROD CLUB' hero and narrative treatment of the spring and early summer 1836 numbers in favour of exploring a modified humorous mode. This process is somewhat obscured for us nowadays by *Pickwick*'s status as a 'book', rather than as a long-drawn-out monthly entertainment. The single entity *Pickwick Papers* never really existed: its materialization (at the end of the serial run) as a single block of 600 pages between hard covers in 1837 was a clever illusion by the publishers, bestowing cosmetic coherence on a rambling entertainment that astutely kept pace with the changing seasons and with cultural climate change over a year and a half, and then stopped. As a test-bed for humour, for gauging what ingredients and what narrative manner would make people laugh in 1836 and 1837, *Pickwick* was invaluable. This protracted experiment eventually secured Dickens his readership, helped to refine his techniques for raising laughter, and determined the distinctive character of his humour.

2

Staging Comic Anecdotes

*'he looked at all things
and people dramatically'*

The President got up, and said, 'Is *this* Mr. Dickens?' – 'Sir', returned
Mr. Dickens – 'It is.' 'I am astonished to see so young a man Sir', said
the President. Mr. Dickens smiled, and thought of returning the compliment – but he didn't; for the President looked too worn and tired,
to justify it. 'I am happy to join with my fellow citizens in welcoming
you, warmly, to this country,' said the President. Mr. Dickens thanked
him, and shook hands. Then the other Mr. Dickens, the secretary,
asked the President to come to his house that night, which the President said he would be glad to do, but for the pressure of business, and
measles. Then the President and the two Mr. Dickenses sat and looked
at each other, until Mr. Dickens of London observed that no doubt
the President's time was fully occupied, and he and the other
Mr. Dickens had better go. Upon that they all rose up; and the President invited Mr. Dickens (of London) to come again, which he said
he would. And that was the end of the conference.

This is a record of an historic meeting between the young Charles
Dickens and the President of the United States, John Tyler, during
Dickens's first visit to America in 1842 (the President's Secretary is
also, confusingly, called Dickens). It is an objective account of a
somewhat underwhelming encounter in which the two world
celebrities fail to strike any spark of energy. In spite of the impassive
third-person manner of the report, it is by Dickens himself, in a letter
to a friend: he boasted that this 'private interview' was 'considered a
greater compliment than the public audience' with the President.

Dickens has the ability to detach himself from his own involvement and to objectify the occasion as a scene he is watching, and he

re-stages it for his correspondent more or less without comment. The humour is in the bathos of the great event, reflected in the flat, dull manner of the narration. The keynote is the incongruity of an enervated President of America, a man apparently with such colossal worldly power who yet has so little personal energy. This bathetic discrepancy between public power and personal frailty is comically miniaturized in the President's declining the social invitation because of pressure of business—'and measles'. Added to that is his awkwardness, occasioned by fatigue (in his *American Notes* account of this audience, Dickens gives a more favourable impression of the 'remarkably unaffected, gentlemanly, and agreeable' Tyler).

Dickens doesn't just describe a desultory encounter; he reproduces the whole strange occasion by embodying in his prose the stilted rhythms of the interview as it struggles to sustain itself, until the meeting eventually runs out of energy altogether. The politely distanced reporting style is all the funnier because of the formal constraints which Dickens observes in his own narrative, curbing any impulse he might have to fly off into rumbustious conceits and caricature.

This is very common practice in Dickens's formal as well as informal story-telling. He doesn't narrate comic anecdotes so much as 'project' them. In his mind's eye he puts them up on stage so that he can watch them and, when he is part of the action, listen to himself participating in them. The degree to which all of Dickens's writing was shaped by histrionic impulses has been subtly analysed by Robert Garis many years ago. I am here considering Dickens's histrionic sensibility in the context of how he generates laughter from apparently everyday incidents.

The epigraph to this essay comes from an obituary notice of Dickens by his friend Arthur Helps. Here is the fuller version of that observation: 'he looked at all things and people dramatically. He assigned to all of us characters; and in his company we could not help playing our parts [...he] brought all that he saw and felt into a magic circle of dramatic creation'. The corollary to this (though Helps doesn't mention it as a 'corollary') was that 'he lived a great deal with the creatures of his brain [...] and found them very amusing society [...]. Such men live in two worlds, the actual and the imaginative; and he lived intensely in both'. Dickens brought those two worlds closer together; he fictionalized the 'actual' world by drawing it into the 'magic circle of dramatic creation' (a phrase reminiscent of Ruskin's remark that Dickens worked his fiction in a 'circle of stage fire'). His imaginary characters in all their theatricality were distinctly real to him, and his real acquaintances were converted by him into theatrical 'characters'.

This need to look at all things and people dramatically drove not only his own writing, but also his editorial policy. There's an example of this in the advice he gave to a would-be contributor to *Household Words*:

> It is necessary for such a purpose, to present some special evil in an animated life-like manner—as a thing *seen* by the writer, or going on before the reader [...] the aim of such pages is to shew a striking instance *as a play might shew it*. (my emphasis)

He gave this advice because his own experience had told him that the most powerful effects of story-telling were those that assimilated him into the action and characters, as on the occasion of his reading Lady De Lancey's account of tending her dying husband after the battle of Waterloo:

> To say that the reading that most astonishing and tremendous account has constituted an epoch in my life—that I never shall forget the lightest word of it—that I cannot throw the impression aside and *never saw anything so real*, so touching, and *so actually present before my eyes*, is nothing. I am husband and wife, dead man and living woman, Emma and General Dundas, doctor and bedstead,—everything and everybody (but the Prussian officer—damn him) all in one. (my emphasis)

When Dickens wants particular vividness of description the example always before him is the theatre, where a live demonstration for spectators is performed and the event, historical or fictional, is 'actually present before my eyes'—'as a play might shew it'. That is evidently the practice he observed when telling comical anecdotes. He would mimic the voices and gestures down to the last detail in order to bring the reported event to life. Here is one example, recalled by his friend Mary Cowden Clarke:

> One of the stories he recounted to us [...] was that of a man who had been told that slips of paper pasted across the chest formed an

> infallible cure for sea-sickness; and that upon going down into the
> cabin of the steamer, this man was to be seen busily employed cut-
> ting up paper into long narrow strips with the gravest of faces, and
> accompanying the slicing of the scissors by a sympathetic movement
> of the jaw, which Dickens mimicked as he described the process.

Dickens reproduces not just the paper-cutting but the moving jaw.
That last detail is not superfluous theatricality; it makes the scene all
the funnier by vividly illustrating the concentration of the man as he
prepares this daft remedy. It forces the listener into *visualizing* the
scene ('a thing *seen* by the writer'). Up to that point in the narrative
it hadn't been wholly necessary—the sense of the absurdity was
enough—but that extra touch suddenly illuminates the head bent on
its task, the furrowed brow and the working jaw. His listeners'
scepticism at the idea of paper strips as a sea-sickness remedy is
comically intensified by the spectacle of the man's utter conviction
of its efficacy.

   The scrupulous reproduction of physical detail which Dickens
loves to mimic is rehearsed descriptively in his writing, and becomes
a trademark of Dickens's humour. For instance in *Pickwick* he represents the way Sam Weller (in Chapter 33) puts pen to paper for his
Valentine letter: 'it being always considered necessary [...] for the
writer to recline his head on his left arm, so as to place his eyes as
nearly as possible on a level with the paper, while glancing sideways
at the letters he is constructing, to form with his tongue imaginary
characters to correspond'. That extra touch of gesture is
quintessentially Dickensian. Without it the account would have been
amusing; but its inclusion heightens concentration on the comical
moment and the obsessive behaviour.

   I will be looking at a number of examples of this process in which
Dickens brings what he experiences as a funny event 'into a magic
circle of dramatic creation' and thereby heightens the comedy.

Some *Dramatis Personae*

In a letter home from Ireland, during one of his Readings tours,
Dickens sets out in playscript format an authentic dialogue he
enjoyed with a perky little Irish boy, about 6 years old. In setting the
scene for his dialogue, he remarks that it really 'requires imitation'.

In other words, it needs to be enacted with the appropriate pronunciation (which one can just imagine Dickens performing); so he is careful to reproduce that pronunciation phonetically:

INIMITABLE. Holloa, old chap.

YOUNG IRELAND. Hal-loo!

INIMITABLE (*In his delightful way*). What a nice old fellow you are. I am very fond of little boys.

YOUNG IRELAND. Air yer? Ye'r right.

INIMITABLE. What do you learn, old fellow?

YOUNG IRELAND (*very intent on Inimitable, and always childish, except in his brogue*). I lairn wureds of three sillibils, and wureds of two sillibils, and wureds of one sillibil.

INIMITABLE (*gaily*). Get out, you humbug! You learn only words of one syllable.

YOUNG IRELAND (*laughs heartily*). You may say that it is mostly wureds of one sillibil.

INIMITABLE. Can you write?

YOUNG IRELAND. Not yet. Things come by deegrays.

INIMITABLE. Can you cipher?

YOUNG IRELAND (*very quickly*). Wha'at's that?

INIMITABLE. Can you make figures?

YOUNG IRELAND. I can make a nought, which is not asy, being roond.

INIMITABLE. I say, old boy, wasn't it you I saw on Sunday morning in the hall, in a soldier's cap? You know—in a soldier's cap?

YOUNG IRELAND (*cogitating deeply*). Was it a very good cap?

INIMITABLE. Yes.

YOUNG IRELAND. Did it fit uncommon?

INIMITABLE. Yes.

YOUNG IRELAND. Dat was me!

Commentary from Dickens is much slighter here than in the President Tyler account: just a few stage directions. He knows that it is the dialogue on its own that carries the humorous energy, so the effort here goes into carefully reproducing its rhythms, and the twists and turns that invert the initial pattern of seniority between a man and a child, into one where the child becomes the dominant figure, not the famous 'Inimitable'. He can hear those rhythms reprised in his mind's ear as he reconstructs it for the reader. The child's precocious self-assurance is teased into full prominence, impressing the older man, and that oddity is developed as the main source of humour, reinforced ironically in the Inimitable's addressing the child as 'old fellow', 'old boy', like a familiar equal. The pacing is beautifully judged, especially in the final exchanges about the soldier's cap. The cautious and profoundly serious lead-up to the triumphant admission turns the inquisitor–interviewee relationship inside out. Such incongruities, or reversals of expectations, account for most of the hilarity in these encounters, with Tyler and Young Ireland, and Dickens plays on them with delight. In the Presidential interview it was the farcical actuality of a portentous encounter, and in Young Ireland it was the earnestness of engagement with trivia.

The speeches and interplay of different characters that Dickens has here constructed so carefully for his correspondent 'requires imitation'. I wonder how much of Dickens's fiction, its specificity of gesture and speech style, also 'requires imitation' from his readers? Dickens provides the script for silent internal performing by his reader.

The Young Ireland exchange runs a little like another Dickens–child encounter, recorded in 'Travelling Abroad' (1860), one of the Uncommercial Traveller series of papers. In this Dickens imagines himself travelling by coach from London to France. As he approaches Rochester he notices on the roadside 'a very queer small boy':

> 'Halloa!' said I, to the very queer small boy, 'where do you live?'
>
> 'At Chatham,' says he.
>
> 'What do you do there?' says I.
>
> 'I go to school,' says he.
>
> I took him up in a moment, and we went on. Presently, the very queer small boy says, 'This is Gadshill we are coming to, where Falstaff went out to rob those travellers, and ran away.'
>
> 'You know something about Falstaff, eh?' said I.
>
> 'All about him,' said the very queer small boy. 'I am old (I am nine), and I read all sorts of books. But *do* let us stop at the top of the hill, and look at the house there, if you please!'
>
> 'You admire that house?' said I.
>
> 'Bless you, sir,' said the very queer small boy, 'when I was not more than half as old as nine, it used to be a treat for me to be brought to look at it. And ever since I can recollect, my father, seeing me so fond of it, has often said to me, "If you were to be very persevering and were to work hard, you might some day come to live in

it." Though that's impossible!' said the very queer small boy, drawing a low breath, and now staring at the house out of window with all his might.

The house turns out to be Dickens's own (Gad's Hill) home, and the small boy is his memory of himself as he was in the Chatham childhood days. As in the Young Ireland dialogue Dickens shows his extraordinary insight into and empathy with the state of childhood: he can be the child or the man (in this particular case they are the same person), and thereby can generate a dialogue between the two which has a strikingly quirky authenticity. As with the earlier exchange, Dickens genially humours a small child's earnest precociousness of manner and invites the reader to smile. There is some adult condescension in the process, of course, but also a genuine respect for the identity of the child's feelings and his expression of them. Dickens's ability to impersonate that child, the comically distanced version of his former self, is as deft as was his reproduction of the personality and idiom of Young Ireland. It is an act of impersonation in both cases, and so much more than a matter of just reporting a conversation with a child. 'What he desired to express he became', wrote Forster of Dickens's imaginative self-projection into other characters. These scenes come alive as dialogue because Dickens can, almost, inhabit both participants. This was his distinctive way of telling anecdotes, especially comical episodes, so as to reproduce the experience as a performance. He cast his friends as *dramatis personae*, 'he assigned to all of us characters', and so it proves in these encounters. The little Irish boy plays his role as 'Young Ireland'. The Gad's Hill child also becomes a role: repetition of the phrase describing him congeals the compounded epithets into a theatrical sobriquet—the 'Very Queer Small Boy'.

Let us look at a couple of longer set-piece comic anecdotes, more narrative than dialogue. Both of them are from Dickens's letters (though the first was also reproduced, in slightly modified form, for *Pictures from Italy*), and both feature the English abroad. Dickens comes across a touring couple, the Davises, during his stay in Italy in 1845:

There was one Mrs Davis—I know her name from her being always in great request among her party, and her party being everywhere—who was in every part of every scene of every ceremony; and who for a fortnight before, had been in every tomb, and every Church, and every Ruin, and every Picture Gallery: and who never for one instant held her tongue. Deep underground, high up in St. Peter's, out on the Campagna, and stifling in the Jews Quarter, Mrs. Davis turned up all the same. I don't think she saw anything or ever looked at anything; and she had always lost something out of a straw hand-basket, and was trying to find it with all her might and main, among an immense quantity of English halfpence which lay, like sands upon the seashore, at the bottom of it. There was a Cicerone always attached to the party (which had been brought over from London, fifteen or twenty strong, by contract I believe); and if he so much as looked at Mrs. Davis, she invariably cut him short by saying, 'there! God bless the man, don't worrit me: I don't understand a word you say, and shouldn't if you was to talk 'till you was black in the face!' Mr. Davis always had a snuff-colored great coat on, and an umbrella in his hand: and had a sort of slow curiosity always devouring him: which prompted him to do extraordinary things, such as taking the covers off Urns, and looking in at the ashes as if they were Pickles—and tracing out Inscriptions with his umbrella, and saying with intense thoughtfulness, 'here's a B, you see—and an R—And this is the way we goes on in!' His antiquarian habits occasioned his being frequently in the rear of the rest; and one of the agonies of Mrs. Davis and the party in general, was, an ever-present fear that Davis would be lost: causing them to scream for him in the strangest places and at the most improper seasons. And when he came slowly emerging out of some Sepulchre or other, like a peaceful Ghoul, saying 'Here I am!'—Mrs. Davis invariably replied 'You'll be buried alive in a foreign country Davis; and it's no use trying to prevent you!'

Once again Dickens lifts the episode beyond plain reportage, in a number of ways, so that the experience brims with comic energy and vivid detail. He doesn't just report the hideous ubiquity of Mrs Davis, he re-enacts it in his repetitive prose patterns—'always in great request ... being everywhere ... in every part of every scene ... every tomb, and every Church, and every Ruin ... every Picture Gallery ... deep underground, high up in St. Peter's ...'. This suffocating experience is compounded by her relentless gar-rulousness, carrying to a climax the rhythmical momentum of the first sentence.

The expressive pacing became rather different when Dickens wrote up the episode for *Pictures from Italy*, for which he drew on his own letters (retrieved from friends and family for the purpose) and modified them:

> It was impossible not to know Mrs Davis's name, from her being always in great request among her party, and her party being everywhere. During the Holy Week, they were in every part of every scene of every ceremony. For a fortnight or three weeks before it, they were in every tomb, and every church, and every ruin, and every Picture Gallery; and I hardly ever observed Mrs Davis to be silent for a moment.

Dickens is now more detached from the frustrations of the moment, and the cooling down shows in the more ventilated punctuation. While the narrative here is largely verbatim from the original text (except the last clause), the letter's single, long, exasperated crescendo has now become three sedate sentences, with a distinct break in the last. His complaint in the letter that Mrs Davis couldn't hold her tongue is now more politely phrased; and, given the woman's ghastly volubility, the contrasting dry politeness makes it rather funnier. To compound his irritation, in spite of witnessing all these wonderful tourist sights, Mrs Davis is neurotically incapable of concentrating on anything outside herself and her hand-basket. Her hysterical behaviour in coping with lost items assumes comically epic proportions. The final anecdote about her in this sequence, her shrill frustration with the poor guide's pidgin English, makes her surplus aggressive energy into something almost pathological.

Dickens works his humorous material by heightening contrasts. All this attention on Mrs Davis has been partly designed so as to show her in sharp relief against her husband, the 'peaceful Ghoul', with his atrophied energy and his absorption in funerary urns and ashes. Mrs Davis's crazed hyperactivity stops her looking at any of the magnificent sights they've travelled all this way to see; whereas poor Mr Davis, with his understandably empathic relationship with those who are peacefully dead, can't be dragged away from them. The wonderful comic energy is generated by the friction between these two utterly opposite personalities, each of whom, over the years of their marriage, has probably driven the other to his or her extremes of behaviour. The climax to this anecdote of frustration and incompatibility intensifies the incongruities with sharp dramatic vividness ('as a thing seen by the writer, or going on before the reader'). Dickens's prose slackens its pace to mimic Mr Davis's ponderous manner, and draws out its vowel sounds—'came slowly emerging...peaceful Ghoul...'—as almost a deliberate provocation to his partner's manic impatience and idiotic threats.

The spectacle of people driven to extremes of behaviour, often on fairly trivial provocation, brings them into the kind of histrionic spotlight that gives Dickens his great comic opportunities. The second anecdote bears this out. It comes in a letter to Thomas Beard from Geneva in 1846, when Dickens was writing *Dombey and Son*. For reasons which I'll explain later, I first give a matter-of-fact summary of the episode.

While writing his letter on the balcony of his hotel Dickens sees below him a small Englishman in company with a large Frenchman. The Englishman has no French but is now and again helped out by the Frenchman who can manage a little English; but the Englishman in return shows less gratitude than mocking condescension at the Frenchman's pidgin English. Dickens recalls having seen them together on a couple of other occasions when this behaviour was repeated. One incident in particular amused him, when he watched the two disembarking from the Lake steamer into small boats so they could be rowed ashore. A sailor on board the steamer discovered the Englishman had left his coat behind, and called the news across to the departing boat, in French. The Englishman called back that he would collect it later, and became very testy when the sailor didn't understand him. His French companion intervened, shouting to the sailor to keep the coat, and then reassured his friend that he had told him to 'cap' it. At which the Englishman burst into laughter at the Frenchman's mispronunciation, and kept chuckling all the way to the shore.

This is an amusing recollection of a relationship that must have been repeated across Europe, wherever the Victorian English had opportunities to flex their arrogant insularity. Here now is Dickens's account:

> There are two men standing under the balcony of the hotel in which
> I am writing, who are really good specimens, and have amused me

mightily. An immense Frenchman, with a face like a bright velvet pincushion—and a very little Englishman, whose head comes up to about the middle of the Frenchman's waistcoat. They are travelling together. I saw them at Mont Blanc, months ago. The Englishman can't speak a word of French, but the Frenchman can speak a very little English, with which he helps the Englishman out of abysses and ravines of difficulty. The Englishman instead of being obliged by this, condescends, good humouredly, to correct the Frenchman's pronunciation—patronizes him—would pat him on the head if he could reach so high—and screeches at his mistakes.—There he is now, staggering over the stones in his little boots, and falling up against a watchmaker's window, in perfect convulsions of joy, because the beaming Giant, without whom he couldn't get a single necessary of life, has made some mistake in the English language! I never saw such a fellow. The last time I met them was at the other end of the Lake by Chillon, disembarking from the steamer. It is done in little boats: the water being shallow, close in shore: and in the confusion, the Giant had gone into one boat, and the dwarf in another. A hairy sailor on board the steamer found the Dwarf's great coat on deck and gave a great roar to him; upon which the Dwarf, standing up in the boat, cried out (in English): 'Put it down. Keep it. I shall be back in an hour.' The hairy sailor of course not understanding one word of this, roared again and shook the coat in the air. 'Oh you damned fool!' said the Dwarf (still in English) 'Oh you precious jackass! Put it down, will you?' The Giant, perceiving from the other boat what was the matter, cried out to the hairy sailor what it was necessary for him to know, and then called out to the Dwarf, 'I have tell him to cap it.' I thought the dwarf would have died with delight. 'Oh my God!' he said to himself, 'You're a nice man! Tell him to cap it, have you? Yes, yes. Ha ha ha!—Cap it, indeed! Oh Lord!'—and never left off chuckling 'till he landed.

My own matter-of-fact summary was designed to throw into sharper relief the manner in which Dickens here has amplified the comedy of the scenes involving these two characters. There are two main ways in which he has done this. In the first place, he converts two human beings into two pantomime characters, the Dwarf and the Giant. (Again, remember Helps's remark about Dickens's casting everyone as 'characters'.) They begin to slip slowly into these roles soon after Dickens has introduced them and caricatured their physical differences with near-superlatives—the Frenchman has to be 'immense' and the Englishman 'very little'. Here are the grotesque contrasts on which Dickens so often relies in building his humorous set-pieces. In the second place, all of their actions and the actions of those around them are inflated and hyper-energized, as was Mrs Davis, to match the often frenetic pantomime mode. Thus the Dwarf 'screeches' at the Frenchman's mistakes, and 'staggers' and falls about in 'convulsions' of laughter. The steamer sailor, who becomes cast (almost) as 'The Hairy Sailor' bit-part, 'roars', and the Dwarf nearly 'dies' with delight. Dickens's staging techniques so often gravitate towards this mode, exaggerating sounds and actions to high levels of shrillness and knock-about violence. I shall return to this issue of comic violence later.

The Pantomime of Ordinary Life

Dickens is fascinated by the public behaviour of private people— another kind of exercise in contrasts: it is his ideal material for staging comic anecdote. He is particularly drawn to the performance antics of naively self-conscious people. There are two rich examples of this in his early sketch 'Astley's' (1835), one near the beginning and one near the end. He introduces the sketch by confessing that he has become more amused by the audience than by the show itself—a famous theatre-cum-circus entertainment. He fastens our attention on a family who have taken a box at the theatre. The father and mother have about ten children, the oldest, George, being about fourteen (and 'evidently trying to look as if he did not belong to the family'), and they are accompanied by a sycophantic governess. Their having taken a box puts them almost as much on display to the audience as is the performance on stage—and they are aware of this.

> The first five minutes were occupied in taking the shawls off the little girls, and adjusting the bows which ornamented their hair; then it was providentially discovered that one of the little boys was seated behind a pillar and could not see, so the governess was stuck behind the pillar, and the boy lifted into her place. Then pa drilled the boys, and directed the stowing away of their pocket-handkerchiefs, and ma having first nodded and winked to the governess to pull the girls' frocks a little more off their shoulders, stood up to review the little

troop—an inspection which appeared to terminate much to her own satisfaction, for she looked with a complacent air at pa, who was standing up at the further end of the seat. Pa returned the glance, and blew his nose very emphatically; and the poor governess peeped out from behind the pillar, and timidly tried to catch ma's eye, with a look expressive of her high admiration of the whole family. [...]

The play began, and the interest of the little boys knew no bounds. Pa was clearly interested too, although he very unsuccessfully endeavoured to look as if he wasn't. As for ma, she was perfectly overcome by the drollery of the principal comedian, and laughed till every one of the immense bows on her ample cap trembled, at which the governess peeped out from behind the pillar again, and whenever she could catch ma's eye, put her handkerchief to her mouth, and appeared, as in duty bound, to be in convulsions of laughter also. Then when the man in the splendid armour vowed to rescue the lady or perish in the attempt, the little boys applauded vehemently, especially one little fellow who was apparently on a visit to the family, and had been carrying on a child's flirtation, the whole evening, with a small coquette of twelve years old, who looked like a model of her mamma on a reduced scale; and who, in common with the other little girls (who generally speaking have even more coquettishness about them than much older ones), looked very properly shocked, when the knight's squire kissed the princess's confidential chambermaid.

When the scenes in the circle commenced, the children were more delighted than ever; and the wish to see what was going forward, completely conquering pa's dignity, he stood up in the box, and applauded as loudly as any of them. Between each feat of horsemanship, the governess leant across to ma, and retailed the clever remarks of the children on that which had preceded: and ma, in the openness of her heart, offered the governess an acidulated drop, and the governess, gratified to be taken notice of, retired behind her pillar again with a brighter countenance: and the whole party seemed quite happy, except the exquisite in the back of the box, who, being too grand to take any interest in the children, and too insignificant to be taken notice of by anybody else, occupied himself, from time to time, in rubbing the place where the whiskers ought to be, and was completely alone in his glory [...]

Each member of the family, including the governess, seems to be playing to the other members as well as sometimes to the Astley's audience. They project a façade of worldliness which is endearingly fragile and transparent, and fall into roles—precocious coquett-ishness, adolescent dandyism, grown-up sophistication (hard to sus-tain) and condescension. The poor governess strains to deserve the patronage of the whole family, and strenuously performs the sycophancy that is to endear her to her employers. The whole sequence could be schematized as a wonderful tangle of intersecting gazes, invited and spurned, according to the degrees of self-consciousness energizing (or paralyzing) each of the players. They are a self-constituted spectacle, amateur auditioners for the *beau monde*, and as such they are prime comic material for Dickens. Dickens's own gaze has turned away from the professional spectacle going on down in the Astley's Circle towards this unofficial spectacle, precisely in order to activate the theatre of everyday life. This is the essence of his staging of comic anecdote.

At the end of the 'Astley's' sketch, after he has finished describing some of the equestrian and clown performances, Dickens turns his attention to an off-stage show of another kind, the groups who hang around outside the theatres, talking 'and attitudinising'. These are usually actors idling the time away between shows. They have 'a kind of conscious air', he writes, and 'They always seem to think they are exhibiting; the lamps are ever before them'.

> That young fellow in the faded brown coat, and very full light green trousers, pulls down the wristbands of his check shirt, as ostentatiously as if it were of the finest linen, and cocks the white hat of the summer-before-last as knowingly over his right eye, as if it were a purchase of yesterday. Look at the dirty white Berlin gloves, and the cheap silk handkerchief stuck in the bosom of his threadbare coat. Is it possible to see him for an instant, and not come to the conclusion that he is the walking gentleman who wears a blue surtout, clean collar, and white trousers, for half an hour, and then shrinks into his worn-out scanty clothes: who has to boast night after night of his splendid fortune, with the painful con-sciousness of a pound a-week and his boots to find; to talk of his father's mansion in the country, with a dreary recollection of his own two-pair back, in the New Cut; and to be envied and flattered as the favoured lover of a rich heiress, remembering all the while that the ex-dancer at home is in the family way, and out of an engagement?

[...]
We could not believe that the beings of light and elegance, in milk-white tunics, salmon-coloured legs, and blue scarfs, who flitted on sleek cream-coloured horses before our eyes at night, with all the aid of lights, music, and artificial flowers, could be the pale, dissipated-looking creatures we beheld by day.

'The lamps are ever before them' in their own minds. But even if these characters were not constantly imagining their self-esteem irradiated by the footlights, Dickens's comic sensibility would be habitually shining lamps on human ordinariness. His unwitting actors from ordinary life flare into sharp visibility, with that slightly unreal, luminescent quality that harsh gaslight gives to faces and figures, and they throw huge, grotesque shadows. They are lit for performance.

It has often been remarked that pantomime or cognate forms of popular entertainment provided a model for much of Dickens's work. George Bernard Shaw saw *Pickwick Papers* as a novelistic harlequinade, with Pickwick himself as 'the king of pantaloons'. Paul Schlicke showed in detail how pantomime and popular theatre permeated the content and mode of a number of the novels. Edwin Eigner proposed even more systematic correspondences between the characterization and incident in *Pickwick* and the conventional characters of pantomime:

> If we think of Miss Rachel as a burlesque Columbine, then Mr. Tupman becomes the foppish Lover, and Jingle plays the agile but penniless trickster, Harlequin. Once Columbine and Harlequin run off together, both Pickwick and Mr. Wardle fall into place as Pantaloons and are soon joined in their awkward pursuit by the body servant, Clown, Sam Weller.

These habits of perception—reflex adaptations of theatrical modes to scenes of real life—developed early in Dickens's career. In one of the papers he wrote for *Bentley's Miscellany*, 'The Pantomime of Life' (1837), he openly confessed that his fondness for pantomime was not because of its traditional attractions—its dazzle of tinsel, its associations with childhood and that world of wonder—but because it was 'a mirror of life'. It mirrored life in its formal and informal moments. Consider the following comical scene in which an elderly gentleman, who has just been dining at the expense of a young man-about-town, stands shaking hands with his host as they part outside the tavern. We are asked to observe 'That affected warmth of the shake of the hand, the courteous nod, the obvious recollection of the dinner, the savoury flavour of which still hangs upon his lips'. Then the old gentleman parts company:

> He hobbles away humming an opera tune, and twirling his cane to and fro, with affected carelessness. Suddenly he stops—'tis at the milliner's window. He peeps through one of the large panes of glass; and, his view of the ladies within being obstructed by the India shawls, directs his attentions to the young girl with the band-box in her hand, who is gazing in at the window also. See! He draws beside her. He coughs; she turns away from him. He draws near her again; she disregards him. He gleefully chucks her under the chin, and, retreating a few steps, nods and beckons with fantastic grimaces, while the girl bestows a contemptuous and supercilious look upon his wrinkled visage. She turns away with a flounce, and the old gentleman trots after her with a toothless chuckle.

Is that a scene Dickens is reporting from a pantomime or from real life? It could be either, and that is Dickens's point. In fact he presents it as something he actually witnessed in the Haymarket (the London street, not the Theatre Royal of that name). What he is trying to demonstrate is that the old gentleman is naturally a real-life version of pantomime's Pantaloon character, the lascivious old man who prompts the clown into mischief and ogles young ladies in the street. He could not avoid 'playing his part' (as Arthur Helps might have put it), with a little assistance from Dickens's imagination. In the street scene just described, so many of Dickens's future comic characters are adumbrated: Mantalini's mincing philandering, Micawber's humming and cane-twirling, Bagstock's grimaces and chuckles.

Comic Violence

Dickens worked in near-pantomime mode on many occasions when he infused comical situations with the extra, somewhat manic energy that is such a distinctive feature of his humorous writing. Everything in the Geneva anecdote about the Englishman and the Frenchman was, bit by bit, grotesquely amplified to high levels of energy, behaviourally and acoustically, that correspond to pantomime knockabout and pantomime characterization. I want to examine this a little more closely, and specifically in the context of comic violence.

J. Hillis Miller, in discussing pantomime and hyperbole in *A Christmas Carol*, drew attention to Baudelaire's essay on laughter, *L'Essence du Rire* (1855). In the course of his essay Baudelaire described a performance of an English pantomime which he had seen in Paris in 1842:

> The distinguishing mark of this variety of the comic, it seemed to me, was its violence [...]. The English Pierrot came onto the stage like a hurricane, and tumbled like a buffoon. When he laughed, the whole theatre appeared to rock on its foundations [...]. The whole action of this extraordinary piece was played on a sustained note of fury. The atmosphere was one of dizzy and bewildering exaggeration [...]. At once a sense of dizzy bewilderment took charge of the stage. It filled the air. One could breathe it. It distended the lungs and renewed the blood in the ventricle [...]. It came from the presence of the absolutely comic. It seemed to possess each of the characters presented to our view [...]. [The characters in the pantomime] made a number of extraordinary gestures which indicated clearly that they were conscious of having been forced into an entirely new form of existence. They whirled their arms round and round; they looked like windmills in a gale.

This 'dizzy bewilderment' is the medium in which much of Dickens's high comedy is immersed, and ordinary incidents and characters are refracted into grotesque human performances: it becomes indeed 'an entirely new form of existence', the world of Dickensian laughter. The Geneva anecdote is a good example of this strange transmutation whereby 'two men standing under the balcony' become a Giant and a Dwarf engaged in a farcical knockabout. Farce is a domesticated version of pantomime, but it can generate a similar level of dizzying energy: doors slamming, trousers dropping, people dashing into each other, frenzied double-takes. Dickens knew the mode well: 'that wild abandonment which alone can carry a farce off'.

The reader of Dickens's pantomime or farcical scenes is somehow lured in to share this intoxication or dizziness that Baudelaire described ('it filled the air. One could breathe it'). It is like a compression chamber preparing for the ignition of the comedy, and the reader *must* be drawn into its atmosphere. Without proper induction we might find the spectacle as Dickens describes it as something happening behind the bars of a lunatic asylum. What Dickens has to break down is the sober detachment in his readers that might indeed render the comic incidents too wildly extravagant (as they seem to have struck the foreigner, Baudelaire).

However, there is this problematic difference between pantomime and Dickens's humorous anecdotes in the letters or novels: one chooses to go to a pantomime or farce and accordingly one is prepared for its zanily playful mode. But one opens a novel or starts to read a newsy letter in a different frame of mind. One starts from neutral, as it were. Thus Dickens has to go to work to rouse his reader's sensibility into near pantomime responsiveness before staging his comical performance; he has to seize his audience and warm them up quickly, and this entails a degree of violence. Just as it can damage the body to undertake violent exercise without properly warming up, so Dickens has to find a way to induct us into the frenetic mode of much of his comedy.

Once we are warmed up and fully engaged, the comic pantomime mode, like violent exercise, can prove physiologically beneficial. Baudelaire suggests that it does indeed have a therapeutic effect as it distends the lungs and renews the blood. Laughter agitates the whole system and can be a violently tonic exercise. When we think about the spectacle of hearty, helpless laughter objectively, we see that it can throw us too (normally sober readers, listeners, spectators) into strangely grotesque pantomimic behaviour: involuntarily we start heaving and spluttering, and emitting cackling or braying sounds. Something is tugging us out of everyday sobriety and we become momentarily, apparently, intoxicated. The tugging comes from Dickens's insistent, energetic engagement of us as readers; he is putting on a show and we *have* to join in. He did precisely this at festive social gatherings. His daughter Mamie recalled his behaviour at family dancing parties. Even when he was not dancing, 'He would insist upon the sides keeping up a kind of jig step, and clapping his hands to add to the fun, and dancing at the backs of those whose enthusiasm he thought needed rousing, was himself never still for a moment'.

Comedy that heightens kinetic energy to the point of violence has great attraction for Dickens, and its affinities with pantomime are clear. English pantomime, for Baudelaire, was 'the absolute comic':

Illustration 5: George Cruikshank, 'A Skaiting Party' and 'A Skaiting Academy'. Print (1841).

violent in itself, it causes 'a true and violent laughter [...] an insane
and excessive mirth'. Baudelaire saw its presence also in England's
popular comic illustrators, such as Seymour and Cruikshank:

> I should say, that the essence of Cruikshank's grotesque is an extrava-
> gant violence of gesture and movement, and a kind of explosion, so
> to speak, within the expression. Each one of his little creatures mimes
> his part in a frenzy and ferment, like a pantomime actor.

There could hardly be a better description than that quotation of
how Dickens goes to work to stage so many of his comic anecdotes.
'Like a pantomime actor': he was explicit in making a similar analogy on one occasion, when he and his family had taken a house in
Boulogne. Two neighbouring cats were taking a predatory interest
in Dick, the family's pet canary, as Dickens reports in a letter:

> it is impossible to shut them out, and they hide themselves in the
> most terrific manner: hanging themselves up behind draperies, like
> bats, and tumbling out in the dead of night with frightful caterwaul-
> ings. Hereupon, French [Dickens's manservant] borrows Beaucourt's
> gun, loads the same to the muzzle, discharges it twice in vain and
> throws himself over with the recoil, exactly like a clown.

'Exactly like a clown'; the addition of that phrase at the end modi-
fies the episode, landing its violence safely in comic territory. Violence with safety is the key. Dickens was fully alert to the value of
this histrionic formula for raising laughter. He expressed his views
on it in a letter of 1849 to Mary Elizabeth Tayler, a Nonconformist
who had written to him expressing her disgust at public Punch and
Judy shows (she had witnessed her first one from 'behind a venetian
blind in lodgings one evening at a quiet watering place'). She hoped,
she wrote, that Dickens might consider giving 'England and the
World a *new Punch* and please give no praise to the liquor that cheats
into intoxication'. Dickens, as might be expected, reacted strongly to
her criticism of Punch, which he regarded as 'one of those extravagant reliefs from the realities of life' and as 'harmless in its influence'
as pantomime violence. He enlarges on this: 'One secret source of
the pleasure very generally derived from [...] the more boisterous
parts of a Christmas Pantomime, is the satisfaction the spectator
feels in the circumstance that likenesses of men and women can be
so knocked about, without any pain or suffering'. Some three years

later Dickens returned to the issue, in a *Household Words* article co-written with W. H. Wills, 'A Curious Dance Round a Curious Tree' (January 1852). He discusses 'the jocund world of Pantomime, where there is no affliction or calamity that leaves the least impression':

> [W]here a man may tumble into the broken ice, or dive into the kitchen fire, and only be the droller for the accident; where babies may be knocked about and sat upon, or choked with gravy spoons, in the process of feeding, and yet no Coroner be wanted, nor anybody made uncomfortable; where workmen may fall from the top of a house to the bottom, or even from the bottom of a house to the top, and sustain no injury to the brain, need no hospital, leave no young children; where every one, in short, is so superior to all the accidents of life, though encountering them at every turn, that I suspect this to be the secret (though many persons may not present it to themselves) of the general enjoyment which an audience of vulnerable spectators, liable to pain and sorrow, find in this class of entertainment.

Dickens reiterated his theory in another *Household Words* article written in October of that same year, 'Lying Awake':

> It always appears to me that the secret of this enjoyment lies in the temporary superiority to the common hazards and mischances of life; in seeing casualties happen through a very rough sort of poetry without the least harm being done to any one—the pretence of distress in a pantomime being so broadly humorous as to be no pretence at all.

He had occasion to test this theory unexpectedly at a Christmas pantomime at Covent Garden in 1860. Quite suddenly the scenery collapsed. In the ensuing chaos a stage-hand rescued one of the clown's props, a preposterously huge drinking vessel, and dumped it on the ledge of one of the proscenium boxes, to the mortification of the couple in the box:

> The moment the House knew that nobody was injured, they directed their whole attention to this gigantic porter pot in its genteel position (the lady and gentleman trying to hide behind it), and roared with laughter. When a modest footman came from behind the Curtain to clear it, and took it up in his arms, like a Brobdingnagian Baby, we all laughed more than we had ever laughed in our lives. I don't know why.

The lavish laughter comes in two waves. The audience, deprived of the show they had come to see, but still sitting expectantly in their seats, eventually all tune into another, impromptu spectacle, the giant pot incongruously sitting on the edge of a posh box, to the excruciating embarrassment of its genteel occupants. The second wave, the one that puzzled Dickens by its intensity, must have been heightened by relief from anxiety as well as the after-effects of shock. The laughter, though, on both occasions comes after and is conditional upon the reassurance that the real, violent catastrophe hasn't hurt anyone.

It is a precarious borderline. We laugh at some sudden disaster that we know, with relief, won't have real, painful consequences; we thus relax our normal guard. James Kincaid has an acute observation to make on this (as he has on so many issues bearing on Dickens's humour) when he discusses what he terms the 'combined immunity-vulnerability' which laughter creates. He makes the point that 'Having released the energies ordinarily used to guard our hostilities, inhibitions, or fears, we are especially unprotected if the promised safety which allowed us to laugh proves to be illusory'. He then suggests by way of illustration some chilling scenarios: 'Imagine the fat old man who slipped on the banana peel being suddenly identified as our brother, now seriously hurt; the custard pie containing sulphuric acid; the train really hitting the funny car and killing the Keystone Cops'. I read this out to a group of students on one occasion. Most of them winced, as might be expected, but one of them became helpless with laughter at these gruesome comic-scenarios-gone-wrong. Counter-intuitively, but not unreasonably perhaps, the raising of the shock-value heightened the comic fall-out.

Generally speaking, laughter at violence can happen only when there's a sense that the victim is not going to experience real pain (as mentioned earlier), or when real pain is inflicted on someone who is not a real person: notice how Dickens when discussing the boisterous violence of pantomime in that letter to Tayler spoke of the *likenesses* of men and women who were being knocked about without pain. They are not quite human. They are facsimiles. This slight touch of artifice in the victim is all that is needed to allow laughter at sudden violent upsets. The idea is related to Bergson's thesis that '*we laugh every time a person gives us the impression of being a thing*'. This is something that happens conventionally on stage, when a real person has become a role. But it can also happen when an ordinary character in everyday life is amplified into stage mode, in ways we have seen Dickens do as he works up his comic anecdotes.

We might test this out in the following scene from *Nicholas Nickleby* (Chapter 4). We have just been introduced to Mr Squeers at the Saracen's Head, where he is receiving the new intake of boys destined for Dotheboys Hall. One very small boy is already with him, sitting miserably on his school trunk:

> ...the little boy on the top of the trunk gave a violent sneeze.
>
> 'Halloa, sir!' growled the schoolmaster, turning round. 'What's that, sir?'
>
> 'Nothing, please sir,' replied the little boy.
>
> 'Nothing, sir!' exclaimed Mr Squeers.
>
> 'Please sir, I sneezed,' rejoined the boy, trembling till the little trunk shook under him.
>
> 'Oh! sneezed, did you?' retorted Mr Squeers. 'Then what did you say "nothing" for, sir?'
>
> In default of a better answer to this question, the little boy screwed a couple of knuckles into each of his eyes and began to cry, wherefore Mr Squeers knocked him [...] off the trunk with a blow on one side of his face, and knocked him on again with a blow to the other.
>
> 'Wait till I get you down into Yorkshire, my young gentleman,' said Mr Squeers, 'and then I'll give you the rest. Will you hold that noise, sir?'
>
> 'Ye—ye—yes,' sobbed the little boy, rubbing his face very hard with the Beggar's Petition in printed calico.

If one abstracts the bare events from this narrative, the cruelty is painful: a brute of a grown man hitting a child around the head. But two things are happening within the narrative to make the scene funny as well as cruel. One of these is the subtle point made by Paul Schlicke in discussing the vicious but also hilarious Dotheboys Hall episodes: 'Entertainment and moral conviction work together as comedy lifts the villainy into a sphere of ethical certainties, in which we can laugh heartily at the wickedness because we know it will be defeated'. Squeers is *such* a transparent villain, sadist and hypocrite, and treated from the start by Dickens as a comic grotesque, that we *know* he will be crushed eventually. The brutality, wretched though it is, is temporary only. We sense this about Squeers's villainy because of the very different way in which the novel's other principal villain, Ralph, is presented with no humour and with sinisterly obscure motives for his cruelties. While he can strike certain stylized melodramatic postures, there is a degree of human complexity about Ralph that is absent in the representation of Squeers, whose malice, sadism and hypocrisy seem more playful, more lightweight (and, as I say, temporary). Ralph's is a melodramatic villainy, whereas Squeers's is a pantomimic villainy. Squeers's hypocrisy is crudely unintelligent. He seems almost to be deceived himself by his own efforts to delude others with his pious sincerities, as we are told in Chapter 8: '[he] covered his rascality, even at home, with a spice of his habitual deceit; as if he really had a notion of some day or another being able to take himself in, and persuade his own mind that he was a very good fellow'. That perception of this characterization plays a part in our responses to the Saracen's Head scene.

Another reason why, perhaps, Squeers's brutality has a comical effect is the way in which casual violence mutates into a slapstick routine: '[Squeers] knocked him off [...] with a blow on one side [...] knocked him on again with a blow to the other'. The choreographed symmetry of the action seems to undermine any squeamishness we may have. Suppose there had been only the first blow, knocking the crying child to the ground; would that have been comical at all? Yet another simple technique for sustaining the predominantly comic mode when dealing with dangerous violence is rapidly to divert attention from the immediate consequences of the violence. That way no one seems hurt, or at least we are not noticing it. Thus as soon as the knocking-off and knocking-on action has happened, we are pulled away from concern about the bruised child and straight into hearing Squeers's threat—' "Wait till I get you down into Yorkshire..." '. When we next return to the child, we find him sobbing and rubbing his face with 'the Beggar's Petition in printed calico'. The absurd fulsomeness of the handkerchief detail (the Beggar's Petition was a pious poem often printed on 'moral pocket handkerchiefs') jostles with the pathos, and induces laughter through the incongruity of juxtaposing such leisurely, superfluous detailing so closely to the violent moment. Throughout this episode of human brutality we have been quickly whisked away from pain and pathos each time it threatens to do violence to the prevailing comic mode.

That comic mode approximates to pantomime, where the violence is a part of the robust knock-about in which we assume a peculiar resilience in both perpetrator and victim. In the scene with Squeers, this mode has been set by the introduction to his character the page before, and we become aware we are watching a comically outrageous performance in Squeers's histrionic hypocrisies. The little boy becomes just a stooge in this performance, not a little boy whose feelings we are invited to share or reflect on (it would be very different if the child were Little Paul Dombey). It is another instance of Dickens's habit of manipulating material into comical theatrical routine.

The ambivalent mixture of vicious sadism and clownishness in Squeers seems to have been reflected in Dickens's impersonation of him in his public readings. When preparing his reading 'Nicholas Nickleby at the Yorkshire School' in the summer of 1861, Dickens was evidently interested in playing up the humour in Squeers, as he told Forster: 'I have also done *Nicholas Nickleby* at the Yorkshire school, and hope I have got something droll out of Squeers, John Browdie, & Co'. The reviewer for the Edinburgh paper *The Courant* commented on Dickens's Squeers impersonation during a reading performance: 'One scarcely knows whether to take Mr Squeers for a mere ruffian or a humorist in disguise. Certainly the author has imparted to him a kind of grim humour, though it sits rather clumsily upon him'. Another spectator at a reading of 'Nickleby' remarked that Dickens's Squeers 'impresses us with the belief that he enjoys being a brute and is not an actor trying to be brutal'. Dickens was playing Squeers for laughs, but with an odd gusto in the man's brutality.

When Dickens the public reader took his final bow to his audience on the night of 15 March 1870, he made a farewell speech. He announced that he was relinquishing the 'garish lights' of his gaslit stage-set, and would resume his usual task of writing fiction for his readership. But as a writer Dickens had always carried that preternaturally bright stage lighting with him and cast it on scenes of ordinary life, bringing 'all that he saw and felt into a magic circle of dramatic creation'. Those garish lights were integral to his sensibility as a humorist.

3

Comic Timing

*'The secret of great comedy is—wait
for it—timing'*

This sentence announces and enacts one of the most elusive techniques for triggering laughter. With a well-scripted joke timing can make the difference between raising half a smile and triggering gusts of laughter. But what exactly is this comic timing to which so many performers will refer when asked about their craft? How is the comic writer, working in solitude and silence, to handle such a thing as timing without any audience rapport? Can comic timing be exercised on a printed page? Does the reader, who is the one who must deliver the comic material (to himself, to herself), have to have an instinct for comic timing in order to bring it off? Before examining Dickens's practice I would like to explore the idea of comic timing itself.

The Mystery of Comic Timing

Comic timing is a puzzle as much to its practitioners as to its theorists. Oliver Double, a professional comedian and writer on the craft of stand-up comedy (and author of the epigraph), assembles a number of attempted definitions in his book *Getting the Joke* (2005). They are drawn from fellow practitioners and other writers and include the following: the ability to anticipate the audience's reaction to a line; control over tempo of delivery of new information; and knowing just the right moment to pause. He and others place particular emphasis on the pause just before the punchline or pay-off; the skilled stand-up must know 'the instant to hit a line like punching a button to detonate laughter', as the American comedian Joan

Rivers put it. According to another, you 'light the fuse' by 'taking a pause before you deliver the punch line'. Notice the language commonly used to describe the impact of the joke—explosions and punches. One of the Italian words for 'joke' is 'battuta', a beating. A joke is a kind of violence, both to language and to the auditor: it so often involves a linguistic torsion, and it violates the expectations of the listener. Timing its build-up is crucial.

Timing, then, is a matter of the distribution of pauses, distribution of the elements of the text, and interaction with other speakers. This definition is offered in a recent essay on 'Timing in the Performance of Jokes', in the course of which the authors become sceptical about the conventional emphasis on the timing of the pause just before the punchline, suggesting that its practice is not as common as supposed. They draw their conclusions from a small-scale but significant controlled experiment with college students who were asked to deliver scripted and unscripted jokes. Another theoretician, Neal Norrick, wisely cautions against 'reifying timing as a unitary notion' and expands the idea of timing to encompass 'the overall tempo of the performance, the ebb and flow of given and new information highlighted by repetition and formulaic phrasing along with rhythms of hesitation and more fluent passages'. That broader definition is the one that particularly helps in approaching Dickens's feel for comic timing.

Nearly all the definitions mentioned above assume the presence of an audience and imply that the comedian must work the audience just as much as he or she works on the joke. Timing in this context is a three-way dynamic, engaging the comedian, the material and the audience. That third element is a mysterious mass to confront. It contains all those deep deposits of laughter, the fossil fuel for high-performance comedy, and the comic has to find the mechanisms to bring it bubbling up. 'Comic timing happens in [...] the feedback loop between [comedian] and each individual audience', according to Greg Dean. That stress on 'each individual audience' is deliberate. Timing is understood as a near instinctual sensitivity in the performer to the mood and responsiveness of this audience—and I mean *this* audience: this particular audience, on this particular evening, in this particular venue. Tomorrow night—same place, same performer, much the same material, but a new audience—the dynamic will have to be reworked all over again as the comedian negotiates a new relationship. The material may be a constant in the sense of a given script, but it needs to be very elastic in performance.

A novel is a fixed script; the readership is the elastic element. Few knew the mercurial nature of audiences and readership better than Dickens himself. He called on all his skills as a comic actor when he performed his public readings. The same material that on one night could reduce the stalls to helpless laughter, on the next might provoke only stifled giggles. He was doing 'stand-up'. However, we are here discussing Dickens the writer, not Dickens the public reader; we are examining the literary performer who delivers comic material to an unseen readership, not to a listening and watching audience. What for the stand-up comic is a three-way dynamic, where each night involves a retuning of that relationship, for the writer becomes a two-way process, writer and material, with the readership only imagined and, at the point of composition, hardly nuancing the 'delivery' in any active way.

Every sentence is an act of timing. Take the epigraph to this essay, about timing and great comedy. The sentence transmits a simple piece of information. But try switching its components around. 'Timing is the secret of great comedy'—that gives exactly the same information; but 'The secret of great comedy is timing' has a new tension in it, a suspense introduced by opening with 'the secret...' and thereby giving a greater resonance to 'timing', because the turn of the sentence means we have had to 'wait for it'. And then the addition of the explicit, teasing call, 'wait for it', stretches the delay and enhances the moment of discovery of the 'secret'. Timing, both on the micro- and macrocosmic scale, is an exercise in calculating the pace of delivery of information, how to prepare for it, where to position it, what kind of manoeuvring has to be done through the punctuation pauses. Comic timing in live performance is a matter of enacting those comical hesitations, phrasing the text of the joke sometimes against the grain of the written punctuation, pulling up for millisecond pauses ('wait for it...') at unpredictable points. How is the silent, solitary reader to begin to enact those lines of print on a page so as to approximate the funny scene to a live performance? How is the writer to help in that?

Let us take the question of pauses. When a writer wants to introduce a significant and perhaps unnerving pause in a conversation in
direct speech, he has to write it down: 'A sudden silence fell upon
the company'. That gives us the information, but does it have any
visceral effect on our engagement with the drama of the scene? The
sentence introducing 'silence' paradoxically fills that silence with the
same graphic 'noise' as the surrounding text; it doesn't open a sudden gap in that text; it doesn't unsettle as a sudden performed
silence might. Different readers will absorb the impact of that 'sudden silence' in different ways, no doubt, and to different degrees. I
use the example only to suggest how difficult it might be for the
novelist to exercise comic timing in the sense in which we are familiar with it in live performance. The fact that Dickens was an actor
as well as a novelist, and that (as we saw in the previous essay) he
was also a lively comic anecdotalist in conversation and correspondence, makes him a particularly interesting writer to explore in this
context. He had an actor's trained instinct for comic timing: how
does he reproduce or translate this in his comic writing?

The Warm-up

At the beginning of his most famous story, *A Christmas Carol*, Dickens
assumes the persona of an entertainer warming up his audience just
before the story starts. Here is his opening patter:

> Marley was dead: to begin with. There is no doubt whatever about
> that. The register of his burial was signed by the clergyman, the
> clerk, the undertaker, and the chief mourner. Scrooge signed it. And
> Scrooge's name was good upon 'Change, for anything he chose to
> put his hand to. Old Marley was as dead as a door-nail.
>
> Mind! I don't mean to say that I know, of my own knowledge, what
> there is particularly dead about a door-nail. I might have been inclined,
> myself, to regard a coffin-nail as the deadest piece of ironmongery in
> the trade. But the wisdom of our ancestors is in the simile; and my
> unhallowed hands shall not disturb it, or the Country's done for. You
> will therefore permit me to repeat, emphatically, that Marley was as
> dead as a door-nail.
>
> Scrooge knew he was dead? Of course he did. How could it be
> otherwise? Scrooge and he were partners for I don't know how many

years. Scrooge was his sole executor, his sole administrator, his sole assign, his sole residuary legatee, his sole friend, and sole mourner. And even Scrooge was not so dreadfully cut up by the sad event, but that he was an excellent man of business on the very day of the funeral, and solemnised it with an undoubted bargain.

The mention of Marley's funeral brings me back to the point I started from. There is no doubt that Marley was dead. This must be distinctly understood, or nothing wonderful can come of the story I am going to relate. If we were not perfectly convinced that Hamlet's Father died before the play began, there would be nothing more remarkable in his taking a stroll at night, in an easterly wind, upon his own ramparts, than there would be in any other middle-aged gentleman rashly turning out after dark in a breezy spot—say Saint Paul's Churchyard for instance—literally to astonish his son's weak mind.

What is going on here, in this apparently bumbling preamble? 'Listeners expect hesitation and disfluency in the build-up of a joke, especially in the opening sentences', writes Neal Norrick. Dickens is not telling a joke, in spite of a pervasive jokiness in his patter, but he certainly does adopt this meandering self-reflexive manner for his opening. He elaborates a fussy self-consciousness about his task as a story-teller and teasingly spins out what amounts to a shaggy-dog story (about the importance of knowing that Marley *was dead*). He does this with a number of facetious diversions and jokes. In these opening paragraphs he very strongly projects not only his own presence as story-teller ('I am standing in the spirit at your elbow', he tells the reader later, in Stave Two), but also the co-presence of the reader/listener whom he is button-holing energetically. He crowds the reader's space. It must be the closest he comes in his fiction to conjuring that three-way dynamic I earlier described as the stand-up comic's routine situation. No wonder he chose the *Carol* as the first item to deliver in his 'stand-up' public readings.

The story-teller toys with the reader. He has a sensationally brief, blunt opening—'Marley was dead'. OK...but why is Marley's death so significant? Who is or was Marley anyway? Presumably we will find out in a sentence or two...but we don't. We are just coaxed further into a narrative where we have yet to get our bearings. Short, prodding sentences are followed by longer ones formally confirming the death as wholly authentic, but a paragraph goes by and we still don't know who Marley was or why his death matters so much. To add to the frustration, in the next paragraph our story-teller swerves off into a long, jokey exploration of the cliché 'dead as a door-nail'. It's difficult to gauge both the narrative trajectory and the story-teller's register. This latter is an odd weave of slang and cliché—'dead as a door-nail', 'the country's done for', 'cut up' (by the death)—crossed with a fussy formality; an apparent narrative urgency counterpoints a rambling side-tracking. Where exactly is this whimsical narrator leading us? We are coaxed towards the imminent story one moment, and then have to mark time while he drifts off in order to over-elaborate unimportant points. Scrooge is introduced as a trusted signatory (but with no other role) in paragraph one, forgotten in paragraph two, back in paragraph three as an important partner, shelved in paragraph four, and back again in paragraph five.

Paragraph four takes the diversionary teasing almost too far, with its protracted *Hamlet* analogy. As with so much of his comic writing Dickens can push a joke to the point where he teeters on the edge of overdoing it, and he admitted as much: 'I have such an inexpressible enjoyment of what I see in a droll light, that I dare say I pet it as if it were a spoilt child'. Dickens must have realized at this point that he was beginning to over-tax the reader's patience, since the manuscript shows that he cut a further four or five lines of facetious chat about the problems of having a son like Hamlet. A sense of timing in this crucial warm-up section is exactly what is propelling Dickens's quill as he scratches out all that material.

Even so, it will take a further five paragraphs before we finally arrive at the Christmas story's traditional beginning, 'Once upon a time...'.

This whole opening of nine paragraphs is a carefully tuned exercise in comic timing. Dickens creates the illusion of being a live entertainer. His main purpose in the first few paragraphs of this meandering preamble is to introduce neither Marley nor Scrooge, but himself, or rather the projected self of this whimsical story-teller. Through the erratic pacing, the narrative swerves and the switches of register Dickens tactically disorients his reader (who was sitting comfortably initially and waiting for the *story* to begin) so as

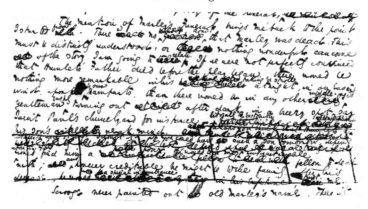

Illustration 6: Detail of manuscript page from *A Christmas Carol*, Pierpont Morgan Library, New York.

to induce a dependency on his narrator self. And that narrator develops a voice with a personality almost as distinctive as one or another of his famous, exuberant characters, to whom we might now turn.

The Monologue Tempo

The great comic characters such as Micawber, Pecksniff and Mrs Gamp, and many of the minor ones such as Podsnap, Mrs Nickleby and Flora, are born not just with their peculiar catch-phrases but also with a signature tempo to their speech. They are not conversationalists, in the sense of adapting their tone and pace to their different interlocutors; they are essentially monologue specialists, and conversation with them is often reduced to a matter of making periodic interruptions. The interlocutor's function is to be little more than a sounding board. One of the greatest of such characters, Mrs Gamp, has conveniently devised a permanent, portable interlocutor wholly under her control—Mrs Harris. Thus when Mrs Gamp is engaged in speaking with a real character it is less a dialogue than a three-way conversation, where Mrs Harris's role is often to pre-empt the responses of the real interlocutor the better to enable Mrs Gamp to monopolize the conversation.

These characters don't need other people, except as audiences. The sound of their own voices and the soothing effect of hearing their own sentiments melodically phrased can be company enough. They are consummate soloists, and once they ease into their rhythm it is mighty hard to knock them off their stroke. Much of the comedy they generate comes from the manifest futility of efforts to do so, and from the fractured and recovered rhythms as they ride the interruptions from others. Pecksniff, for example, in prime mellifluous form throughout most of *Martin Chuzzlewit*, can be wholly unruffled by the occasional daft interventions which would disconcert most people in full flow. Here he is presiding serenely over a very fractious Chuzzlewit family meeting (Chapter 4). He is well into his oratorical stride when he is apparently brought up short, first by a hostile interruption, and then by forgetting a name:

> '...Now,' said Mr Pecksniff, crossing his two forefingers in a manner which was at once conciliatory and argumentative; 'I will not, upon the one hand, go so far as to say that she deserves all the inflictions which have been so very forcibly and hilariously suggested;' one of his ornamental sentences; 'nor will I, upon the other, on any account compromise my common understanding as a man, by making the assertion that she does not. What I would observe is, that I think some practical means might be devised of inducing our respected, shall I say our revered—?'
>
> 'No!' interposed the strong-minded woman in a loud voice.
>
> 'Then I will not,' said Mr Pecksniff. 'You are quite right, my dear madam, and I appreciate and thank you for your discriminating objection—our respected relative, to dispose himself to listen to the promptings of nature, and not to the—'
>
> 'Go on, Pa!' cried Mercy.
>
> 'Why, the truth is, my dear,' said Mr Pecksniff, smiling upon his assembled kindred, 'that I am at a loss for a word. The name of those fabulous animals (pagan, I regret to say) who used to sing in the water, has quite escaped me.'
>
> Mr George Chuzzlewit suggested 'swans.'
>
> 'No,' said Mr Pecksniff. 'Not swans. Very like swans, too. Thank you.'
>
> The nephew with the outline of a countenance, speaking for the first and last time on that occasion, propounded 'Oysters.'

    'No,' said Mr Pecksniff, with his own peculiar urbanity, 'nor oys-
ters. But by no means unlike oysters; a very excellent idea; thank you,
my dear sir, very much. Wait! Sirens. Dear me! sirens, of course.
I think, I say, that means might be devised of disposing our respected
relative to listen to the promptings of nature, and not to the siren-like
delusions of art.....'

The comic shock comes from the bathetic incongruity of the 'swans'
and 'oysters' with the ornate mythological world that Pecksniff is
conjuring. It would have been much less funny, I think, had these
interventions simply done what might have been expected, that is
terminally to puncture this oratorical afflatus. But no—Pecksniff's
self-possession is indomitable, and the jarring 'oysters' are absorbed
into the stately idiom and pacing of his ingratiating address. His
signature rhythm is that of the English church sermon at its most
bland. It consists typically of long, elaborate periods ('ornamental
sentences' as the narrator observes) in which one can almost hear
the gentle sliding of the voice up and down the scale to achieve
those sanctimonious cadences. The symptom of his being at all
ruffled appears only in a temporary shortening of his usual sentence-
lengths or periods—'...nor oysters. But by no means unlike oysters;
a very excellent idea; thank you...'—before he can resume his usual
pace and poise.

    The timing of interruptions to the magnificent monologues con-
structed by such characters is carefully judged by Dickens for comic
effect. Here is another example—the grand dinner party in *Our
Mutual Friend* (Book 1, Chapter 11) given by Mr and Mrs Podsnap,
to which a Frenchman has been invited. Although not formally a
monologue, it is in effect one. It is one of Dickens's funniest scenes
and I reproduce it at length:

    'How Do You Like London?' Mr Podsnap now inquired [of the
Frenchman] from his station of host, as if he were administering
something in the nature of a powder or potion to the deaf child;
'London, Londres, London?'
    The foreign gentleman admired it.
    'You find it Very Large?' said Mr Podsnap, spaciously.
    The foreign gentleman found it very large.
    'And Very Rich?'
    The foreign gentleman found it, without doubt, enormément riche.

'Enormously Rich, We say,' returned Mr Podsnap, in a condescending manner. 'Our English adverbs do Not terminate in Mong, and We Pronounce the "ch" as if there were a "t" before it. We say Ritch.'

'Reetch,' remarked the foreign gentleman.

'And Do You Find, Sir,' pursued Mr Podsnap, with dignity, 'Many Evidences that Strike You, of our British Constitution in the Streets Of The World's Metropolis, London, Londres, London?'

The foreign gentleman begged to be pardoned, but did not altogether understand.

'The Constitution Britannique,' Mr Podsnap explained, as if he were teaching in an infant school. 'We Say British, But You Say Britannique, You Know' (forgivingly, as if that were not his fault). 'The Constitution, Sir.'

The foreign gentleman said, 'Mais, yees; I know eem.'

A youngish sallowish gentleman in spectacles, with a lumpy forehead, seated in a supplementary chair at a corner of the table, here caused a profound sensation by saying, in a raised voice, 'ESKER,' and then stopping dead.

'Mais oui,' said the foreign gentleman, turning towards him. 'Est-ce que? Quoi donc?'

But the gentleman with the lumpy forehead having for the time delivered himself of all that he found behind his lumps, spake for the time no more.

'I Was Inquiring,' said Mr Podsnap, resuming the thread of his discourse, 'Whether You Have Observed in our Streets as We should say, Upon our Pavvy as You would say, any Tokens—'

The foreign gentleman, with patient courtesy entreated pardon; 'But what was tokenz?'

'Marks,' said Mr Podsnap; 'Signs, you know, Appearances—Traces.'

'Ah! Of a Orse?' inquired the foreign gentleman.

'We call it Horse,' said Mr Podsnap, with forbearance. 'In England, Angleterre, England, We Aspirate the "H," and We Say "Horse." Only our Lower Classes Say "Orse!"'

'Pardon,' said the foreign gentleman; 'I am alwiz wrong!'

'Our Language,' said Mr Podsnap, with a gracious consciousness of being always right, 'is Difficult. Ours is a Copious Language, and Trying to Strangers. I will not Pursue my Question.'

But the lumpy gentleman, unwilling to give it up, again madly said, 'ESKER,' and again spake no more.

'It merely referred,' Mr Podsnap explained, with a sense of meritorious proprietorship, 'to Our Constitution, Sir. We Englishmen are

Very Proud of our Constitution, Sir. It Was Bestowed Upon Us By Providence. No Other Country is so Favoured as This Country.'

'And ozer countries?—' the foreign gentleman was beginning, when Mr Podsnap put him right again.

'We do not say Ozer; we say Other: the letters are "T" and "H;" You say Tay and Aish, You Know; (still with clemency). The sound is "th"—"th!"'

'And OTHER countries,' said the foreign gentleman. 'They do how?'

'They do, Sir,' returned Mr Podsnap, gravely shaking his head; 'they do—I am sorry to be obliged to say it—AS they do.' [...] So it is. It was the Charter of the Land. This Island was Blest, Sir, to the Direct Exclusion of such Other Countries as—as there may happen to be. And if we were all Englishmen present, I would say,' added Mr Podsnap, looking round upon his compatriots, and sounding solemnly with his theme, 'that there is in the Englishman a combination of qualities, a modesty, an independence, a responsibility, a repose, combined with an absence of everything calculated to call a blush into the cheek of a young person, which one would seek in vain among the Nations of the Earth.'

This is, of course, a travesty of hospitality, grotesquely funny as it steadily exposes the pretensions and contradictions in cultural prejudices. Podsnap's gentility is all surface show and noise; it is the Frenchman, with his 'patient courtesy', who has the true gentlemanly instinct graciously to put others at their ease. It is, ironically, he who embodies that 'combination of qualities' which Podsnap appropriates as exclusively the characteristic of the Englishman—modesty, independence and repose—and this is, in effect, the punchline of this extended joke.

If we examine this scene more closely, its comic pacing and distinctive rhythms come through clearly. The dinner-table exchange can hardly be called a conversation (as the formal occasion conventionally requires). Podsnap engages the foreign gentleman only in order to condescend to him and give him an unsolicited tutorial in English usage. His opening questions are rhetorical, not any kind of invitation to the guest to offer his independent opinions on London; and since Podsnap and the rest of the company have already decided to infantilize the visitor ('as if he were a child who was hard of hearing'), his opinions would anyway be of little interest to them.

To keep our comic distance on the scene, the narrator ironically preserves the victim in the amber of Podsnappian prejudice by fixing him throughout as 'the foreign gentleman', with no significant human individuality, not even a name. These initial positions are established and sustained throughout the scene, and from them Dickens creates a comic routine, with refrain and repetition, in a series of exchanges, all of much the same kind: Podsnappian sallies and jingoistic bluster counterpointed by the calm, courteous compliance of the Frenchman. It amounts to a discontinuous monologue by Podsnap on Britishness and the English language, with the rest of the company cast as audience. There are occasional minor interruptions from the Frenchman, but these are ignored or seized on as cues for correcting anything that is 'not 'English', linguistically or culturally.

Podsnap dominates, sonorous and pedantic. The play between the muted, fragmentary responses of the guest and the measured tread of Podsnap's heavily capitalized sentences, with the repeated reproof 'We Say…', establishes a rhythmical pattern. This is temporarily interrupted by two sensational disturbances in the course of the dinner, when the gentleman with the lumpy forehead makes an abortive overture to the foreign guest: 'ESKER…'. These riveting interventions are finely timed within the routine so that it doesn't become too 'routine'. They punctuate the near-monologue *just* short of the points where Podsnap's overbearing corrections might become a little too repetitive.

'Oysters' and 'ESKER': these idiotic intrusions on the dignity of Pecksniff and Podsnap jolt the stately occasion and break the routine in order to refresh it. Dickens's monologue specialists develop a special kind of rhythmical monotony in their speech. It is an expression of their comical rigidity as characters. That is why coarse interruptions can be so funny, the conversational counterpart to watching their ponderous gait being tripped up in the street. This is typified in Mr Podsnap. Unlike Micawber and Pecksniff, he is designed to represent a national type: his outlook epitomises an arrogant insularity and conventionality which is infecting the cultural life of the country and bullying the creative arts into compliance with a dull, rigidly routinized domestic realism:

> Elsewhere, the world got up at eight, shaved close at a quarter-past, breakfasted at nine, went to the City at ten, came home at half-past five,

and dined at seven. Mr Podsnap's notions of the Arts in their integrity might have been stated thus. Literature; large print, respectfully descriptive of getting up at eight, shaving close at a quarter past, breakfasting at nine, going to the City at ten, coming home at half-past five, and dining at seven. Painting and Sculpture; models and portraits representing Professors of getting up at eight, shaving close at a quarter past, breakfasting at nine, going to the City at ten, coming home at half-past five, and dining at seven. Music; a respectable performance (without variations) on stringed and wind instruments, sedately expressive of getting up at eight, shaving close at a quarter past, breakfasting at nine, going to the City at ten, coming home at half-past five, and dining at seven. Nothing else to be permitted to those same vagrants the Arts, on pain of excommunication. Nothing else To Be—anywhere!

This formidable paragraph is a test for gauging the limits of repetition for comic purposes (and again Dickens can sometimes misjudge repetitiousness). Three gettings-up-at-eight is just about right; to add a fourth would be excessive. The first run, 'Literature...', establishes the Podsnappian prescription. The second, 'Painting and Sculpture...', reinforces it, complete again in all its verbatim dullness. The third, 'Music...', is an inspired risk (probably only Dickens would have gone for it), since the reader would not have expected the whole detailed routine to be repeated *yet again*.

Having given readings of this episode on many occasions, I have been aware of the fairly consistent patterns of laughter (if I am lucky), as follows. The Literature sentence usually gets a subdued chuckle or two as the Podsnappian definition is first absorbed. The Painting and Sculpture deadpan repetition gets laughter steadily throughout. The Music sentence has a teasingly protracted overture compared with the other two; by the time one is on the verge of the 'getting-up-at-eight...' one can sense the audience squirming slightly—oh no...not *again!*...—and a slight pause just at that point milks it nicely: '...wind instruments, sedately expressive of [—wait for it—] getting up at eight....'. This often gets the biggest laugh, close to that 'squirm' point of the routine, but it is short-lived. Thereafter, through the rest of the sentence it steadily peters out, and it is clear that the comic motif has peaked. A fourth run would not trigger laughter.

Dickens has made his comic-timing calculations here, just as he did in his manuscript cutting away of those superfluous sentences in the *Carol*'s facetious observations on *Hamlet*. In the case of the

Podsnap view of the Arts, three samples are enough to work the joke. Stand-up comedy is familiar with a timing technique known as 'rule of three', as Oliver Double explains:

> The classic version of the three-part list joke has been defined as 'Establish, Reinforce, Surprise!' A lot of comedy works by deviating from an expected pattern. The first part of the list establishes the pattern, the second reinforces it and the third subverts it.

Dickens works the three-part list in the paragraph just quoted. The 'Surprise' on the third is not the 'deviation from an expected pattern', but its repetition; however, that repetition surprises expectations that surely he would not dare to run the whole thing *yet again*.

We turn now to one of the supreme monologue specialists, Mrs Gamp. In the following scene from *Chuzzlewit*, Chapter 19, Pecksniff has arrived at Mrs Gamp's house to ask her to attend the laying out of the body of Anthony Chuzzlewit prior to the funeral. She greets him with her standard speech of stoical commiseration—'But it's what we must all come to...'

> 'You have become indifferent since then, I suppose?' said Mr. Pecksniff. 'Use is second nature, Mrs. Gamp.'
>
> 'You may well say second natur, sir,' returned that lady. 'One's first ways is to find sich things a trial to the feelings, and so is one's lasting custom. If it wasn't for the nerve a little sip of liquor gives me (I never was able to do more than taste it), I never could go through with what I sometimes has to do. "Mrs. Harris," I says, at the very last case as ever I acted in, which it was but a young person, "Mrs. Harris," I says, "leave the bottle on the chimley-piece, and don't ask me to take none, but let me put my lips to it when I am so dispoged, and then I will do what I'm engaged to do, according to the best of my ability." "Mrs. Gamp," she says, in answer, "if ever there was a sober creetur to be got at eighteen pence a day for working people, and three and six for gentlefolks—night watching,"' said Mrs. Gamp with emphasis, '"being a extra charge—you are that inwallable person." "Mrs. Harris," I says to her, "don't name the charge, for if I could afford to lay all my feller creeturs out for nothink, I would gladly do it, sich is the love I bears 'em. But what I always says to them as has the management of matters, Mrs. Harris:"' here she kept her eye on Mr. Pecksniff: '"be they gents or be they ladies, is, don't ask me whether I won't take none, or whether I will, but leave the bottle on the chimley-piece, and let me put my lips to it when I am so dispoged."'

This is effectively Mrs Gamp's business card, a well-rehearsed ('what I always says to them...') self-introduction and indication of her 'terms and conditions' of work. It has the sound of a refrain, even in the reported exchange between herself and Mrs Harris. She has to strike the right balance, the appropriate register, in both observing the solemnity of the occasion and at the same time detailing her professional expectations. Much of this is to do with the pacing of her speech, organized around those solemn repetitions—'leave the bottle on the chimley-piece', '"Mrs Harris" I says...', 'I always says...'. Like the monologue style of Pecksniff or Podsnap, once her speech gets into its stride, it has a sublime, impregnable monotony in its delivery. Mrs Gamp's sanctimonious cadences have become ritualized as part of her professional identity, and she seems unable to adapt her register to the circumstances of ordinary conversation. She is relentlessly self-centred: 'I have to say [...] I have been [...] I hope I knows [...] I have seen [...] I am not [...]'. The monotony of her phrasing is matched by the thematic monotony, and both contribute to her signature music:

> 'It is not much as I have to say, when people is a-mourning for the dead and gone,' said Mrs. Gamp; 'but what I have to say is *to* the pint and purpose, and no offence intended, must be so considered. I have been at a many places in my time, gentlemen, and I hope I knows what my duties is, and how the same should be performed: in course, if I did not, it would be very strange, and very wrong in sich a gentleman as Mr. Mould, which has undertook the highest families in this land, and given every satisfaction, so to recommend me as he does. I have seen a deal of trouble my own self,' said Mrs. Gamp, laying greater and greater stress upon her words, 'and I can feel for them as has their feelings tried: but I am not a Rooshan or a Prooshan, and consequently cannot suffer Spies to be set over me.'

Part of what Dickens is expecting us to laugh at is, of course, her mangled English ('Who deniges of it, Betsey?'), but her full comic presence is carried in the dirge-like music of her speech, which drags those mutilations along in its wave-like rhythms. It is all the funnier—on the incongruity principle of laughter—to witness these deformed passengers in such a splendid, solemn equipage.

How did Dickens hear Mrs Gamp's speech? He said that 'every word uttered by his characters was distinctly *heard* by him before it was written down'. Interesting evidence of this comes from a report, by Kate Field, of Dickens's public reading, 'Mrs Gamp':

> Take a comb, cover it with tissue paper, and attempt to sing through it, and you have an admirable idea of the quality of Mrs. Gamp's vocal organ, provided you make the proper allowance for an inordinate use of snuff [...]. There is an intellectual ponderosity about her that renders an exclamation impossible [...]. She scorns staccato passages, and her vocalization may be said to be confined to the use of semi-breves, on which she lingers as if desirous of developing her voice by what is technically known as 'swelling.' She holds all notions of light and shade in contempt, and with monotonous cadence produces effects on her hearers undreamed of by her readers [... and she addresses Mrs Harris] with a pendulum wag to her head in the *tempo* of a funeral march.

Mrs Gamp's 'snuffy, husky, unctuous' voice (as another witness to these readings described it) organizes its speech metronomically. She 'scorns staccato passages', and leaves these to those who might interrupt her. Like Pecksniff and Micawber, her musical mode is legato.

Micawber is another sublime monologue specialist, but with a difference. He doesn't have an imaginary interlocutor to punctuate his elaborate addresses, but he endearingly interrupts himself, breaking the dominant legato patterns and 'swellings' of his own speech.

> [David is introduced to Mr Micawber with whose family he is to lodge in London] 'Under the impression,' said Mr. Micawber, 'that your peregrinations in this metropolis have not as yet been extensive, and that you might have some difficulty in penetrating the arcana of the Modern Babylon in the direction of the City Road,—in short,' said Mr. Micawber, in another burst of confidence, 'that you might lose yourself—I shall be happy to call this evening, and install you in the knowledge of the nearest way.' (*Copperfield*, Chapter 11)

> 'The twins no longer derive their sustenance from Nature's founts—in short,' said Mr. Micawber, in one of his bursts of confidence, 'they are weaned...'
> ... 'I have no scruple in saying, in the presence of our friends here, that I am a man who has, for some years, contended against the pressure of pecuniary difficulties.' I knew he was certain to say something of this kind; he always would be so boastful about his difficulties.

'Sometimes I have risen superior to my difficulties. Sometimes my
difficulties have—in short, have floored me. (Chapter 17)

The sharp, explosive discrepancies in register between ornate
formality and blunt vernacular are funny in the same way that
shocking incongruity can trigger laughter (as we shall see in the
next essay): the sudden bathetic relief from the strain or tension
generated by elevated language. Usually in Dickens this takes the
form of one character, or the mischievous narrator, puncturing
the pomposity of another character. But in Micawber's speeches,
he does this shock switch himself as he suddenly reins in his
stately, 'swelling' polysyllabics with 'in short,...'; and that 'in
short' ushers in a blunt monosyllable—'lose [yourself]', 'weaned',
'floored'. It seems that Micawber himself is relieved to escape the
strain of his own magniloquence, because the 'in short...' pull-up
is usually accompanied by a 'burst of confidence'. As I have
argued elsewhere, Micawber's discourse is the perfect linguistic
analogue to the character's shabby-gentility: his ornately-dressed
speech seems unable to support itself for long in the manner to
which it aspires.

What I have discussed so far in his speech-style is a matter of the
register, the linguistic switch. The timing, however, is key to making
this linguistic jolt comically effective. There are seldom more than
half a dozen lines of orotund speech before Micawber abruptly
checks his flow, just enough to establish the impressive movement of
his swelling periods—his signature rhythm. When Dickens in his
public readings impersonated Micawber, he tipped backward and
forward, first on his heels and then on his toes. That rocking motion
underscored the signature rhythms, much as Mrs Gamp's 'pendulum
wag' of her head helped to conduct her speech rhythms. David Copperfield, when first introduced to Micawber, noticed 'a certain condescending roll' in Micawber's voice, and that deftly characterizes
the tempo of his formal address. His legato swell hits the breakwater
just as it seems to be gathering full momentum, and just at the point
where the reader has fully tuned into its stately music, because that
is precisely when the comic jolt is best positioned. Were Micawber to
run on for a dozen lines or more in his high genteel style, it would
have a very different effect; he would be a different character (he

might become Mr Dorrit). In which case it would have to be up to another character to make the comic-bathetic interruption.

All four soloists, Pecksniff, Gamp, Micawber and Podsnap, are great performers. They have a theatricality about them, as has often been observed. Though they may not all derive from stock theatrical types (as Sam Weller, for instance, is supposed to have done), they nonetheless play their roles in the novels with a consciousness of projecting a part, and this is evident in their carefully crafted speeches which are designed to 'hold the stage'.

Cross-Talk Rhythms

Another comic technique in which timing is crucial originated again probably from Dickens's saturation in popular theatre. This is the cross-talk act, a rapid exchange between two characters often involving ridiculous misunderstandings (two befuddled drunks on a train stopping at Wembley Station: 'Is this Wembley?' 'No, it's Thursday.' 'So am I—let's go and have a drink'). Timing in the performance of the cross-talk act is vital. Dickens has a fine ear for the tempo of such episodes, and he will sometimes use the cross-talk mode to accentuate the comical misunderstandings between different classes. In the following scene from *Dombey and Son* (Chapter 2) the genteel Miss Tox introduces the working-class Toodle family (the father, the 'apple-faced' man, works on the railways) to the formidable Mrs Chick, Mr Dombey's sister:

> '...Five children. Youngest six weeks. The fine little boy with the blister on his nose is the eldest. The blister, I believe,' said Miss Tox, looking round upon the family, 'is not constitutional, but accidental?'
>
> The apple-faced man was understood to growl, 'Flat iron.'
>
> 'I beg your pardon, Sir,' said Miss Tox, 'did you?—'
>
> 'Flat iron,' he repeated.
>
> 'Oh yes,' said Miss Tox. 'Yes! quite true. I forgot. The little creature, in his mother's absence, smelt a warm flat iron. You're quite right, Sir. You were going to have the goodness—inform me, when we arrived at the door that you were by trade, a—'
>
> 'Stoker,' said the man.
>
> 'A choker!' said Miss Tox, quite aghast.

'Stoker,' said the man. 'Steam ingine.'

'Oh-h! Yes!' returned Miss Tox, looking thoughtfully at him, and seeming still to have but a very imperfect understanding of his meaning.

'And how do you like it, Sir?'

'Which, Mum?' said the man.

'That,' replied Miss Tox. 'Your trade.'

'Oh! Pretty well, Mum. The ashes sometimes gets in here;' touching his chest: 'and makes a man speak gruff, as at the present time. But it *is* ashes, Mum, not crustiness.'

Miss Tox seemed to be so little enlightened by this reply, as to find a difficulty in pursuing the subject.

The pacing is exquisite. It needs to be so constructed as to ensure that we can hear and see the diffidence and delicacy, the stumbles and hesitations, of Miss Tox as she struggles to mediate the rough-and-ready Toodles to the imperious Mrs Chick. Miss Tox, hampered in this assignment by the socially narrow world in which she lives, is slow on the uptake and over-deliberate in her genteel speech; and that makes for a hilarious counterpointing with Toodle's gruff, clipped responses. Out of this comes the whole comic tempo of the piece, and it is just this tempo that Dickens wants to exploit to the full at this juncture, so that the reader gets the immediate shock impact and embarrassment of it. It is important to the dynamics of the scene for the rhythm of the exchange between the voices to determine the tempo, and this entails minimal interruption from narratorial 'stage directions'; i.e. the minimum of mediation by the narrator.

The Tox–Toodle exchange is funny in its zig-zag moments of mutual incomprehension conducted in a staccato conversation. Another example of Dickens's exploitation of the comic rhythms of conversation is one where the two participants are not so far apart socially. In *Our Mutual Friend* the Golden Dustman, Mr Boffin, has the idea of employing someone to read to him and his wife, and (in Book 1, Chapter 5) approaches the rogue Silas Wegg with the proposition, after he has calculated (on Wegg's stool, with a piece of chalk) what he thinks an appropriate fee:

'…and you mount up to thirty long'uns. A round'un! Half a crown!'

Pointing to this result as a large and satisfactory one, Mr Boffin smeared it out with his moistened glove, and sat down on the remains.

'Half a crown,' said Wegg, meditating. 'Yes. (It ain't much, sir.) Half a crown.'

'Per week, you know.'

'Per week. Yes. As to the amount of strain upon the intellect now. Was you thinking at all of poetry?' Mr Wegg inquired, musing.

'Would it come dearer?' Mr Boffin asked.

'It would come dearer,' Mr Wegg returned. 'For when a person comes to grind off poetry night after night, it is but right he should expect to be paid for its weakening effect on his mind.'

'To tell you the truth Wegg,' said Boffin, 'I wasn't thinking of poetry, except in so fur as this:—If you was to happen now and then to feel yourself in the mind to tip me and Mrs Boffin one of your ballads, why then we should drop into poetry.'

'I follow you, sir,' said Wegg. 'But not being a regular musical professional, I should be loath to engage myself for that; and therefore when I dropped into poetry, I should ask to be considered so fur, in the light of a friend.'

At this, Mr Boffin's eyes sparkled, and he shook Silas earnestly by the hand.

The tempo of this sequence of stages in the delicate negotiation is finely judged. It rocks gracefully to and fro (nudged into that rhythm by Wegg), and with each rock it advances just a shade further towards securing the wishes of the wily Wegg. Boffin is bluff and affable, but becomes increasingly anxious as Wegg manoeuvres around him (Wegg indeed 'had stimulated this anxiety by his hard reserve of manner, and […] had begun to understand his man very well'). The two participants are thus strongly contrasted in manner (open and impulsive vs close and calculating), but are drawn into tighter relationship by the distinctive rhythm of the exchange. This is generated by the repetitions, as Wegg consistently echoes each of the key terms introduced by Boffin, and then mock-reflectively draws him further into his snares: 'half a crown…per week…dearer…drop into poetry…'. It epitomizes that description given by Neil Norrick of comic timing in its broader scope: 'the ebb and flow of given and new information highlighted by repetition and formulaic phrasing along with rhythms of hesitation and more fluent passages'.

Repetition and formulaic phrasing is part of Dickens's trademark in his comic narratives and characters' speech styles. But he can also fall into the same patterns when representing strong passions, just as he modulates into blank verse sometimes when he is emotionally stirred by his subject (as in his apostrophizing the death of Little Nell). An example of the former comes in *Great Expectations* when the grown-up Estella harshly confronts Miss Havisham with the consequences of her upbringing (Chapter 38), and, as in the Wegg–Boffin exchange, each party picks up on the salient words or phrases of the other:

> 'Soon forgotten!' moaned Miss Havisham. 'Times soon forgotten!'
>
> 'No, not forgotten,' retorted Estella. 'Not forgotten, but treasured up in my memory. When have you found me false to your teaching? When have you found me unmindful of your lessons? When have you found me giving admission here,' she touched her bosom with her hand, 'to anything that you excluded? Be just to me.'
>
> 'So proud, so proud!' moaned Miss Havisham, pushing away her grey hair with both her hands.
>
> 'Who taught me to be proud?' returned Estella. 'Who praised me when I learnt my lesson?'
>
> 'So hard, so hard!' moaned Miss Havisham, with her former action.
>
> 'Who taught me to be hard?' returned Estella. 'Who praised me when I learnt my lesson?'
>
> 'But to be proud and hard to *me*!' Miss Havisham quite shrieked, as she stretched out her arms. 'Estella, Estella, Estella, to be proud and hard to *me*!'

The incantatory manner here, structured by repetition and refrain, sounds unnatural to modern ears, especially in speech that is supposedly generated by raw tempestuous feelings. Dickens seems to have assumed the artificial conventions of melodrama in such oratorical posturings and formalized rhythms of dialogue. The usual critical line is that Dickens writes much more freely in his comedy, where he can relax from this strained register into his natural rhythm and into more naturalistic language. But, as Edgar Rosenberg has pointed out, evidence from Dickens's manuscript of *Great Expectations* indicates that passages such as the one just quoted have hardly any erasures: 'these things, one feels, Dickens could do in his sleep'. Whereas, for example, the composition of the magnificent comedy of Wopsle's *Hamlet* 'roused Dickens to the most finicky and fastidious exertions and [...] he blotted a thousandfold in an effort to get them quite right'.

Dickens's comedy, then, for all its apparently anarchic spontaneity, can be the result of very painstaking composition indeed. It can also, as we have seen in the examples from Podsnap, Gamp and Micawber, be fashioned in quite a stylized manner in terms of pacing and rhythm, whether in a monologue or brisk dialogue, not unlike the rhetorical choreography of his moments of pathos and passion.

Repetition and Timing in Action

The public readings give us some examples of how Dickens elaborated his comic timing, how he heard what he wrote. One such comes from his reading of 'Bob Sawyer's Party', containing Jack Hopkins's preposterous anecdote of the boy who swallowed his sister's necklace beads (all twenty-five of them) and could then be heard rattling. Here is the episode in *Pickwick*, Chapter 32:

> 'A few days afterwards, the family were at dinner—baked shoulder of mutton, and potatoes under it—the child, who wasn't hungry, was playing about the room, when suddenly there was heard a devil of a noise, like a small hailstorm. "Don't do that, my boy," said the father. "I ain't a doin' nothing," said the child. "Well, don't do it again," said the father'.

In performing this as a reading, Dickens stylized the inflections in the father's two speeches. It was represented diagrammatically as follows by one who witnessed the reading:

                                                          boy!"

            "*Don't*   my

                Do that,

The boy says he wasn't doing anything, and the father replies:

                                                      gain!"

                                              a-

            "Well,   do it

                don't

Absurdly rigid repetition both of language and delivery mode can
be as funny as persistent rigidity of character (Bergson's key source
of laughter). Dickens can use insistent patterns of repetition, carefully crafted, to structure both his comic and melodramatic writing.
We have seen one example of the comical repetition in Podsnap's
notion of the Arts ('getting up eight...'). A more elaborate instance
comes in the well-known description of the Circumlocution Office
in Chapter 10 of *Little Dorrit*:

> It is true that How not to do it was the great study and object of all
> public departments and professional politicians all round the Circum-
> locution Office. It is true that every new premier and every new gov-
> ernment, coming in because they had upheld a certain thing as
> necessary to be done, were no sooner come in than they applied their
> utmost faculties to discovering How not to do it. It is true that from
> the moment when a general election was over, every returned man
> who had been raving on hustings because it hadn't been done, and who
> had been asking the friends of the honourable gentleman in the oppo-
> site interest on pain of impeachment to tell him why it hadn't been
> done, and who had been asserting that it must be done, and who had
> been pledging himself that it should be done, began to devise, How it
> was not to be done. It is true that the debates of both Houses of
> Parliament the whole session through, uniformly tended to the pro-
> tracted deliberation, How not to do it. It is true that the royal speech
> at the opening of such session virtually said, My lords and gentlemen,
> you have a considerable stroke of work to do, and you will please to
> retire to your respective chambers, and discuss, How not to do it.

'HOW NOT TO DO IT' (meaning how to avoid doing anything,
rather than how to mis-do it) is the mission statement of the Circumlocution Office. That is the basic joke: the executive branch of
government has developed a serious policy of not executing anything at all. The satirical novelist might have given a paragraph to
that joke and then got on with the plot. But typically Dickens plays
this out at great length, now and again exploiting the manner of
high-toned statesmanship to give gravitas to this abysmal mandate.
Thus a single witty stroke, intellectually appealing, becomes more
broadly funny by expanding itself luxuriously within the solemn
ceremonials that give legislative authority to this policy, through
party-manifesto declaration and the Queen's speech in opening

Parliament. A whimsical, surreal, satirical conception is thereby actually rooted and begins to flower preposterously in the novel's social reality. The sustaining of this through several paragraphs of variations on a theme is breathtaking.

But again, even this splendid burlesque wouldn't be so *viscerally* funny without the exquisite timing. Dickens uses a mélange of authorial description, free indirect discourse, and ('virtually') direct speech, and all this is developed within a framework of sonorous anaphora and epistrophe—'It is true that [...] How not to do it', over and over. It is an elaborate oratorical orchestration. In this he is aping the conventional inflections of parliamentary oratory, with its repetitive soaring and diving, generating a kind of music to which he was hilariously sensitive. 'Why, why, above all,' he asks in his 1851 essay for *Household Words* (28 June), 'A Few Conventionalities', 'in either house of Parliament must the English language be set to music—bad and conventional beyond any parallel on earth—and delivered, in a manner barely expressible to the eye as follows:

		night	
	to		
Sir when I came do	this house		
	o		
	o		
wn to			

		ters	
	Minis		
	ty's		
I found Her	jes		
Ma			

Most of Dickens's great monologue characters suffer from verbal superfluity cast into a musical form. They are inordinately long-winded, but that verbosity is carefully orchestrated, and—as this diagram suggests—they were probably more finely tuned in Dickens's mind's ear in terms of patterns of cadence and inflection than he could represent on the page. If as narrator he wants to point up such characteristics in the delivery of his characters' speeches, he has to interrupt them in mid flow to provide the stage directions: and that can disturb as much as it might illuminate style and momentum.

This raises another issue to do with comic timing: when is the precisely right moment for inserting into a scene or speech a detail that upsets the projection of dignity? Because prose has to be sequential, segmental, the undercutting detail cannot happen synchronically, in the way that it can with a visual joke. Take for instance a pantomime scene where a dignitary is strutting about condescending to the townsfolk and unaware that a prankster has attached a sign to his back saying 'I am an ass—please kick me'. On stage, the discrepancy between his self-importance and the rude sign can fuel laughter all the time he is giving himself airs; both are seen simultaneously. But the writer cannot reproduce this simultaneity. A decision has to be made when first to introduce the sign once the character appears, and then when and how often to remind the reader of its ridiculing presence. If the two (the character and the placard) are introduced more or less simultaneously, in, say, the opening sentence, then the comic shock of the irreverent sign is proportionately decreased, since that shock depends on the sudden humiliation of someone whose self-importance we have had time to accept. The revelation of the sign can be delayed until the end of the description, allowing that self-importance to be fully established and *felt*. Or the revelation can interrupt the performance of self-importance in midflow. The judgement about such timing is crucial. Here is an example from *Nicholas Nickleby* (Chapter 29).

Nicholas, who has been playing in Crummles's productions, receives a formal letter from Mr Lenville, the chief tragic actor in the troupe, who has been consistently upstaged by Nicholas, to his mortification. The letter summoning Nicholas to appear in public to have his nose pulled is delivered by Mr Folair, whose theatrical hauteur is accentuated by a very tall hat and a glass-handled cane (very much in the foppish mode of Osric delivering Laertes's challenge to Hamlet). Mr Folair hands over the letter and then, while Nicholas reads, sits 'knitting his brow and pursing up his mouth with great dignity [...] with his eyes steadily fixed upon the ceiling'.

'Do you know the contents of this note, sir?' [Nicholas] asked, at length.

'Yes,' rejoined Mr Folair, looking round for an instant, and immediately carrying his eyes back again to the ceiling.

'And how dare you bring it here, sir?' asked Nicholas, tearing it into very little pieces, and jerking it in a shower towards the messenger. 'Had you no fear of being kicked downstairs, sir?'

Mr Folair turned his head—now ornamented with several fragments of the note—towards Nicholas, and with the same imperturbable dignity, briefly replied 'No.'

'Then,' said Nicholas, taking up the tall hat and tossing it towards the door, 'you had better follow that article of your dress, sir, or you may find yourself very disagreeably deceived, and that within a dozen seconds.'

'I say, Johnson,' remonstrated Mr Folair, suddenly losing all his dignity, 'none of that, you know. No tricks with a gentleman's wardrobe.'

By the end, Folair's fragile dignity is in tatters along with his dismantled 'wardrobe'. But the funniest part of that process comes in the fourth paragraph where the shower of letter scraps lands on him. Here timing is executed with precision. Dickens could have used the preceding paragraph to describe this effect in the same moment as the letter is torn up and thrown: for instance, 'jerking it in a shower towards the messenger *where it floated down onto his head...*'. That is how we would *see* it happening in performance. But the mind's eye in reading is controlled adroitly by the writer. Dickens delays the comic information just a fraction longer, in order to sustain Folair's dignity with a further theatrical inclination of his head towards Nicholas—a head wholly unaware that it is now wearing odd shreds of paper. Dickens times the introduction of the humiliation so that it runs right up against that stage-gesture of dignity; and it is all the funnier in its quietly devastating effect by being delivered in a low-key manner, parenthetically.

Throughout writing this essay I have wondered how much Dickens might have tried these effects *viva voce*, in his study, in order to test the timing before writing. We know he composed out loud and made faces and mutterings into mirrors as he developed characters and stories, but that's not the same as trying it out on an audience (like a stand-up comic). The occasional anecdotes from his middle and later years suggested that he did practise this, at least from time to time. For instance, Wilkie Collins recalled Dickens reading parts of the manuscript of *Bleak House* to his household, 'speaking the dialogue [...] and dramatically as if he was acting [...] and making his audience laugh and cry with equal fervour'. With such an ear and eye for delivery of humorous speech and action it would be surprising if he didn't try out his written timing 'live'.

4

Laughter and Incongruity

'I think it is my infirmity to fancy or perceive relations in things which are not apparent generally.'

Dickens made this confession of his constitutional 'infirmity' in the course of a letter to his fellow novelist, Bulwer Lytton. He is responding probably to some gentle criticism of his writing by a friend whose judgement he respects. A little later in the letter there is another wry confession: 'I have such an inexpressible enjoyment of what I see in a droll light that I dare say I pet it as if it were a spoilt child'. What he is here describing in an apparently apologetic manner are two of his greatest gifts as a writer. The perception of relations between apparently unlike things is the key to Dickens's extravagant metaphorical practices. It is also fundamental to his comic technique, in all its petted extravagance, as I hope to show in the present essay.

The zestful shock of incongruity has long been recognized as one of the prime triggers of laughter, and I want to spend a bit of time on the various theories of humorous incongruity before exploring Dickens's dependence on it.

Incongruity and 'Bisociation'

> [Suitor] 'Sir, I would like to ask for your daughter's hand.'
> [Prospective father-in-law] 'Why not? You have already had the rest.'

This exchange comes from a film script and is quoted by Arthur Koestler in order to illustrate his theory of 'bisociation', the comical effect of an abrupt incongruity in the process of being resolved. Bisociation, according to Koestler, is 'the perceiving a situation or idea in two self-consistent but mutually incompatible frames of reference or associative contexts':

> [It is] the sudden clash [or 'delightful mental jolt'] between [...] two mutually exclusive codes of rules—or associative contexts, or cognitive holons—which produces the comic effect. It compels us to perceive the situation in two self-consistent but incompatible frames of reference at the same time; it makes us function simultaneously on two different wave-lengths.

Thus, in the film dialogue already quoted, 'the daughter's "hand" is perceived first in a metaphorical frame of reference, then suddenly in a literal, bodily context'. This abrupt juxtaposition triggers the laugh. As Bergson remarked, 'once our attention is fixed on the material aspect of a metaphor, the idea expressed becomes comic.' The suddenness of the transition between the two—the having to hold the two in a bisociative relation which recognizes the incongruity at the same time as the grotesque logical continuity—constitutes a kind of shock: laughter is the physiological expression of that shock. It doesn't last long; the sting goes out of it after the first delivery, and on repetition the laughter subsides into a chuckle or just a smile.

Whatever one thinks of the theory (and it acquired extra currency and authority when Koestler featured it in his entry for 'Humour and wit' in the *Encyclopaedia Britannica*) the nature of the effect of calculated incongruity on humour has preoccupied many writers. The eighteenth-century Scottish philosopher Alexander Gerard expressed its function and scope with methodical clarity in his *Essay on Taste* (1756): '[Ridicule's] object is in general *incongruity*, or a surprising and uncommon mixture of *relation* and *contrariety* in things. More explicitly [sic]; it is gratified by an *inconsistence* and *dissonance* of circumstances in the *same* object; or in objects nearly *related* in the main; or by a *similitude* or *relation* unexpected between things on the whole *opposite* and *unlike*'. Precisely the symptom of Dickens's 'infirmity'.

A century after Alexander Gerard, Sidney Smith continued to accept incongruity as the key element in humour: 'the discriminating cause [of laughter] is *incongruity*, or the conjunction of objects and circumstances not usually combined'. Another writer transferred the emphasis more on to the laugher's own mental state: 'Humour is a sense of incongruous emotions' (this, we shall see later, is especially pertinent to Dickens's treatment of funerals). Leigh Hunt associated calculated incongruity with Wit: 'Wit is the clash and reconcilement of incongruities; the meeting of extremes round a corner; the flashing of an artificial light from one object to another, disclosing some unexpected resemblance or connection'.

Today, laughter and its triggers have come to be studied more clinically. Where the scientist Duchenne de Boulogne in the nineteenth century had used primitive electrodes to manipulate the muscles on his subjects' faces into expressions of laughter, experiments now conduct the subjects through fMRI scanners where brain activation can be monitored and analysed in response to laughter stimuli. According to a 2005 synthesizing article on the evolution and function of humour, 'What emerges from the literature [on these studies] is something of a consensus that incongruity and unexpectedness underlie much of formal laughter-evoking humor'. The incongruity that stimulates laughter is restricted to 'a sudden unexpected change in events that is perceived to be at once not serious and in a social context—that is, *nonserious social incongruity*'. Incongruity continues to be invoked in analyses of the phenomenon of mental 'frame-shifting' in reception of jokes, in the work of Seana Coulson and others. Humour theoreticians have been concerned to distinguish whether it is the perception of incongruity on its own that is the laughter stimulus or whether the effect is caused by incongruity *resolution*, that 'more subtle aspect of jokes which renders incongruity meaningful or appropriate by resolving or explaining it'. Thus humour is described as 'resolvable or meaningful incongruity', as against nonsense, which is 'pure or unresolved incongruity'.

Unresolved incongruity can be daunting. Nonsense is a form of chaos, which at a certain pitch can be terrifying as well as funny. John Bowen has some very shrewd observations on the relationship between humour and the sublime (the overwhelming and unrepresentable):

> Both humor and sublimity are concerned with the inadequacy or failure of human consciousness or reason, with the inability of the human mind to 'impose analytic and systematic projections on the

essentially irrational, instinctual, contingent flux of human affairs'
[quoting George Steiner]. It can be terrifying not to understand or
be able to express something; it can also be ludicrously funny [...].
Both the sublime and the ludicrous [...] take the mind outwards to
extreme things beyond ourselves, and resist reason and analysis. Our
bosoms throb; our sides split. They are two of the most distinctive
reflexes or modes of Dickens's writing.

Dickens takes extravagant risks of just this kind and readers do well
sometimes to take the brace position when flying with him 'to
extreme things beyond ourselves'. Bowen is absolutely right: Dickens's humour is intimately related to his power to move us in non-
humorous ways with his passionate imagination.

Koestler introduced his concept of 'bisociation' in his book *The
Act of Creation* (1964) where he treated its potential for conceptual
blending of apparent incongruities as fundamental to creativity in
general. What he called 'previously unconnected matrices of experience' are brought together, but the nature of that bringing-together
has different results. This was summed up by Alan Partington: 'If
the process of their connection is a *collision* then humour will ensue,
if a *fusion* intellectual understanding, if a *confrontation*, an aesthetic
experience'. Koestler returned to the topic again in his 1978 book,
Janus: A Summing Up. His theories continue to be much invoked in
subsequent discussions of the workings of laughter, though he has
not been treated kindly by some more recent analysts of humour: in
a 2006 issue of *Humor*, Salvatore Attardo referred to his 'journalistic
vulgarization' of incongruity theory.

Most of Koestler's examples of humorous bisociation are jokes,
such as the one cited earlier, about the suitor and father-in-law.
These jokes usually involve some narrative of degradation. Steven
Pinker summarizes:

> Humor [...] begins with a train of thought in one frame of reference
> that bumps up against an anomaly: an event or statement that makes
> no sense in the context of what has come before. The anomaly can
> be resolved by shifting to a different frame of reference, one in which
> the event does make some sense. And within *that* frame, someone's
> dignity has been downgraded.

The connections between incongruity, its bisociative function, and
ridiculous degradation was explored at some length in 'The Physiology

of Laughter' (1860) by the Victorian philosopher Herbert Spencer. Spencer argues that laughter is a release from strain or tension: 'the nervous excitement at any moment present to consciousness as feeling, must expend itself in some way or other [...] of the three classes of channels open to it, it must take one, two, or more, according to circumstances [and] the closure or obstruction of one, must increase the discharge through the others'.

After explaining the physiological phenomenon of laughter as a complex muscular spasm involving the sudden release of nervous tension under pressure, Spencer investigates what it is that might prompt such a reaction. As a practical illustration he suggests imagining ourselves watching a play in which a pair of lovers have been reconciled after a long and painful misunderstanding:

> The sentiments these fictitious personages have for the moment inspired you with, are not such as would lead you to rejoice in any indignity offered to them; but rather, such as would make you resent the indignity. And now, while you are contemplating the reconciliation with a pleasurable sympathy, there appears from behind the scenes a tame kid, which, having stared round at the audience, walks up to the lovers and sniffs at them. You cannot help joining in the roar which greets this contretemps.

So, what has happened to all that feeling generated by sympathetic engagement with the loving couple and their trials? It is still there, backed up in the nervous system:

> But now, this large amount of nervous energy, instead of being allowed to expend itself in producing an equivalent amount of the new thoughts and emotions which were nascent, is suddenly checked in its flow. The channels along which the discharge was about to take place, are closed. The new channel opened—that afforded by the appearance and proceedings of the kid—is a small one; the ideas and feelings suggested [by the kid] are not numerous and massive enough to carry off the nervous energy to be expended. The excess must therefore discharge itself in some other direction; and in the way already explained, there results an efflux through the motor nerves to various classes of the muscles, producing the half-convulsive actions we term laughter.

The spectator has been charged with powerful feelings—sympathy, hope, fear, romantic identification—generated by lofty actions and sentiments. These have to be channelled, and would have been channelled by the ensuing drama had it developed in the same key. But instead comes the shock confrontation with the reverse, with a sudden degrading incongruity: 'laughter naturally results only when consciousness is unawares transferred from great things to small—only when there is what we call a *descending* incongruity', as Spencer puts it. The pressure of those powerful feelings, blocked in their expected channels, needs release; and so they burst out in laughter. That, anyway, is the theory—the so-called 'relief theory'—which strongly influenced other thinkers on the subject: Freud, for example, in his ideas on laughter as the discharge of repressed psychic energy; and John Dewey, who believed that laughter was like 'the sigh of relief': 'this sudden relaxation of strain, so far as occurring through the medium of the breathing and vocal apparatus, is laughter'.

We can see how Spencer's scenario and his interpretation might relate to Koestler's 'bisociation' example. The drama of Spencer's lovers broadly corresponds to the elevated mode of the suitor's request for his beloved's hand in marriage. The arrival of the kid—the accidental intrusion of the lower mode—corresponds to the father's crudely deflationary response to the suitor. The suddenness of the switch the audience/listener has to make between the two frames of reference causes the jolt that creates laughter—the laughter of 'descending incongruity'.

Laughter can also be triggered by the sudden descent from the drama of high consequence not to coarseness, but to sheer inconsequentiality. In this context it accords with Kant's remark in the *Critique of Judgement*: '*Laughter is an affection arising from the sudden transformation of a strained expectation into nothing*'. Let us try out an example from Dickens. The following passage from *Martin Chuzzlewit* involves strained expectation meeting a bathetic conclusion. The pompous Dr Jobling is regaling an acquaintance with his own knowledge of anatomy and one of his former patients' ignorance of quite where his stomach was located:

> 'There was a patient of mine once [...] a gentleman who did me the honour to make a very handsome mention of me in his will—"in testimony," as he was pleased to say, "of the unremitting zeal, talent, and attention of my friend and medical attendant, John Jobling, Esquire, M.R.C.S.,"—who was so overcome by the idea of having all

his life laboured under an erroneous view of the locality of this important organ, that when I assured him, on my professional reputation, he was mistaken, he burst into tears, put out his hand, and said, "Jobling, God bless you!" Immediately afterwards he became speechless, and was ultimately buried at Brixton.' (Chapter 27)

The 'strain' is generated by the high formal style of Jobling's narrative underlining the human gravity and professional dignity of the incident. It is also generated by the length of the sentence, a long periodic sentence that increases suspense as it coils itself up ready for the weighty conclusion. But it is 'Brixton' that triggers the laugh. The specific name is so utterly inconsequential, just when we've been geared up for a solemn ending of high consequence. Think for instance how different it would be if this gentleman were to have been buried in 'Westminster Abbey', or even if the last sentence had ended '...became speechless, and died some months later'. Theories of comic technique in literature recognize this kind of strategy in terms like bathos or travesty.

Dickens and 'Descending Incongruity'

Let us now test these incongruity-based theories of laughter more broadly in Dickens's comic practices. It should be noted again that Koestler's ideas are based on examples of short jokes. He argues that bisociation depends upon the *simultaneous* functioning in the mind of two separate frames of reference, not just the sudden drop into the low. It would be difficult to sustain this idea of simultaneity in anything other than a short joke, such as the two-liner already cited, because the initial frame of reference should still be reverberating in the reader's mind as the new frame takes over. Recent debates in the theorization of humour as well as neuroscientific research into the laughter response have continued to rely on jokes or cartoons as experimental stimuli. Such material, self-evidently, is of limited use in examining Dickensian laughter, even though he could deploy quick-fire jokes such as Wellerisms. My examples of Dickens's humour that follow are not jokes. Nonetheless they do, I think, draw on the mechanism of bisociation, incongruity-resolution and Spencer's '*descending* incongruity' in order to trigger laughter.

During the Trial scene in *Pickwick Papers* (Chapter 34), Serjeant
Buzfuz solicits the jury's pity for Mrs Bardell's situation:

> 'The plaintiff, gentlemen,' continued Serjeant Buzfuz, in a soft and
> melancholy voice, 'the plaintiff is a widow; yes, gentlemen, a widow.
> The late Mr Bardell, after enjoying, for many years, the esteem and
> confidence of his sovereign, as one of the guardians of his royal rev-
> enues, glided almost imperceptibly from the world, to seek elsewhere
> for that repose and peace which a custom-house can never afford.'
>
> At this pathetic description of the decease of Mr Bardell, who
> had been knocked on the head with a quart-pot in a public-house
> cellar, the learned serjeant's voice faltered, and he proceeded with
> emotion.

The comic effect comes precisely from a 'delightful mental jolt'
occasioned by the clash between Buzfuz's grandiloquent, euphemis-
tic description of Mr Bardell's death, and the narrator's blunt version of the reality. This is a species of travesty; and travesty is one
of the main comic ingredients throughout *Pickwick Papers*.

The gross discrepancy between the two versions of the circumstances in which Bardell died is the main joke. But that joke is
reinforced in the linguistic incongruity between Buzfuz's idiom and
the narrator's, just at that point where the narrator reveals the true
version of Bardell's death. Buzfuz delivers a funereal panegyric and
elevates the solemnity of the occasion with a long complex Latinate
sentence form and elaborate vocabulary. The narrator dispatches
Bardell's death in a short relative clause, with a coarser, Anglo-
Saxon vocabulary. Buzfuz's verbal music is carried by mellifluous
liquids and sibilants and long plaintive vowel-sounds. The narrator's
jolting, brutal version is carried in plosives and short vowels. Think
how different it would be if the narrator's language were different—
as in, for example: 'At this pathetic description of the decease of
Mr Bardell, *who had been fatally injured in a tavern by a blow from a
tankard*'. The greater the stylistic homogeneity the less the shock of
incongruity, and therefore the more subdued the laughter.

The dissonant juxtaposition of Buzfuz and Boz 'compels us [if we
adopt Koestler's formulation] to perceive the situation in two self-
consistent but incompatible frames of reference at the same time; it
makes us function simultaneously on two different wave-lengths.

While this unusual condition lasts, the event is not, as is normally the case, associated with a single frame of reference, but *bisociated* with two'. It is not a matter of relief from strain, though that may play some part; it is that juxtaposition, that simultaneity of discrepant accounts of the same event, and incongruous registers. The effect might be the same if we heard and saw Buzfuz delivering his panegyric, with, simultaneously, Boz's version running as a subtitle.

He might have backed his deflationary version right up against the end of Buzfuz's, and opened that new paragraph directly with the coarsely narrated facts of the death, and that closer juxtaposition would certainly have amplified the dissonance. However, the creation of a second paragraph to challenge the Buzfuz paragraph would have formally separated the two versions and reduced that simultaneous holding together of the 'mutually incompatible frames of reference' on which the humorous shock depends. So instead Dickens opens the new paragraph in language that ironically continues to endorse Buzfuz's mournful eulogy—'At this pathetic description of the decease...'—and then slides in the squalid reality with its jolt into the vernacular, and immediately after resumes his ironically respectful Trial report—'...the learned serjeant's voice faltered, and he proceeded with emotion'. This construction intensifies the juxtaposition, increases the near simultaneity of reception, and thus heightens the bisociative humorous incongruity.

The next example is somewhat similar. It comes from the 'The Tuggses at Ramsgate', one of the *Sketches by Boz*. The nouveaux-riches Tuggses arrive at Ramsgate off the steamer from London and are besieged by cabmen touting for business:

> 'Nice light fly and a fast trotter, sir,' said another: 'fourteen mile an hour, and surroundin' objects rendered inwisible by ex-treme weloc-ity!' [...]
>
> 'Here's *your* fly, sir!' shouted another aspiring charioteer, mounting the box, and inducing an old grey horse to indulge in some imperfect reminiscences of a canter. 'Look at him, sir! – temper of a lamb and haction of a steam-ingein!'

There's humour first of all in the extravagance of the cabmen's claims as they jostle for custom, in effervescent vernacular. The first one slips briefly into a more formal advertising register (Extreme

Velocity), rendered in cockneyfied accent—thereby giving us the comical incongruity of a dignified proclamation being delivered in mutilated form. The second cabbie is introduced in overdone mock-Homeric as the 'aspiring charioteer'. The funniest part is when the narrator intervenes drily with what amounts to a brief stage direction: '... inducing an old grey horse to indulge in some imperfect reminiscences of a canter'. The precise comic effect of this can best be identified by trying an alternative phrasing; thus that facetiously grandiloquent clause might have gone: 'prodding his old horse into a wobbly canter'. The comic focus would then have been wholly on the *action*'s incongruousness with the commercial boast ('haction of a steam-ingein'). But Dickens's switch of register into polite pedantry ('imperfect reminiscences', etc.) compounds that incongruity with a linguistic one that imparts an additional jolt, and thereby provokes the laugh. It's an inversion of the method in the *Pickwick* Trial episode: there the coarse actuality behind the posh euphemisms was delivered in low language (travesty); here the pathetic reality is delivered in elevated language (burlesque). In this binary model neither component, neither the incident nor the linguistic register, is particularly funny on its own, but only when suddenly exposed in dynamic and close counterpoint. That is bisociation.

Rosemary Bodenheimer has written eloquently of the questionable extent of Dickens's self-knowledge in his commuting between elevated and low language registers, sometimes with a deliberately parodic agenda, at other times apparently unself-consciously. Dickens seems instinctively bilingual, sometimes ironically, sometimes not. He is also instinctively bisociative, as I shall suggest later. The principle behind Koestler's bisociative colliding of two different 'frames of reference' could be extended from joke material to apply to these two different linguistic modes.

A more extended example of the fun Dickens can have with burlesque incongruity comes in three letters announcing the death of his pet raven in March 1841. The most fully detailed and comically developed account is in his letter to Daniel Maclise (12 March), written on the day the bird died:

> You will be greatly shocked and grieved to hear that the Raven is no
> more.

He expired to-day at a few minutes after Twelve o'Clock at noon. He had been ailing (as I told you t'other night) for a few days, but we anticipated no serious result, conjecturing that a portion of the white paint he swallowed last summer might be lingering about his vitals without having any serious effect upon his constitution. Yesterday afternoon he was taken so much worse that I sent an express for the medical gentleman (Mr. Herring) who promptly attended, and administered a powerful dose of castor oil. Under the influence of this medicine, he recovered so far as to be able at 8 o'Clock p.m. to bite Topping. His night was peaceful. This morning at daybreak he appeared better; received (agreeably to the doctor's directions) another dose of castor oil; and partook plentifully of some warm gruel, the flavor of which he appeared to relish. Towards eleven o'Clock he was so much worse that it was found necessary to muffle the stable knocker. At half past, or thereabouts, he was heard talking to himself about the horse and Topping's family, and to add some incoherent expressions which are supposed to have been either a foreboding of his approaching dissolution, or some wishes relative to the disposal of his little property—consisting chiefly of halfpence which he had buried in different parts of the garden. On the clock striking twelve he appeared slightly agitated, but he soon recovered, walked twice or thrice along the coachhouse, stopped to bark, staggered, exclaimed 'Halloa old girl!' (his favorite expression) and died.

He behaved throughout with a decent fortitude, equanimity, and self-possession, which cannot be too much admired. I deeply regret that being in ignorance of his danger I did not attend to receive his last instructions. Something remarkable about his eyes occasioned Topping to run for the doctor at Twelve. When they returned together our friend was gone. It was the medical gentleman who informed me of his decease. He did it with great caution and delicacy, preparing me by the remark that 'a jolly queer start had taken place', but the shock was very great notwithstanding.

As Dickens warms to his task, his tone changes and gradually resembles first the manner of a formal inquest report and eventually a *Times* obituary. He detaches himself from the pain of rehearsing the loss by finding a register that gives him distance on the event, and that distance lets the humour seep in. The vet gave the bird some castor oil: 'under the influence of this medicine, he recovered so far as to be able at 8 o'Clock p.m. to bite Topping'. The

dry pedantic language and meticulous recording of the time prepare the reader for some such clinically dignified conclusion as 'to
be able...to take a little nourishment'. Instead, the newly fortified
bird bites Dickens's groom. This small shock of the unexpected is
compounded by Dickens's inflating expectations in one register
and then pricking them in another. That slight comic shock of
informality—'...to bite Topping'—is less effective when Dickens,
in another account of exactly the same incident, writes: 'so far
recovered...as to be enabled to bite the groom severely'; for
there, though the comic event remains, he sustains the formality
through to the end.

By the time the patient is described as partaking plentifully of
some warm gruel and appearing to relish its flavour, the bird has
become a human subject and the narrative of its last moments is
conducted in the full dignity of highly dressed language. Some
incoherent expressions from the patient are overheard by the
anxious owner, who understands them 'to have been either a
foreboding of his approaching dissolution, or some wishes relative to the disposal of his little property', at which Dickens pre-
tends to furrow his brow with regret that he 'did not attend to
receive his last instructions'. The solemnities of death are fully
observed in this idiom, and then undermined by the reported last
words of the bird—'Halloa old girl!' The bird's exclamation is
exactly the same in the other two letters reporting the death. It
is funny simply left as it is, in all its dissonance amidst the pious
mourning. But in another letter Dickens cannot resist a facetious
gloss on the speech: '—which I take to be an apostrophe to
death, which is feminine in Latin'. Too clever-clever? The
strained elaboration highlights how well Dickens has controlled
his sustained exercise in humorous incongruity in the Maclise
letter.

Finally there is the speech of Mr Herring as he breaks the news
to Dickens. Here are the three different versions, in chronological
order of letter-writing:

> [to Maclise] He did it with great caution and delicacy, preparing me
> by the remark that "a jolly queer start had taken place," but the
> shock was very great notwithstanding.

[to Latimer] He did it with great delicacy, preparing me with the remark that 'a jolly queer start as ever he know'd had took place back'ards there' (the stable is in the rear of the premises) but the shock was very great of course.

[to Hall] The medical gentleman broke out the fact of his decease to me with great delicacy, observing that 'the jolliest queer start had taken place with that 'ere knowing card of a bird, as ever he see'd'— but the shock was naturally very great.

Between the sober framing remarks about the delicacy of the news-breaking and the final reflection on the real shock of the event, Dickens gradually stretches Herring's picturesque speech, playing up its vernacular incongruity with his own adopted solemnity. He is writing essentially the same piece of news to three different people: Daniel Maclise, the painter was a close friend, with whom Dickens could relax playfully; Thomas Latimer was a witty, caustic journalist, not part of Dickens's inner circle; Basil Hall was a distinguished naval officer, on the edge of that circle. In the letter to Hall Dickens notably restrains that preposterously solemn and formal manner that he had developed for Maclise. The letter to Latimer gives a much briefer account of the episode altogether. Otherwise the main difference is Dickens's insertion, for Latimer, of that strained joke about the bird's apostrophe to death—presumably thinking the jokey pedantry might appeal to a fellow writer with a sharp pen (he and Latimer had been rival apprentice reporters in their early years).

Dickens carefully calibrates his play of the incongruity ratio of vernacular to formal in accordance with his sense of his known correspondents. This makes one wonder how he decided to play his humorous games of stylistic incongruity when faced with an unknown readership; that is, when writing his novels. Perhaps after *Pickwick*'s triumph he was confident enough in his cultural assumptions about his collective readership and their tastes in this particular kind of humour—tastes which, after all, he had largely shaped. Bergson suggested that this particular form of stylistic incongruity became distinctly English, partly due to Dickens's practice: 'To express in respectable language some disreputable idea [...] some lower-class calling or disgraceful behaviour, and describe them in terms of the utmost "*Respectability*", is generally comic [...]. The practice itself is characteristically English. Many instances of it may be found in Dickens and Thackeray'.

Incongruity in a Subtler Mode

My final examples illustrate a more complex playing out of these comical incongruities, and they come from Dickens's two first-person narratives, *Great Expectations* and *David Copperfield*. The incongruities are indeed bound up with that narrative format.

In Chapter 31 of *Great Expectations* Pip and Herbert go to see Mr Wopsle's conspicuously low-budget *Hamlet*. As the famous first act unfolds, Pip and the audience are struck by the eccentric behaviour of the Ghost of Hamlet's father:

> Several curious little circumstances transpired as the action proceeded. The late king of the country not only appeared to have been troubled with a cough at the time of his decease, but to have taken it with him to the tomb and to have brought it back. The royal phantom also carried a ghostly manuscript round its truncheon, to which it had the appearance of occasionally referring, and that too, with an air of anxiety and a tendency to lose the place of reference which were suggestive of a state of mortality. It was this, I conceive, which led to the Shade's being advised by the gallery to 'turn over!'—a recommendation which it took extremely ill [...]. Whenever that undecided Prince had to ask a question or state a doubt, the public helped him out with it. As for example: on the question whether 'twas nobler in the mind to suffer, some roared yes, and some no, and some inclining to both opinions said 'toss up for it;' and quite a Debating Society arose.

As John Carey has pointed out, Dickens's 'hearty literalism' is very often the chief source of humour when it comes to theatre, and so it is here. Carey's 'hearty literalism' takes us to the threshold of Spencer's 'descending incongruity'. Let me try to unravel the entwined strands. Simple 'descending incongruity' would point to the collision between the gravity of 'To be or not to be—that is the question' (like the suitor's asking for the daughter's hand in marriage) and the levity of 'toss up for it' (like the father's crude response). But we have three compacted levels, codes or discourses here enriching the seam of comedy. Level one is that supposedly fostered by any play, involving the suspension of disbelief; the audience's tacit agreement to accept the illusion for a reality, and to accept the currency of an archaic language—in this case accepting the Ghost as a ghost, the tragic reality of Hamlet's predicament, and its articulation in a dignified register. Level two is Pip's somewhat rueful inability to sustain any such illusion because the production quality is so hopelessly threadbare; he is here a reluctant literalist, politely deflationary, because, as he confessed, he and Herbert 'had sat, feeling keenly for him [Wopsle], but laughing, nevertheless [...] I laughed in spite of myself all the time'. Level three is the gallery knockabout, taunting the poor Ghost to attend to his script or helping Hamlet with his existential dilemmas. Unlike Pip, the audience is uncompromised by any familiarity with Wopsle personally, and wholly unable or unwilling to suspend disbelief in this illusion. (Pip the blacksmith's boy as well as the newly-minted gentleman is perhaps a hybrid of levels two and three.)

Pip's prosy literalism is conveyed in a very different register both from Shakespeare's original and from the audience's raillery, and his manner helps to throw the latter into sharper relief. His narrative style, conscientiously grave (and all the funnier for it), mediates between the lofty aspirations of the production and the philistine response of the crowd; it articulates a point of view that represents a sophisticated scepticism, one that is sympathetic with but also at some distance from the gallery's crudely bathetic puncturing. His dry, mock-tentative description both exposes the failed dignity of this *Hamlet* and at the same time, in the politeness of its register, gives almost a burlesque elevation to the production's crude flaws, which themselves amount to an unintentional travesty of an elevated original. This—one of the funniest scenes in all Dickens—is a delicious and finely orchestrated symphony of comic effects, in which Dickens conducts exquisitely the various interwoven linguistic registers. And they are all held in suspension, mutually interacting. Take Pip out of the equation and you'd have the much simpler confrontation—Spencer's 'descending incongruity', hurtling downwards on a steeper gradient (the characteristic contour of Dickens's early comic landscapes).

A no less intricate weave of humorous incongruities between a style of narration and the events narrated happens in Dickens's other

novel featuring a first-person narrator, *David Copperfield*. In the opening chapters the adult, mature David is recreating the sensibility and
primitive perceptions of the world experienced by his child self. This
is particularly so in Chapter 2, 'I Observe':

> There comes out of the cloud, our house—not new to me, but quite
> familiar, in its earliest remembrance. On the ground-floor is Peg-
> gotty's kitchen, opening into a back yard [...] and a quantity of fowls
> that look terribly tall to me, walking about, in a menacing and fero-
> cious manner [...]. The sheep are feeding [in the churchyard], when
> I kneel up, early in the morning, in my little bed in a closet within
> my mother's room, to look out at it; and I see the red light shining
> on the sun-dial, and think within myself, 'Is the sun-dial glad, I won-
> der, that it can tell the time again?'
>
> Here is our pew in the church. What a high-backed pew!...
> [Peggotty frowns to me] that I am to look at the clergyman. But I
> can't always look at him—I know him without that white thing on,
> and I am afraid of his wondering why I stare so, and perhaps stop-
> ping the service to inquire—and what am I to do? It's a dreadful
> thing to gape, but I must do something. I look at my mother, but *she*
> pretends not to see me. I look at a boy in the aisle, and *he* makes
> faces at me. I look at the sunlight coming in at the open door
> through the porch, and there I see a stray sheep—I don't mean a
> sinner, but mutton—half making up his mind to come into the
> church [...]
>
> Now I am in the garden at the back [...] where the fruit clus-
> ters on the trees, riper and richer than fruit has ever been since,
> in any other garden, and where my mother gathers some in a
> basket, while I stand by, bolting furtive gooseberries, and trying to
> look unmoved. A great wind rises, and the summer is gone in a
> moment. We are playing in the winter twilight, dancing about the
> parlour.

This is a medley of memories still potent and pungent enough to
have survived the passage of years into the mind of the grown-up
David. The present tense indicates that they are still living presences
in his life, as vividly real to him as they were two decades or so ago.
The gigantic fowls, the forlornly out-of-work sun-dial, the familiar
neighbour who puts on a piece of white cloth on Sundays to become
a 'clergyman': ordinary life is a strange warp. The child can't make
much sense of his world, but accepts it.

Bergson made the point that 'a comic character is generally comic in proportion to his ignorance of himself. The comic person is unconscious'. In *Pickwick Papers* this formula worked to great effect through comical incongruity: Mr Pickwick was a grown man ignorant of himself in crucial respects, yet with an inflated sense of his wisdom and importance. The more he grew into self-knowledge, the more those incongruities subsided, and the more the humour seeped away. Child David is as yet relatively ignorant of himself, and like Pickwick his naivety lands him in comical difficulties. The difference between the two is that the mature narrating David belongs organically to the experiencing child David; part of him still shares that sensibility, feels its bruises. His affectionately ironical commentary on the child's ignorance is therefore very different from Boz's detached, archly ironical commentary on Pickwick's naivety and consequent misadventures.

This is a complex variation on Koestler's bisociation, where the recipient of the joke is asked to 'function simultaneously on two different wave-lengths'. We experience empathically the child David's often surreal or abruptly literalizing reading of the world, while we are also enjoying the distance on it created by the narrator's sophisticated perspective, a distance that allows it to become humorous. In addition the narration throughout these early chapters is both retrospective and immediately present (Chapter 2's opening paragraphs are conducted in the present tense). It is a very complicated balance to strike. Dickens does it with great delicacy and deftness. The child's experience is articulated through a kind of free indirect discourse, the mature narrator projecting himself into the mind of the child and mediating the newly-awakened consciousness thereby. The humorous effects in the passage quoted come often from the awed seriousness with which the infant sensibility experiences what to adults are mundane objects and events—another kind of incongruity. Our laughter depends on the relative detachment we as adult readers, and David as an adult narrator, have on the experiences which are knocking the child back and forth between fear and mystification (the *child* is not laughing or smiling at any of these incidents).

David Copperfield is as a whole—or rather for much of its run—a novel energized by precisely these fine tensions. It engages the empathic imagination very strongly on behalf of the child and the naive young David, and it also forges a comic distance between the adult perspective and those early experiences. We laugh while we feel pangs—whether it's at the Brooks of Sheffield incident or the Yarmouth waiter's beguiling the child out of his meal or David's infatuated courtship of Dora. This is what Dickens wanted from the reader. At the end of the 'Blissful' Chapter 33 (where David becomes engaged to Dora), he comments: 'Of all the times of mine that Time has in his grip, there is none that in one retrospection I can smile at half so much, and think of half so tenderly'. In the manuscript of that chapter there is a sentence that never appeared in print: 'I was in my heart so innocent and pure, so earnest, so impassioned and so true, that while I laugh, I mourn a little; and while I think of the discretion I have gained since then, I remember with a touch of sorrow, what I have lost'.

This chapter, 'Blissful', wonderfully catches the agony and absurdity of intoxicating love, and somehow Dickens does manage a kind of bisociative triumph, making 'us function simultaneously on two different wave-lengths'. It is a long way from those sharp specimen jokes presented by Koestler, but it is working essentially with the same idea. 'Blissful' does not depend on incongruity as crude bathos, as in Spencer's scenario of the goat interrupting a lovers' tryst (though it sometimes sails close to that): the dizzying infatuation is never terminally deflated for comic effect. Laughter as a release is allowed in on several occasions, almost as a safety valve when the pressures of impassioned romance mount too high. This is handled exquisitely by Dickens. Let me offer two examples. David, having made up his mind after the countryside picnic to go to Dora's the next day and propose to her, finds himself eventually alone with her, and is seized with panic:

> I began to think I would put it off till to-morrow.
> 'I hope your poor horse was not tired, when he got home at night,' said Dora, lifting up her beautiful eyes. 'It was a long way for him.'
> I began to think I would do it to-day.
> 'It was a long way for *him*,' said I, 'for *he* had nothing to uphold him on the journey.'
> 'Wasn't he fed, poor thing?' asked Dora.
> I began to think I would put it off till to-morrow.

This has some similarity with Koestler's sample bisociative joke about the suitor asking for his loved one's 'hand' in marriage' ('Why not?' says her literalizing father; 'You've already had the rest'). Dora naively literalizes courtly metaphorical language, and the bathetic shock is very funny.

The other safety valve is the accompaniment of Miss Mills and her maudlin romanticism ('Do not allow a trivial misunderstanding to wither the blossoms of spring [...]. I speak [...] from experience of the past—the remote irrevocable past. The gushing fountains which sparkle in the sun, must not be stopped in mere caprice [...]'). The involvement in the David–Dora courtship of someone whose language is romantically over-inflated siphons off much of the deflationary laughter that might have been prompted by David's sometimes floridly rhapsodic, but no less impassioned language. And that focuses laughter of a more affectionate kind, which still respects the awed, helpless infatuation of young David.

The laughter in the childhood sections of *David Copperfield* is potentially Hobbesian. Thomas Hobbes concluded, in *Treatise on Human Nature* (1650), that 'the passion of Laughter is nothing else but a *sudden Glory* arising from sudden conception of some Eminency in ourselves, by comparison with the Infirmities of others, or with our own formerly: for men laugh at the follies of themselves past, when they come suddenly to remembrance'. The grown-up David invites us, from his present position of 'eminency', to laugh at the follies of his past self. However, it is more complicated than that Hobbesian formula. We are not laughing at those childish follies in the way that, for example, Quinion laughs at the 'Brooks of Sheffield' joke and at the expense of David's naivety. The laughter at the child David is much more of the Carlylean kind, arising from the 'inverse sublimity' mentioned earlier in this book. True humour, he wrote, exalts 'into our affections what is below us, while sublimity draws down into our affections what is above us'. The superiority to David's misfortunes and follies which we share with his narrator is not of the detached kind that might make the laughter fully Hobbesian, or that might make it Bergsonian ('the comic demands something like a momentary anaesthesia of the heart'). It truly exalts into our affections what is below us—when 'us' means the older David and the reader, as we both watch his younger self struggling to make sense of his new world. The man David has no more fully detached his adult self's 'eminence' from his child self than he has experienced anaesthesia of the heart.

This delicate relationship, so finely modulated in the early chapters of *David Copperfield*, determines the mode of the humour. The older man gently deflates the romantic afflatus of his younger self, or exposes the comic literalism of the gullible child. However—and this is the point—that fallible younger self is utterly alive as a presence in the novel and as an internalized survivor within the older David's personality; he is not just an object of the adult's condescending, nostalgic reminiscences. It is the child's sensibility that dominates, and wins our affection and sympathy. The bisociative 'shock' registers the more strongly, as we shift in seconds between the 'two different wave-lengths'—or even exist simultaneously in each. We are taught empathically to respect the loving trust of the child and his rich imagination; and gentle laughter plays its part in this sentimental education.

The comic techniques I've been discussing are, I know, mostly pretty traditional, but they are worked with an extra gusto and extra finesse by Dickens, and with his distinctive comic timing: that is the difference. If bisociation is going to work, that timing is vital, so as to ensure that we 'function simultaneously on two different wavelengths' in order to provoke the richest laughter.

As I mentioned earlier in this discussion, Dickens's perception of 'relations in things which are not apparent generally' (the condition under which bisociation is generated) has further implications when we consider the nature of Dickens's achievement and indeed himself. For there is, I think, something in Dickens's own constitution that corresponds powerfully to the condition of bisociation. It's not just a matter of there being an internalized Lord of Misrule in him, the child whose rebellious literalism always makes him expose the Emperor's new clothes for what they aren't. It goes deeper than that. What Dickens, perhaps ironically, identifies as his infirmity is one of the traits we now most admire in his writing—for instance his scintillating word-play, his magnificent conceits, which are often elaborated Wellerisms in their shock analogies between utterly disparate things. This too is a species of bisociation and belongs at the core of his humour.

Forster in his biography of Dickens glossed this 'infirmity' eloquently: 'To perceive relations in things which are not apparent generally, is one of those exquisite properties of humour by which are discovered the affinities between the high and the low, the attractive and the repulsive, the rarest things and things of everyday, which brings us all upon the level of a common humanity'. This is a most suggestive formulation. It recognizes in Dickens's distinctive brand of humour impulses which we associate with both his social sympathies and his imaginative strategies.

In terms of social sympathies, Dickens spent his career seeking a rapprochement between disparate classes of people by reminding them of, and emotionally educating them into, a sense of their 'common humanity'. In *A Christmas Carol* Scrooge's nephew announced that Christmas was the great occasion when 'men and women [...] open their shut-up hearts freely, and [...] think of people below them as if they really were fellow-passengers to the grave, and not another race of creatures bound on other journeys'. Humour, for Carlyle, was wholly consistent with crusades of this social kind. As we have seen, he elevated the status of humour so that it became part of a humane sensibility. 'True humour springs not more from the head than from the heart; it is not contempt, its essence is love; it issues not in laughter, but in still smiles, which lie far deeper'. His notion of 'inverse sublimity' highlighted the impulse of benign *inclusiveness*. This humorous faculty was marked by 'warm, tender fellow-feeling with all forms of existence', a formulation that is remarkably similar both to Scrooge's nephew's creed and to Forster's declaration that Dickens's humour 'brings us all upon the level of a common humanity'.

In terms of his imaginative strategies, Dickens aimed to fuse fancy with the intractable realities of mundane life, seeking, in Forster's terms, 'affinities between [...] the rarest things and things of everyday' or, perhaps, as Dickens put it, dwelling on 'the romantic side of familiar things'. Bisociation, in Koestler's words, 'compels us to perceive the situation in two self-consistent but incompatible frames of reference at the same time'. The bisociative mind lives with contradictions, with incongruous affinities; it heightens awareness of the incompatibilities, and shocks one into hilarious discoveries of how they might co-habit. Laughter on this basis—Dickens's laughter arising from his 'infirmity' in seeing 'relations in things which are not apparent generally'—can do something quite radical to our sensibilities, something way beyond humorous amusement. As one writer on humour put it in 1872, trying to express the shock effect of 'an original and striking comparison': 'it is as if a partition-wall in our intellect was suddenly blown out; two things formerly strange to one another have flashed together'.

5

Falling Apart Laughing

We use several expressions to indicate our sense that laughter undoes the self. People 'collapse in laughter', or they 'fall apart laughing'; they 'split their sides' and 'burst out' laughing. 'Pull yourself together!' can be the reprimand for someone helpless in the throes of laughter. The self has somehow disintegrated temporarily, and recovery of composure is, idiomatically, to take the form of reconstituting that self as a single compact unit. Laughter benignly threatens individuality; the corollary is that it promotes merging. Laughter's unrestrained physical demonstration of enjoyment has two effects: it disarms the normal reserves, producing a kind of collapse ('falling apart'), and it stimulates and liberates others to share that enjoyment. In this essay I am exploring the former effect, and in the following essay the latter.

Dickens often uses the motif of collapse and disintegration to secure his laughter, which is itself an experience of near collapse. But what exactly is collapsing in such scenarios in Dickens's fiction? Very often it happens in a climactic exposure scene which entails the undoing of an individual, particularly when that individual has developed a distinctive façade to protect his true identity, as in the case of a hypocrite (Pecksniff's come-uppance is a fine example). The laughter at the crumbling of a deceitful façade is partly joyful triumph at a well-deserved retribution. But it can go deeper than this, beyond the dropping of the hypocritical mask, because there can be something comical, perhaps comical-grotesque, in the abrupt unravelling of the jealously guarded single self. At this point, and before concentrating on Dickens's scenarios, I would like to draw in some ideas from two theorists who were particularly concerned with the constitution of selfhood, fragmentation and hybridity—Jacques Lacan and Mikhail Bakhtin. What they suggest about the factitiousness and fragility of the unified self, and the terms they use to describe its defensive strategies, help to illuminate the disintegrative power of laughter.

The Fortress Self

In his 1949 essay, 'The Mirror-Phase as Formative of the Function of the I', Lacan outlines the 'mirror-phase' of the infant's development as follows: 'a drama whose internal impulse rushes from insufficiency to anticipation and which manufactures for the subject [...] the succession of phantasies from a fragmented body-image to a form of its totality [...] to the assumption, finally, of the armour of an alienating identity, which will stamp with the rigidity of its structure the whole of the subject's mental development'. Prior to this 'alienating identity' (a totalized selfhood, the 'I') the subject experiences the 'fragmented body-image', which 'regularly manifests itself in dreams when the movement of the analysis encounters a certain level of aggressive disintegration in the individual'. This fragmented body, according to Lacan, appears in dreams in the form of disjointed limbs, organs growing wings, and generally the monstrous bodily fantasies familiar from the paintings of Hieronymous Bosch. The formation of the 'I', on the other hand, 'is symbolized in dreams by a fortress, or a stadium—its inner arena and enclosure, surrounded by marshes and rubbish-tips, dividing it into two opposed fields of contest where the subject flounders in quest of the haughty and remote inner castle'. The nightmare image of the fragmented body visualizes the grotesque hybridity of the self which may precede or underlie the constitution of the 'I' as a coherent, totalized, bounded entity.

The figurative language used by Lacan throughout this description of the drama of the quest for identity is almost aggressively militaristic: the 'armour', the 'rigidity of its structure', the 'fortress', the 'inner castle'. This formulation links with Bergson's idea of what provokes laughter—excessive and persistent 'rigidity' or 'inelasticity' in the human being—and also with the contention of one of Dickens's contemporaries, Alexander Bain, in his discussion of the 'Ludicrous' in *The Emotions and the Will* (1859): 'It is the *coerced* form of seriousness and solemnity, without the reality [i.e. without sincere respect and earnestness], that gives us *that stiff position*, from which a contact with triviality or vulgarity relieves us to our uproarious delight' (my emphasis). It may also remind one of Spencer's 'descending incongruity', which we touched on in the essay on incongruity. But I want to draw attention to the correspondences in the language of 'stiffness' and containment used by these writers for their rather different purposes.

Bain continues: 'The comic temperament is probably determined by a natural inaptitude for the dignified, solemn, or serious, rendering it especially irksome to sustain the attitude of reverence, and very delightful to rebound from it [...]. The mirthful is the aspect of ease, freedom, abandon, and animal spirits'. This cluster of symptoms of 'the mirthful' as a state of 'animal' abandonment has affinities with Mikhail Bakhtin's diagnoses of the carnival spirit. His vivid and dynamic account of body imagery as allegorizing the individual 'I' (the 'bourgeois ego') and its sprawling antithesis comes in his study *Rabelais and his World* (1965). He famously anatomizes the grotesque body, and images it as obscenely disproportionate and uncontrollably abundant, always in movement, always outgrowing its own self, never completed:

> It is presented not in a private, egotistic form, severed from the other spheres of life, but as something universal, representing all the people [...]. The material bodily principle is contained not in the biological individual, not in the bourgeois ego, but in the people, a people who are continually growing and renewed. That is why all that is bodily becomes grandiose, exaggerated, immeasurable [...]. The leading themes of these images of bodily life are fertility, growth, and a brimming-over abundance. Manifestations of this life refer not to the isolated biological individual, not to the private, egotistic 'economic man', but to the collective ancestral body of all the people.

Bakhtin's concept of the excessive body is associated with the people, and particularly with carnival. It has no boundaries: it is always growing, never complete, shapeless and bulging, and always immeasurable. The antithesis he posits is the bourgeois ego, and in this he anticipates Lacan's 'fortress' imagery of the 'I', representing containment, determinacy, restriction, exclusivity—the armoured single identity.

The Lacanian fragmented body and the Bakhtinian body of the people have certain features in common, in terms of aggressively grotesque disproportion: but they are given different values. Lacanian fragmentation and hybridity is imaged as a negative, a nightmare alternative to the embattled 'I'; whereas Bakhtin's antithesis to the 'bourgeois ego'—the grotesque body—is construed as the image of a rich popular-cultural vitality, most robustly alive in carnival: 'carnival is the people's second life, organized on the basis of laughter'. In contrast to this, according to Bakhtin, what he terms the 'official feast', the traditional formal, ceremonial festivity, 'asserted all that was stable, unchanging, perennial: the existing hierarchy, the existing religious, political and moral values, norms and prohibitions'. The official feast, one might say, takes place in the 'haughty and remote inner castle' of Lacan's psychodrama. Carnival takes place all around. Carnival laughter 'degrades and materializes'; it can be heard ringing around those 'marshes and rubbish tips' from which Lacan's fortress self seeks refuge. Laughter itself is a spectacle of collapsing rigidity.

When we consider manifestations of these principles of disintegration and deformity in Dickens, we find that they are ambivalently valued: fragmentation, hybridity and grotesque abundance are viewed in Dickens both positively and negatively, but they can be vibrant sources of laughter, as I hope to demonstrate. So, I want to explore some aspects of Dickens's humour in the light of these principles of the controlled 'fortress' self as opposed to frag-mentation and indeterminate, over-spilling abundance, and would like to begin with some examples of the humour of language. In the idiosyncratic speech styles Dickens deploys we very often have something like a linguistic analogy to the kind of antithetical relations imaged by Lacan and Bakhtin. That is to say, fragmentation and hybridity, unconstrained fantastic growth, in speech terms, are set in relief from and threaten to destabilize coherence, uniformity, orthodoxy and controlled development. The friction between the two—between the disruptive energy of uncontrol-lable superfluity and a buttoned-up, 'fortress' orderliness—is a chief source of Dickensian laughter; and, of course, it is another species of incongruity.

Speech Order and Anarchy

Here are two episodes from *Pickwick Papers*. The dramatic comedy in *Pickwick* begins with the arrival on the scene of Jingle. It is in the confrontation of Jingle with Pickwick that the book comes comically alive, in the friction generated between two principles: Pickwickian propriety and prosy literalness, and Jingle's racy eloquence and versatility. In Chapter 2 the Pickwickians and Jingle (the 'loquacious stranger') leave the Golden Cross Inn on the Rochester-bound coach:

> 'Head, heads—take care of your heads!' cried the loquacious stranger, as they came out under the low archway, which in those days formed the entrance to the coach-yard. 'Terrible place—dangerous work—other day—five children—mother—tall lady, eating sandwiches—forgot the arch—crash—knock—children look round—mother's head off—sandwich in her hand—no mouth to put it in—head of a family off—shocking, shocking! Looking at Whitehall, sir?—fine place—little window—somebody else's head off there, eh, sir?—he didn't keep a sharp look-out enough either—eh, sir, eh?'
>
> 'I am ruminating,' said Mr. Pickwick, 'on the strange mutability of human affairs.'
>
> 'Ah! I see—in at the palace door one day, out at the window the next. Philosopher, sir?'
>
> 'An observer of human nature, sir,' said Mr. Pickwick.
>
> 'Ah, so am I. Most people are when they've little to do and less to get.'

Jingle's speech, narrating a spectacular episode of literal bodily fragmentation, is itself mesmerizingly *dis*-jointed, fragmented, grotesque in its exaggeration, endlessly prolific: it is hard to distinguish excrescence from fundamental form. In contrast, Pickwick's speech (more broadly in the early part of the novel) is standard educated English, Latinate in vocabulary and syntactically coherent. It is 'fortress' English, with its carefully measured boundaries. You know what a Pickwickian sentence is as it sounds out through the early chapters: it has a clear beginning and end; it is hierarchically structured with principal and subordinate clauses. It has pulled itself together. It is as rationally ordered and primly syntactic as Pickwick himself in the early stages of the book. Jingle's speech is in utter contrast; it would be flattering

even to call it '*para*tactic'. It is described as 'A lengthened string of
[...] broken sentences'. Jingle's speech is a linguistic variation on the
fragmented body image. It never stops long enough to settle into a
coherent shape. But then nor does Jingle himself keep his own identity
constant for long: he is everything to everybody. He is the actor,
whose capacity to change identity is his living. As such, as a polymor-
phous principle expressed in the dizzying energy and adaptability of
his language, Jingle is demonized by the Pickwickians who eventually
recognize that he constitutes a threat. He is the agile free spirit, mon-
arch of the marshes and rubbish tips, until finally he succumbs to
imprisonment by the official world which he has long eluded and
parodied. He becomes a dependent on Pickwick rather than his
antagonist; and the comic energy in their relationship evaporates.

Jingle exploits Pickwick and his colleagues as a comic exploits his
stooge or as a circus clown cheeks the pompous ringmaster; indeed,
his role has often been seen as a nineteenth-century Lord of Misrule or jester (the bell-studded '*jingle*-stick' was traditionally flour-
ished by the jester). But his speech is also internally frictional. His
patter can for a while riffle through a standard, plausible narrative
line, leap-frogging those hiatuses, but then will abruptly veer off
into surreal detail, as in the account of the decapitated mother with
her sandwich still in her hand. This kind of fracturing of standard
speech patterning and sudden eruption of grotesquerie is very
funny, especially, on the incongruity principle, when conducted
before strait-laced, literal-minded innocents.

In the next example, 'official' discourse is absent in the sense that
no character like Pickwick is present in the scene to throw into relief
the more anarchic forms of language from other characters. But
cultivated, posh language is implied and aspired to, and therein lies
the comedy. It is the scene where Sam Weller is trying to compose
a Valentine letter (Chapter 33), and agrees to read out to his father
what he has so far written:

> ' "Lovely creetur i feel myself a dammed"—.'
>   'That ain't proper,' said Mr Weller, taking his pipe from his mouth.
>   'No; it ain't "dammed",' observed Sam, holding the letter up to
> the light, 'it's "shamed," there's a blot there [...] "Feel myself ashamed,
> and completely circ—" I forget what this here word is,' said Sam,
> scratching his head with the pen, in vain attempts to remember.

'Why don't you look at it, then?' inquired Mr Weller.

'So I *am* a lookin' at it,' replied Sam, 'but there's another blot. Here's a "c," and a "i," and a "d." '

'Circumwented, p'haps,' suggested Mr Weller.

'No, it ain't that,' said Sam, 'circumscribed; that's it.'

'That ain't as good a word as circumwented, Sammy,' said Mr Weller, gravely.

'Think not?' said Sam.

'Nothin' like it,' replied his father.

'But don't you think it means more?' inquired Sam.

'Vell p'raps it is a more tenderer word,' said Mr Weller, after a few moments' reflection. 'Go on, Sammy.'

' "Feel myself ashamed and completely circumscribed in a dressin' of you, for you *are* a nice gal and nothin' but it." '

'That's a werry pretty sentiment,[...]Wot I like in that 'ere style of writin',' said the elder Mr Weller, 'is, that there ain't no callin' names in it,—no Wenuses, nor nothin' o' that kind. Wot's the good o' callin' a young 'ooman a Wenus or a angel, Sammy? [...] You might jist as well call her a griffin, or a unicorn, or a king's arms at once, which is werry well known to be a col-lection o' fabulous animals, [...]. Drive on, Sammy,' said Mr Weller [...]

' "Afore I see you, I thought all women was alike." '

'So they are.'

' "But now," ' continued Sam, ' "now I find what a reg'lar soft-headed, ink-red'lous turnip I must ha' been; for there ain't nobody like you, though *I* like you better than nothin' at all." I thought it best to make that rayther strong, [...]. "So I take the privilidge of the day, Mary, my dear [...] to tell you that the first and only time I see you, your likeness was took on my hart in much quicker time and brighter colours than ever a likeness was took by the profeel macheen (wich p'raps you may have heerd on Mary my dear) altho it *does* finish a portrait and put the frame and glass on complete, with a hook at the end to hang it up by, and all in two minutes and a quarter." '

On first impression the dialogue offers us classic comedy according to Aristotelian ideas of the necessary superiority of the spectator or reader to the characters and their exchanges; the laughter is affectionate and condescending, as we watch father and son struggle to achieve a polite and courtly composition. But then we realize that the scene is also a way of ridiculing ornately figurative writing by exposing it to the blunt common sense of the Wellers—'I never knowed a respectable coachman as wrote poetry'. The Wellers are linguistically upwardly aspiring, perhaps out of respect for this solemn Valentine occasion only, and are trying to lift their natural vernacular into an elegantly formal literary register. Words dropped from Sam's pen on to the 'gilt-edged letter-paper' become materialized as courtly dignitaries. These dignified constructions fall to pieces every now and again, and Sam has to reassemble them from the debris—'Here's a "c", and a "i", and a "d"...'. There is an element of carnival in this, in the folk mockery of the 'official feast'. Old Weller's game stab at 'circumwented' is a polysyllabic gesture towards sophistication, towards an awesome linguistic currency that has uncertain value for the two of them. It *sounds* weighty and rich and respectable, even if semantically 'circumwented' is entirely inappropriate. High-flown literary language is coming apart under their hands, even as Sam is aspiring to it. His father's allergy to poetry makes the use of 'Angel' and 'Venus' contemptible, and ridicules them by literalizing their inappropriateness—'might jist as well call her a griffin, or a unicorn...'. In Bakhtin's words, 'Laughter degrades and materializes', a remark similar to Bergson's, 'once our attention is fixed on the material aspect of a metaphor, the idea expressed becomes comic'. That is what is happening in old Weller's reaction to the hackneyed language of courtly love. The laugh is on the Wellers, certainly, but it is also on the conventions they are deriding.

The scene depends on a series of comically unsuccessful efforts to discipline the grotesque body in linguistic terms. Correct grammar and orthography, and a physically elegant manuscript, may be aspired to, but the contrary anarchic impulses keep pulling against it. Thus, as a further example, the Profile Machine simile runs beyond control. It swells out of proportion, way beyond the strictly utilitarian function of the analogy, and thereby becomes contemptible 'poetry'. It obeys an impulse towards elaborated conceits that Dickens himself can seldom resist. The final manuscript of the letter is a comically deformed text, materially and linguistically: spattered with ink blots, syntactically contorted, and as joyously prolific in its waywardness as Sam's idiosyncratic speech itself.

Comical anarchy and the hilarious collapse of bourgeois dignity before the brimming-over forces of life—these are the primary

Illustration 7: Hablot Knight Browne ('Phiz'), (top) 'The Election at Eatanswill', (lower left) 'Mr Bob Sawyer's Mode of Travelling', (lower right) 'The Warden's Room': *The Pickwick Papers* (1836–37).

motifs of *Pickwick Papers*. They are dramatized in many if not most of its illustrations. Time and again Phiz shows us Pickwick's 'fortress' dignity and primness jostled and tousled by the noisy, boisterous world of the poorer classes: in the Pound, at the Eatanswill Elections, in his prison room, on a coach-ride with Bob Sawyer. That last-mentioned illustration is particularly resonant of the Bakhtinian carnival world, with Sawyer's abandoned attitude aloft, food and drink circulating, and below a swarm of boisterous beggars with a teeming family: 'The leading themes of these images of bodily life are fertility, growth, and a brimming-over abundance'. Phiz's vignettes are bursting with such imagery.

Let us look at one more instance of the linguistic version of comically collapsing coherence and uncontrollable superfluity. This is not so much a matter of working-class semi-literacy, in the Weller mode, as of middle-class controls losing their grip. This is not the comedy of transgression against orthography or standard syntax or pronunciation; almost the reverse—its mental dishevelment is all the funnier for the earnest fastidiousness of the language. In *Nicholas Nickleby* (Chapter 27) Mrs Nickleby launches a magnificently inane monologue about her visit to Stratford-on-Avon some years ago, when she was pregnant with her son Nicholas:

> 'I think there must be something in the place,' said Mrs Nickleby, who had been listening in silence; 'for, soon after I was married, I went to Stratford with poor dear Mr Nickleby, in a post-chaise from Birmingham—was it a post-chaise though!' said Mrs Nickleby, considering; 'yes, it must have been a post-chaise, because I recollect remarking at the time that the driver had a green shade over his left eye;—in a post-chaise from Birmingham, and after we had seen Shakespeare's tomb and birth-place, we went back to the inn there, where we slept that night, and I recollect that all night long I dreamt of nothing but a black gentleman, at full length, in plaster-of-Paris, with a lay down collar tied with two tassels, leaning against a post and thinking; and when I woke in the morning and described him to Mr Nickleby, he said it was Shakespeare just as he had been when he was alive, which was very curious indeed. Stratford—Stratford,' continued Mrs Nickleby, considering. 'Yes, I am positive about that, because I recollect I was in the family way with my son Nicholas at the time, and I had been very much frightened by an Italian image boy that very morning. In fact, it was quite a mercy, ma'am,' added Mrs Nickleby, in a whisper to Mrs Wititterly, 'that my son didn't turn out to be a Shakespeare, and what a dreadful thing that would have been!'

Mrs Nickleby's speech is unedited, random association, hopelessly sprawling and undirected, circling around on itself, never settling into any coherent shape. It suppresses nothing, it hierarchizes nothing. It just keeps growing in unstructured ways. It is Jingle's speech without the extravagant, anecdotal plot-line. It is, significantly, partly reported dream, where incoherence is licensed and where we might expect grotesque fragmentation and hybridity. But what is funny in Mrs Nickleby's speech is that there's no difference between dream fantasy-association and waking fantasy-association, as she shows when she refers to her imminent son and the association with an Italian image boy. The image boy, Shakespeare and the embryonic Nicholas—the living and the dead and the unborn—live in a state of fluid exchange in the surreal world of Mrs Nickleby's mind. Her inability to separate delusion from reality makes her susceptible to the imbecile courtship of the gentleman in small-clothes in Chapter 41, who keeps lobbing vegetables over the garden wall in order to win her heart. That episode is a grotesque parody of the serious romances already developing in the novel. Like the Weller Valentine, it is comically subversive of the orderly and idealized procedures of courtship, just as Mrs Nickleby's disoriented mental processes are comically subversive of the orderly patterns of intelligent thought and communication.

In each of these instances, what helps to provoke laughter is the juxtaposition of order and near anarchy—but an anarchy that exposes the fragility of the order that is challenged. Jingle connives with his author to expose the foolishness of the naive pedant that is Pickwick. The Wellers play with polite discourse as if it were partly a foreign language and expose the absurdity of some of its conventional formalities. We laugh at Mrs Nickleby at the same time as we realize that she exposes, in quite the wrong public situation, exaggeratedly deformed processes of thought-association that we might all admit to in private. The shock of invasion of the inchoate and the uncontrollably protean, of vivacious deformity, of incompleteness as a permanent condition, whether it be in terms of Lacanian self-identity or of the Bakhtinian bodily principle, is, to my mind, one of the great sources of humour in Dickens.

The Buttoned-up Self and the Fragmenting Body

The threat to order and reason from bursts of comical anarchy is a familiar feature of Dickens's writing. It is, for example, played out right across *The Old Curiosity Shop* in the persecution of Little Nell by

Quilp. Quilp is the personification of subversively anarchic energy, and indiscriminate in his targets: he is as much a malicious fiend to the saintly Nell as he is to Kit Nubbles, Mrs Quilp, or his own corrupt legal minion Sampson Brass. I want to continue to explore these issues of comic disruption and fragmentation in two more contexts, by looking at narrative episodes (rather than speech or dialogue) from *David Copperfield* and *Our Mutual Friend*.

Just before examining the passages from *Copperfield*, I want to make a few general points about childhood in relation to what I have been discussing. The child can be seen as a focal figure in Lacanian and Bakhtinian thinking about these issues of fragmentation, incoherence and the material bodily principle. It is the *child* after all who is said to experience the mirror stage and those accompanying anxieties about the constitution of the coherent self which can later manifest themselves in dreams of the fragmented body image; and it is the child, in the Bakhtinian context, who has that curiosity and delight in bodily life that knows no shame about its basic functions of ingestion and excretion.

Bakhtin associates the material bodily principle with the aesthetic concept of grotesque realism in opposition to that of high abstract idealism. Grotesque realism and the comedy it generates emerge, as mentioned already, from folk culture, earthy carnivalesque celebrations: 'Laughter degrades and materializes'; seriousness elevates and idealizes. I repeat some of the statements of Bakhtinian principles quoted near the start of this essay:

> In grotesque realism, therefore, the bodily element is deeply positive.
> It is presented not in a private, egotistic form, severed from the other
> spheres of life, but as something universal, representing all the peo-
> ple. As such it is opposed to severance from the material and bodily
> roots of the world; it makes no pretence to renunciation of the earthy,
> or independence of the earth and the body. We repeat: the body and
> bodily life have here a cosmic and at the same time an all-people's
> character; this is not the body and its physiology in the modern sense
> of these words, because it is not individualised. The material bodily
> principle is contained not in the biological individual, not in the
> bourgeois ego, but in the people, a people who are continually grow-
> ing and renewed. That is why all that is bodily becomes grandiose,
> exaggerated, immeasurable.

Applying this to the child, we could suggest that the child represents
the stage before this severing of the self from the 'material and bodily roots'. With these ideas in mind, let us turn to young David
Copperfield.

We cannot easily talk about the 'Rabelaisian' elements in Victorian *David Copperfield*, but David's earliest memories do in some ways
offer illustrations of the material bodily principle, or more precisely
of the beginnings of the severance of the child from that principle.
This happens in Chapter 2, 'I Observe':

> The first objects that assume a distinct presence before me, as I look
> far back, into the blank of my infancy, are my mother with her pretty
> hair and youthful shape, and Peggotty, with no shape at all, and eyes
> so dark that they seem to darken their whole neighbourhood in her
> face, and cheeks and arms so hard and red that I wondered the birds
> didn't peck her in preference to apples.

The differences in the way these two key figures in David's life
are perceived correspond to the antithetical patterns already
outlined. The mother has a shape, is distinctly realized as a
determinate, defined entity. The visual contours separating
mother from non-mother, mother from the environment in which
she exists, are already in place. The description is complimentary
(and distinctly meagre)—'pretty hair', 'youthful shape'.

Peggotty, on the other hand, has a sublime comic indeterminacy.
She has 'no shape at all'. We recall those Bakhtinian phrases about
the material bodily principle: 'grandiose, exaggerated, immeasurable',
'brimming-over abundance'. This is the immanent life principle. 'No
shape at all'. What we perceive of Peggotty through the child's mediating perception is an assemblage of body parts: extraordinary dark
eyes, hard red cheeks and arms, a roughened forefinger. From these
constituent pieces the child will eventually form another, coherent
figure, with discernible contours. The mother is perceived in terms of
(to use Bakhtin's phrases) the 'isolated biological individual', the 'bourgeois ego'. But Peggotty, even after she has for David settled into a
determinate individual, continues to defy attempts to contain or
restrict her incipient shapelessness (like Jingle's speeches, like the
unruly Weller Valentine). We remember how often her buttons
burst off her when she joyfully embraces those she loves. She is the

comic folk principle, the body of the people, and just when she reunites herself with that folk principle, shape-constraining buttons explode in all directions.

Dickens comically literalizes the self-containment of characters, the armoured 'fortress' self, the isolated 'bourgeois ego'. The sartorial antithesis to button-bursting Peggotty is the buttoned-up man who stays buttoned up. A fine example is Mr Tite Barnacle in *Little Dorrit* (Book II, Chapter 12):

> Mr. Tite Barnacle was a buttoned-up man, and consequently a weighty one. All buttoned-up men are weighty. All buttoned-up men are believed in. Whether or no the reserved and never-exercised power of unbuttoning, fascinates mankind; whether or no wisdom is supposed to condense and augment when buttoned up, and to evaporate when unbuttoned; it is certain that the man to whom importance is accorded is the buttoned-up man.

The comical unbuttoning of 'weighty' individuals is a large part of Dickens's agenda. Without their buttons such imposing characters are threatened with falling apart (buttoned-up men don't laugh, of course), with exposure, for better or worse, of their chaotic human hybridity.

What happens to Peggotty? As the folk-rooted, material bodily principle, she is driven from the bourgeois parlour by the invading Murdstones, way off to the kitchen. She's separated from David's mother, with whom she has had an intensely close, almost symbiotic relationship—both are called Clara, and both, together, constituted the full, nurturing maternal support for David. Murdstone scorns what he calls David's 'attachment to low and common company'. From then on David is systematically weaned from the bodily principle, as represented in Peggotty. Low life, in the form of Peggotty, is seen to obstruct the serious process of constituting the bourgeois ego and is relegated to a harmless comic role. Of course low life *would* obstruct such a process, since it is a principle of undiscriminating inclusiveness, of earthy candour, of free spontaneous growth and abundance. The training of David into a bourgeois gentleman is a process of isolating him from this principle in all its manifestations. David at the end of the novel is, in Lacanian terms, the fortress or stadium. Surrounding him—but at a safe distance—in his hard-won, bourgeois, domestic fortress at the end of the novel are the novel's versions of those marshes and rubbish-tips—literally in the foul, dark riverside where Martha nearly ended her life, and metaphorically in that place of punitive exile for ne'er-do-wells, Australia. Death or exile is the destination for those dangerously discordant principles of the 'grotesque body' (whether high- or low-born), the sexually promiscuous Steerforth, Martha and Emily, the effervescent child-wife Dora, and the improvident, chaotic Micawbers with their teeming family.

There is one particular episode in the novel where laughter is directly related to the kind of fissility I have been discussing, where the single buttoned-up self seems to come apart with hilarious results. This is the occasion of David's 'first Dissipation': the term itself is related to 'scattering', 'disintegration'. The coherent fortress self, insulated from any identity confusions, can be comically undone by drink. David in adolescence and early manhood is preoccupied with trying on various selves, as his good and bad models come and go, and one of these selves is the sophisticated man-about-town (in emulation of Steerforth). To mark his genteel independence he hosts a small party in his London lodgings for Steerforth and two of his friends (one of whom, Markham, appropriately in this scenario of alienations, keeps talking about himself in the third person). On this occasion (Chapter 24) David is intensely preoccupied with displaying his savoir-faire and concealing his immaturity, though his hostly arrangements (Mrs Crupp's 'cooking', the delinquency of his serving-man) are always threatening to collapse. But the main collapse, promoted by cigars and wine, happens to David himself. He and his façade self begin to stray from each other:

> Somebody was leaning out of my bedroom window, refreshing his forehead against the cool stone of the parapet, and feeling the air upon his face. It was myself. I was addressing myself as 'Copperfield', and saying, 'Why did you try to smoke? You might have known you couldn't do it.' Now, somebody was unsteadily contemplating his features in the looking-glass. That was I too. I was very pale in the looking-glass; my eyes had a vacant appearance; and my hair—only my hair, nothing else—looked drunk.
>
> Somebody said to me, 'Let us go to the theatre, Copperfield!' There was no bedroom before me, but again the jingling table covered with

glasses [he turns off the lights as they are about to leave]. Owing to
some confusion in the dark, the door was gone. I was feeling for it in
the window-curtains, when Steerforth, laughing, took me by the arm
and led me out. We went downstairs, one behind another. Near the
bottom, somebody fell, and rolled down. Somebody else said it was
Copperfield. I was angry at that false report, until, finding myself on my
back in the passage, I began to think there might be some foundation
for it.

The bewildering fissility of his self, as he and the 'somebody' who is
also called Copperfield lose each other temporarily and then coalesce,
is hilariously rendered. Visual focus goes askew under drink and so
does identity. The Copperfield self visible in the looking-glass comically reverses the process of I-formation Lacan ascribes to the 'mirror-phase', whereby the gazer in the mirror discovers a coherence
and integrity in the self that has otherwise been imagined as more
fragmented. David-in-the-mirror is unaccountably more dishevelled
and lost than David-the-gazer imagined himself to be.

There are two successive stages in this comical dilapidation: David
manifestly failing to command the hospitable occasion as its infra-
structure crumbles around him; and then David himself falling apart,
his various components seeming to drift out of his control (his hair—
'nothing else'—looked drunk). The growing chaos at the core is all
the funnier for being narrated in a mildly phlegmatic manner,
reminding us that drunken David has yet a third self, the older narrator David gazing back at his mirror-gazing younger image.

Bourgeois realism isolates, separates and distinguishes. It purports
to analyse relationships and relate people to environment; it shapes
coherent, chronological narratives. Its debased version is perfectly
exemplified in what Mr Podsnap in *Our Mutual Friend* prescribes as
the proper nature of Literature: 'large print, respectfully descriptive
of getting up at eight, shaving close at a quarter past, breakfasting
at nine, going to the City at ten, coming home at half-past five, and
dining at seven. [...] Nothing else to be permitted to those same
vagrants the Arts'. David, as he grows up, learns to master that realism, to understand the way people relate to each other and how he
relates to them. But as a child, he cannot yet manage this: 'I could
observe, in little pieces, as it were; but as to making a net of these
pieces, and catching anybody in it, that was, as yet, beyond me'.

The child intellectually moves in the same element as that associated with the material bodily principle. Without any sense of his own co-ordination, or any comprehension of the relation of parts of himself to a total self-identity, he sees himself and others fragmentarily, in 'pieces'. This is regarded by the Murdstonian culture as a deficiency. Instead, this chronically unbuttoned condition might be regarded as vitally enabling to the extent that it does not cut him off from others. Prior to the fortress self, the child and his environment, human and material, are composed of miscellaneous fragments, held as it were in common ownership in a kind of fluid element. To fall apart laughing rejuvenates the adult: it restores the laugher to that primitive condition and to the folk principle of shapelessness.

Young David tries on his man-of-the-world personae watched with affectionate amusement by his older narrating self. Few of young David's masks fit well or stay on for very long. The mask of the mature hypocrite is a very different matter. When, in *Martin Chuzzlewit*, Pecksniff gets drunk at Todgers's it is as if his mask, without quite falling off, keeps slipping at a grotesque angle, occasionally exposing something of the real face. The two faces tilt apart and recombine.

There are few more hilarious scenes in all Dickens (yes, I know I keep saying this before presenting excerpts!) than the description in Chapter 9 of the evening at Todgers's when the company all withdraw upstairs after a lavish and bibulous dinner. Pecksniff is very far gone. He swings uncontrollably from maudlin philosophizing to lasciviousness, from pious sententiousness to transparent avarice. He seats himself beside Mrs Todgers with whom he develops a ghastly amorousness. The wine has made him oblivious of the coffee spilt on his trousers and the muffin resting on his knee, and prompts mournful reminiscences of his dead wife. After a few despondent exchanges with Mrs Todgers...

> He suddenly became conscious of the bit of muffin, and stared at it intently; shaking his head the while, in a forlorn and imbecile manner, as if he regarded it as his evil genius, and mildly reproached it.
>
> 'She was beautiful, Mrs Todgers,' he said, turning his glazed eye again upon her, without the least preliminary notice. 'She had a small property.'
>
> 'So I have heard,' cried Mrs Todgers with great sympathy.

'Those are her daughters,' said Mr Pecksniff, pointing out the young ladies, with increased emotion.

Mrs Todgers had no doubt about it.

'Mercy and Charity,' said Mr Pecksniff, 'Charity and Mercy. Not unholy names, I hope?'

'Mr Pecksniff!' cried Mrs Todgers. 'What a ghastly smile! Are you ill, sir?'

He pressed his hand upon her arm, and answered in a solemn manner, and a faint voice, 'Chronic.'

'Cholic?' cried the frightened Mrs Todgers.

'Chron-ic,' he repeated with some difficulty. 'Chron-ic. A chronic disorder. I have been its victim from childhood. It is carrying me to my grave.'

'Heaven forbid!' cried Mrs Todgers.

'Yes, it is,' said Mr Pecksniff, reckless with despair. 'I am rather glad of it, upon the whole. You are like her, Mrs Todgers.'

'Don't squeeze me so tight, pray, Mr Pecksniff. If any of the gentlemen should notice us.'

'For her sake,' said Mr Pecksniff. 'Permit me—in honour of her memory. For the sake of a voice from the tomb. You are VERY like her Mrs Todgers! What a world this is!'

Throughout this episode as Pecksniff in every other capacity falls apart, his speech style continues to comport itself with dignity. The unctuously ornate phrasing still emerges from his now thick and slurred voice. This unruffled manner is in sharp contrast to both the voice and the chaotic lurching from one topic to another, and that contrast is what makes the scene so wonderfully funny.

Pecksniff warms to Mrs Todgers in his drunkenness, but protests it is the spirit of his dead wife that is prompting his wholly decent amorous feelings. So he can reproach her with impiety when she coyly resists his groping advances:

'Has a voice from the grave no influence?' said Mr Pecksniff, with dismal tenderness. 'This is irreligious! My dear creature [...]. Don't suppose it's me: it's the voice; it's her voice.'

That 'dismal tenderness' catches beautifully the comically grotesque mix of emotions in Pecksniff's maudlin lubriciousness. Bakhtin's carnival laughter 'degrades and materializes', and that is just what happens with the 'voice from the grave', invoked reverently by

Pecksniff, when the narrator drily observes that 'Mrs Pecksniff deceased, must have had an unusually thick and husky voice for a lady, [...] and to say the truth somewhat of a drunken voice, if it had ever borne much resemblance to that in which Mr Pecksniff spoke just then'.

After he has collapsed into the fireplace and been carried off to his bedroom, he re-emerges on the landing in his night-wear, completely unembarrassed and with renewed homiletic zeal, calls on the astonished company to 'improve their minds by mutual inquiry and discussion', recommending as an opening topic 'the legs of the human subject'. This impropriety, compounded by his saying that he 'should very much like to see Mrs Todgers's notion of a wooden leg, if perfectly agreeable to herself', is too much for the company, and he is forced back to bed and eventually locked into his bedroom.

Complete collapse would not be so funny. The utterly improbable survival of one faculty, his dignified speech style, while all else is crumbling—*that* has a grotesque comicality. It is like a chicken continuing to stalk around after its head has been cut off; or, for that matter, like a suddenly headless mother with a sandwich in her hand and no mouth to put it into. As has often been noted in Dickens, certain components of a human being can manifest an independent existence and a capacity to survive intact while all the rest of the constitutional make-up seems to have fallen apart.

Jack Bunsby in *Dombey and Son* is a spectacular comic embodiment of the 'fragmented body image'. It was not drink that caused this disconnection between the component parts of himself, but, apparently, a maritime career of head injuries: 'Here is a man [according to Captain Cuttle] that took as many spars and bars and bolts about the outside of his head when he was young, as you'd want an order for on Chatham-yard to build a pleasure-yacht with'. Bunsby's mental defectiveness is made to seem hilarious. His discourse as a result is incomprehensible, but because he delivers his nonsensical opinions in a ponderous and deliberate manner, he has acquired awesome oracular dignity (in Cuttle's eyes, anyway).

His speech, when it amounts to more than a sentence, falls apart into a maze of non-sequiturs. His body parts are equally uncoordinated: he has one stationary eye and one revolving one; his voice comes from somewhere, but not evidently from the vicinity of his expressionless face; his limbs seem to have an agency independent of the rest of him: his 'right hand and arm, emerging from a pocket, shook the Captain's, and went back again'. *He* doesn't shake hands; it is only that limb that goes through the motions.

Cuttle engages Bunsby's oracular gifts in order to find out more about the fate of Walter Gay, whose ship, the *Son and Heir*, is possibly lost at sea, and so, in Chapter 23, takes him proudly to the Wooden Midshipman shop and asks him to deliver his verdict. 'The voice', that detached faculty, obliges:

> Bunsby, whose eye continued to be addressed to somewhere about the half-way house between London and Gravesend, two or three times put out his rough right arm, as seeking to wind it for inspiration round the fair form of Miss Nipper; but that young female having withdrawn herself, in displeasure, to the opposite side of the table, the soft heart of the Commander of the Cautious Clara met with no response to its impulses. After sundry failures in this wise, the Commander, addressing himself to nobody, thus spake; or rather the voice within him said of its own accord, and quite independent of himself, as if he were possessed by a gruff spirit:
>
> 'My name's Jack Bunsby! [...] And what I says,' pursued the voice, after some deliberation, 'I stands to.'
>
> The Captain, with Florence on his arm, nodded at the auditory, and seemed to say, 'Now he's coming out. This is what I meant when I brought him.'
>
> 'Whereby,' proceeded the voice, 'why not? If so, what odds? Can any man say otherwise? No. Awast then!'
>
> When it had pursued its train of argument to this point, the voice stopped, and rested. It then proceeded very slowly, thus:
>
> 'Do I believe that this here Son and Heir's gone down, my lads? Mayhap. Do I say so? Which? If a skipper stands out by Sen' George's Channel, making for the Downs, what's right ahead of him? The Goodwins. He isn't forced to run upon the Goodwins, but he may. The bearings of this observation lays in the application on it. That an't no part of my duty. Awast then, keep a bright look-out for'ard, and good luck to you!'
>
> The voice here went out of the back parlour and into the street, taking the Commander of the Cautious Clara with it, and accompanying him on board again with all convenient expedition, where he immediately turned in, and refreshed his mind with a nap.

The solemn attention with which these mystifying revelations are received makes it all the funnier. Bunsby's auditors are either too polite or too credulous to accept that they are listening to a mind that has crumbled long ago. Imbecility in Dickens is frequently very funny (Mr F's Aunt, is an example), especially when it is set in high relief from strait-laced and earnest behaviour.

The determinedly unitary self conceals its hybridity, buttons itself up over the fault-lines in its constitution, 'pulls itself together' all the time. Laughter arrives to expose those joins; it relaxes rigidity, and its seismic activity threatens those constitutional fault-lines. The other extreme is represented by characters such as Bunsby, a walking shambles who is now unable to pull himself together to constitute a mentally and physically coherent human being. Dickens incites us to laugh at both extremes. These are among his celebrated eccentrics. The term itself is significant: ec-centric, off-centre. To laugh at an eccentric is to pull him or her back into the centre. This is the corrective, normalizing function of laughter, designed to ensure the health of the social body by ridiculing deviancies. Laughter is seen to include this function, by Bergson and other theorists; and, though Bergson doesn't mention it, this function may be seen to have a Darwinian purpose in it, as a way of promoting the survival of the 'fittest' (elasticity of mind and body is best adapted for human life; rigidity isn't, so becomes an object of social ridicule).

'... to collect myself like a genteel person'

The final passage in this exploration comes from *Our Mutual Friend*, a novel which, like *David Copperfield*, is preoccupied with the constitution and dissolution of identity. In one particular scene, in Book I, Chapter 7, this preoccupation is explored in grotesquely material terms and offers the reader hilarious versions of and debates on the nightmare of the fragmented body image. The scene involves Mr Wegg and Mr Venus. Wegg has secured his new position as comfortably ensconced reader to Mr and Mrs Boffin, and now sees his way ahead to social gentility. However, he feels strongly that his social progress towards gentility is hampered by the fact that he has a wooden leg rather than his own leg: he is already, as it were, partially fragmented. So he heads for Mr Venus's shop where that leg resides waiting to find a new skeleton host. From the start he enters a world of bizarre, dark fragmentation and hybridity:

> [I]n a narrow and a dirty street devoted to such callings, Mr Wegg selects one dark shop-window with a tallow candle dimly burning in it, surrounded by a muddle of objects vaguely resembling pieces of leather and dry stick, but among which nothing is resolvable into anything distinct, save the candle itself in its old tin candlestick, and two preserved frogs fighting a small-sword duel. Stumping with fresh vigour, he goes in at the dark greasy entry, pushes a little greasy reluctant side-door, and follows the door into the little dark greasy shop [...]
>
> 'Good evening, Mr Venus. Don't you remember?'
>
> With slowly dawning remembrance, Mr Venus rises, and holds his candle over the little counter, and holds it down towards the legs, natural and artificial, of Mr Wegg.
>
> 'To be *sure!*' he says, then. 'How do you do?'
>
> 'Wegg, you know,' that gentleman explains.
>
> 'Yes, yes,' says the other. 'Hospital amputation?'
>
> 'Just so,' says Mr Wegg.
>
> 'Yes, yes,' quoth Venus. 'How do you do? Sit down by the fire, and warm your – your other one.'
>
> [...] the little shop is so excessively dark, is stuck so full of black shelves and brackets and nooks and corners, that he sees Mr Venus's cup and saucer only because it is close under the candle, and does not see from what mysterious recess Mr Venus produces another for himself, until it is under his nose. Concurrently, Wegg perceives a pretty little dead bird lying on the counter, with its head drooping on one side against the rim of Mr Venus's saucer, and a long stiff wire piercing its breast [...]. As the muffins disappear, little by little, the black shelves and nooks and corners begin to appear, and Mr Wegg gradually acquires an imperfect notion that over against him on the chimney-piece is a Hindoo baby in a bottle, curved up with his big head tucked under him, as though he would instantly throw a summersault if the bottle were large enough.

We approach Venus's shop through Wegg's point of view and what is impressed on us is its surreal indeterminacy. It is visually and commercially obscure in its identity. Its window display, like its interior, presents a muddle of miscellaneous objects. 'Nothing is resolvable into anything distinct'. The constituent elements are unrelated to each other such that it seems impossible to assemble the sense of a coherent shop or commercial practice of any kind; and Dickens here, as he often does, defers identification of the establishment for some time, revelling in grotesque mystery. This is the practice of the novel as a whole, of course.

The duelling frogs, the little dead bird impaled on a long piece of wire, the large-headed Hindoo baby in a bottle—this is like one of the monstrous fantasies of Hieronymous Bosch, which Lacan had invoked in describing the nightmare of bodily fragmentation. The weirdly assorted contents of the shop swim in and out of darkness, in a pageant of floating miscellaneity reminiscent of the child David's earliest memories of his environment.

The motif of indeterminacy carries over into the next stage of the scene and Wegg's polite enquiry after his leg. This leads into a protracted debate about human miscellaneity and homogeneity:

'And how have I been going on, this long time, Mr Venus?'
'Very bad,' says Mr Venus, uncompromisingly.
'What? Am I still at home?' asks Wegg, with an air of surprise.
'Always at home.'
[…] 'I don't know […] to what to attribute it, Mr Wegg. I can't work you into a miscellaneous one, no how. Do what I will, you can't be got to fit. Anybody with a passable knowledge would pick you out at a look, and say,—"No go! Don't match!"'
'Well, but hang it, Mr Venus,' Wegg expostulates with some little irritation, 'that can't be personal and peculiar in *me*. It must often happen with miscellaneous ones.'
'With ribs (I grant you) always. But not else. When I prepare a miscellaneous one, I know beforehand that I can't keep to nature, and be miscellaneous with ribs, because every man has his own ribs, and no other man's will go with them; but elseways I can be miscellaneous. I have just sent home a Beauty—a perfect Beauty—to a school of art. One leg Belgian, one leg English, and the pickings of eight other people in it. Talk of not being qualified to be miscellaneous! By rights you *ought* to be, Mr Wegg.'
[…] Mr Venus takes from a corner by his chair, the bones of a leg and foot, beautifully pure, and put together with exquisite neatness. These he compares with Mr Wegg's leg; that gentleman looking on, as if he were being measured for a riding-boot. 'No, I don't know how it is, but so it is. You have got a twist in that bone, to the best of my belief. *I* never saw the likes of you.'

Mr Wegg having looked distrustfully at his own limb, and suspiciously at the pattern with which it has been compared, makes the point:

'I'll bet a pound that ain't an English one!'

'An easy wager, when we run so much into foreign! No, it belongs to that French gentleman.'

As he nods towards a point of darkness behind Mr Wegg, the latter, with a slight start, looks round for 'that French gentleman,' whom he at length descries to be represented (in a very workman-like manner) by his ribs only, standing on a shelf in another corner, like a piece of armour or a pair of stays.

'Oh!' says Mr Wegg, with a sort of sense of being introduced; 'I dare say you were all right enough in your own country, but I hope no objections will be taken to my saying that the Frenchman was never yet born as I should wish to match. [...] I have a prospect of getting on in life and elevating myself by my own independent exertions,' says Wegg, feelingly, 'and I shouldn't like—I tell you openly I should *not* like—under such circumstances, to be what I may call dispersed, a part of me here, and a part of me there, but should wish to collect myself like a genteel person.'

The endless play on miscellaneous physical identity is hilarious. 'Laughter degrades and materializes'—indeed. In the grotesque realism of this scene many of the novel's prime thematic concerns and satirical targets are degraded and materialized into comical absurdity: the puzzle of identity (chiefly in John Harmon's story); social-class hybridity and the constitution of the gentleman (Veneerings, Charlie Hexam and Headstone); Podsnappian chauvinism and xenophobia. Wegg's conviction that a dispersed body is to be deplored as a serious disqualification for social gentility, let alone for a coherent personal identity, is reminiscent of Peggotty's status in *David Copperfield*. The button-bursting, bodily shapelessness of Peggotty was associated with a joyful folk culture that celebrated, rather than deplored, inclusiveness, unstructured relationship, and that 'brimming-over abundance' that belonged to 'the collective ancestral body of all the people'. In a nightmare of collapsing identity boundaries, Wegg realizes that his dispersed body parts might have contributed to a physiologically cosmopolitan skeleton ('One leg Belgian, one leg English, and the pickings of eight other people in it'), the corporeal epitome of pan-European man.

We have, of course, by now discovered what Venus's profession is, taxidermist and articulator of skeletons. Only he can make articulate sense of the miscellaneous human and animal material in his warehouse. In this respect, as indeed in the respect of their both owning that curious ornament the sword-duelling frogs or toads, Mr Venus improbably resembles his novelist creator. In the Postscript to this novel Dickens made the analogy between his craft and that of the weaver at his loom: only he, from the outset of a novel, could perceive the relations of the finer textual threads to the whole evolving pattern. Dickens's analogy with the weaver is rather like David Copperfield's use of the imagery of the net: his image for the capacity (beyond the reach of the child) to articulate a web of relationships in which individuals can be placed and given specific relational significance. Like the weaver, the serial novelist has to articulate miscellaneous textual components, over a year-and-a-half's work, into a coherent fictional body. Likewise it is Venus alone who can give articulate form and coherent identity to the obscure, heterogeneous components swimming in the darkness of his shop.

Articulateness in linguistic terms—whether it be tested in writing a Valentine letter or in conversation or in meandering monologue— is the equivalent to Mr Venus's work on the human body once it is reduced to skeletal parts. It is the same principle of making syntactical sense of random components. Syntactical dismemberment (if one can call it that) is one of the richest sources of comedy in Dickens, all the funnier when set off in relief from articulate, buttoned-up prose, as in the encounters between Pickwick and Jingle. In order to 'get on in life' (to revert to Wegg's way of putting it) one would not want one's speech to be 'dispersed' (like Mrs Nickleby's, like the epistolary struggles of the Wellers)—a part of it here and a part of it there—but one would want to collect oneself, syntactically, like a genteel person, or like the rigid Lacanian fortress-self.

The centripetal force militating against dispersal, against syntactical formlessness, against the fragmented body-image is the articulator: the articulator of bones and of words, phrases and sentences. The laughter in Dickens explodes again and again when that battle is joined.

6

Laughter and Laughers in Dickens

'There is nothing in the world so irresistibly contagious as laughter and good humour'—so the narrator of *A Christmas Carol* tells us in Stave 3. What exactly is this odd affliction, laughter, and what is the nature of its contagiousness? Before looking at Dickens's laughers we might reflect on laughter itself in its social context.

In the early 1970s a carefully controlled experiment was conducted into the effects of canned laughter on responses to a series of taped jokes. Each member of two groups of subjects (university students aged between 18 and 21) was tested separately, with a set of exactly the same ten jokes, delivered by the same person. One of the two groups was given tapes of the jokes accompanied by canned laughter. Overt responses were measured on a four-point 'mirth-scale' (from 'no response', through half-smile and full smile, to audible laughter), and on the subjects' rating of the quality of the jokes. The results showed clearly a higher mirth rating for those who had the canned laughter tapes, and also a higher 'intellectual appreciation' rating of the quality of the jokes from that same group. The canned laughter clearly enhanced the humorous value of the material. Why? Social conformity might have been one possible explanation for the results. The authors, however, were sceptical about that explanation, since each subject was isolated, and not conscious of being directly observed. This dismissal of social conformity seems to me an odd conclusion. The subject may have been as physically isolated as the circumstances could allow, but surely the very presence of the laughter track introduced, albeit synthetically and illusorily, a larger social context for each participant, and thereby both encouraged conformity as well as providing an extra stimulus for the laughter?

The result of the experiment, anyway, confirms what humour theorists, psychological, anthropological and lay, have long taken for granted, that laughter happens best in company. Other laughers help to disinhibit one's own responses in giving vent to laughter. More than that, the presence of other laughers consciously or unconsciously encourages *audible* laughter. As we have already heard from Bergson, 'Laughter always implies a kind of secret free-masonry, or even complicity, with other laughers, real or imaginary', and, had it been invented then, he might have felt canned laughter was a useful synthetic hybrid of the real and imaginary. Laughter (as long as it is benign laughter) and smiles disarm one's own inhibitory defences and also those of others. Henry Kissinger deliberately made humour a tool of diplomacy. In his Cold War negotiations with the Russians and other world powers, his humorous banter 'inspired banter in others and usually led to a more relaxed atmosphere [...] and created a more propitious climate for making accommodation'.

Laughter changes the social climate. It is a signal for gregariousness. This is borne out by recent research into the neurological mechanism of the brain. When the brain is monitored for responses to different emotional sounds there is a double reaction, according to the neurobiologist Sophie Scott. Under brain-scanning tests the subject is given a variety of recorded emotional noises made by other people. There is auditory activation in that part of the brain where one would expect to detect it; however, 'we also find activation in the parts of the brain to do with actually producing movement, say of the face, or if you were going to make a sound yourself'. So, for the people lying silently in the scanner listening to these sounds 'part of their brain is getting ready to produce those sounds'. The effects are different in scale for different emotions. There is relatively little effect for 'disgust' sounds, but an enormous effect from the sound of laughter. 'This response in the brain, automatically priming us to smile or laugh, provides a way of mirroring the behavior of others, something which helps us interact socially,' observes Scott. 'It could play an important role in building strong bonds between individuals in a group'. Laughter generates responsive laughter, almost as a demonstrative reflex, and thereby signals community of feeling.

Laughter feeds off laughter. In Bergson's words, it needs an echo: 'Listen to it carefully; it is not an articulate, clear, well-defined sound; it is something which would fain be prolonged by reverberating from one to another, something beginning with a crash, to continue in successive rumblings, like thunder in a mountain'. Laughter prolongs itself (assuming that 'freemasonry' of other laughers) by its peculiar contagiousness, and the echo is a kind of auditory contagion. Dickens testified to this when he reported on the success of a public reading of 'Nicholas Nickleby at the Yorkshire School' in Dover:

> The audience with the greatest sense of humour, certainly is Dover. The people in the stalls set the example of laughing, in the most curiously unreserved way; and they really laughed when Squeers read the boys' letters, with such cordial enjoyment, that the contagion extended to me. For one couldn't hear them without laughing.

Laughter here has relaxed the often rather reserved atmosphere of these events (reserved, at least, at the outset) and has supplied that sense of 'complicity with other laughers'. This 'example of laughing' was the trigger for that chain reaction, which, once initiated, relied on natural contagiousness to sustain it; and even Dickens's iron self-control was vulnerable to mass laughter. Indeed, it might be more accurate to say that he had no wish at all to build an immunity to such contagion.

The laughter at Dover was 'curiously unreserved', Dickens notes. That qualifier 'curiously' indicates Dickens's awareness of English inhibitions about audible laughter in public situations. This was a class phenomenon. In the cheap popular theatres, where audiences were predominantly working class or lower-middle class, there was a rowdy participation in the performance—jeers, cheers, and loud laughter. Dickens gives us several descriptions of such occasions, such as the Nubbles family's outing to Astley's in *The Old Curiosity Shop*, and Wopsle's *Hamlet* in *Great Expectations*, where (as we have seen) the audience throughout offers boisterous, irreverent advice to the hesitant prince. Audience laughter at such venues would be raucous. But theatre culture changed, partly to propitiate and win back genteel middle-class audiences who were offended by what they felt to be its rowdy bohemianism and patronage by prostitutes and other forms of 'low life' licentiousness. Such prejudices stigmatized theatre in the early nineteenth century (as was clear in *Mansfield Park* during the episode of the theatricals). Audiences in the changed theatre climate responded more obediently to specific laughter cues, otherwise the auditorium became an increasingly silent place during a performance.

Dickens's public readings were rather different from conventional theatre, in that they had been designed as drawing-room entertainments amplified for large audiences, rather than stage performances. He hardly ever gave readings in a theatre, preferring assembly rooms, town halls, concert rooms and other municipal venues; and he always wore formal evening dress, and read from behind his neat velvet-covered reading desk. These were occasions designed to distance themselves from theatrical performances and thereby recruit audiences from those milieux alienated by the theatre. Newspaper reports often remarked on the 'respectable' social composition of the readings, sometimes counting the numbers of clergymen present in the audience. These were the respectable people Dickens was particularly keen to set laughing, and to encourage to feel at ease in communal laughter. But it was not a simple matter.

Once everyone is laughing, then laughter in public can be unembarrassed. The converse situation is very trying. We have all experienced the exquisite embarrassment of helpless laughter when no one else around is laughing. Laughter is a 'spontaneous impulse', as Hazlitt remarked, and the trouble is that 'we laugh the more at any restraint upon the impulse. We laugh at a thing merely because we ought not'. My own worst memory of this was during a generally excellent Stratford-on-Avon production of *Macbeth* decades ago, when there was a dismally inept actor playing Macduff. At least, he became dire for me and my brother (we were barely in our teens at the time), though evidently impressive enough for most of the rest of the audience. He could not manage pathos in any way that carried conviction for us. The more he was stricken with grief the funnier his dreadfully forced contortions of voice and body became. The climax (nadir?) came as he received the news of his slaughtered family. When he cried 'What! all my pretty chickens and their dam/At one fell swoop?', with his face buried in his Tam o' Shanter, we were writhing in our stalls seats, trying to stifle laughter while several people around were frowning and clicking tongues. Perhaps canned *sobbing*, discreetly released into the auditorium at such points, would have helped to discourage that reaction?

Canned laughter playing in the Dover auditorium for Dickens's 'Nickleby' reading might well have 'set the example of laughing' from the outset and thereby relieved any inhibitions the audience may have had; but that mechanical aid was a century away. The laughter track was invented by the American sound engineer Charles Douglas just after the Second World War. He crafted what he called his 'sweetening machine', a contraption which was operated like an organ with a keyboard to select the style, sex and age of the laugh as well as a foot pedal to time the length of the reaction. It could artificially prolong live audience laughter as well as control excessive guffawing.

Canned laughter, as borne out by the experiment mentioned earlier, exploits the powerfully contagious nature of laughter and manipulates the responses of TV and radio audiences. However, such audiences are a ready-made, primed community: knowing that they are settling down to a comedy show, they are prepared specifically for laughter. But what about the solitary book reader, with no collateral aids to prompt response to the material? (*Electronic* books, of course, may be able to harness the technology as an optional 'app': imagine the scenario—as one strokes over the Kindle pages of *Pickwick*, the screen detects the eye's arrival at the Weller Valentine…fade in a lightly audible laughter-track to accompany the scene. That technology might at least ease the burden of solitary laughter for those who feel squeamish about giving way to it). That solitary reader is really the principal issue in this study of Dickens and laughter: the mystery of the individual, private reader's sudden unaccompanied laughter, prompted just by a page of text. This strange reaction can break out unexpectedly from one's silent neighbour reading on a tube train, from one's companion stretched out, book in hand, on a beach, or from oneself at the dead of night under a discreet reading lamp. Private reading is supposed to be a quiet activity. No one else is disturbed as the reader drifts away from present company to wrap himself or herself in another world, silently. Except, that is, where laughter erupts.

Dickens has long provoked helpless laughter at inconvenient times and in inconvenient places. *Pickwick* has been responsible more than the other novels. In the Preface to this book I mentioned the sheep-ish accounts by Edmund Gosse and John Middleton Murry of their 'hysterical abandonment' to the humour of *Pickwick*, both when they were children and in their later years. As Murry recorded in *Pencillings* (1923):

> I was persuaded that the behaviour Mr Pickwick induced in me at the age of eight and nine was a clear proof of a peculiar madness [...]. I have never been able to read more than a few pages since then, because the helpless feeling of unquenchable Achaean laughter takes hold of me. I dare not let go my sanity; I am afraid of a second childhood.

The language used to pathologize laughter is arresting: 'hysterical abandonment', 'a peculiar madness' and loss of 'sanity', 'second childhood'. Murry's sense of shame at having surrendered to laughter had come early, perhaps because the climate of late Victorian England (this would have been in the 1890s) was not favourable to that degree of abandoned laughter. This raises the question about laughter's status in a changing cultural climate (a topic I return to briefly in the Afterword).

In the winter of 1838 Dickens and Hablot Knight Browne, young men in their twenties on a tour in England and Wales, enjoyed an evening at a theatre where a farce was being performed by some very funny actors. Dickens reported on the evening: 'Browne laughed with such indecent heartiness at one point of the entertainments that an old gentleman in the next box suffered the most violent indignation'. The Victorian reserve about giving way to hearty laughter, implied in Dickens's ironic use of 'indecent', has been attributed variously to the puritanical strain in the culture of its middle classes, to its concern with earnestness and emotional self-discipline (especially for men), and to the residue of eighteenth-century polite etiquette. The latter was enshrined in Lord Chesterfield's maxims, which included censure of laughter: 'In my mind there is nothing so illiberal, and so ill-bred, as audible laughter', he wrote in his correspondence to his son.

> Observe it, the vulgar often laugh, but never smile, whereas well-bred people often smile, and seldom or never laugh. A witty thing never excited laughter, it pleases only the mind and never distorts the countenance.

Dickens was well aware of the prejudices against 'audible laughter', and there is a hint of his defiance of that when he once confessed how funny he found one of his own creations, at which immodesty, he told Forster, he had 'always roared in the most unblushing manner'. To laugh out loud risked social embarrassment.

The puritanical and class-conscious revulsion from laughter in the Victorian period is well represented in George Vasey's rather sour book *The Philosophy of Laughter and Smiling* (1875; a second and enlarged edition appeared in 1877). He sees robust laughter as a symptom of idiocy and a display of revolting physical deformity. He is fortified in these views (as he sees it) by Darwin's recent *The Expression of the Emotions in Man and Animals* (1872), where Darwin cites the psychiatrist Chrichton-Browne's findings that 'with idiots laughter is the most prevalent and frequent of all the emotional expressions'. This, incidentally, would fit the amiable shambolic Sloppy in *Our Mutual Friend*, who disconcertingly bursts into laughter for no obvious reason. But whereas Vasey is contemptuous of what he judges revolting behaviour, Dickens encourages his readers to accept the good-natured humanity in his idiot, whose laughter indicates a sympathetic emotional intelligence, however mentally retarded he might otherwise be.

Vasey continues: 'The laughing propensity gradually increases, in the same proportion as the weakness of mind increases, until we arrive at the lowest stage of mental vacuity, in which the habit of laughing becomes permanent and incessant'. For Vasey, fits of laughter are 'morally annoying to any one possessing the least dignity of character or thoughtful reflection', and 'the gentle, the most amiable, the most intelligent, the most virtuous are rarely prone to laughter'. Smiling, on the other hand, is dignified, 'free from all these violent and painful emotions—no convulsions—no distortions— no violent distension of the vocal organs'. Laughter is the symptom of a coarsely primitive mind: it comes either from those whose mind has degenerated, or from those who have barely set foot on the first rung of the evolutionary ladder. Vasey's is not a conduct book or disinterested philosophical or anthropological study; he sees laughter as pernicious and pathologically threatening. His project belongs with a number of publications late in the century which promoted fears of degeneration in the English race.

The Hearty Laugh of the Gentler Sex.   The Superlative Laugh, or Highest Degree of Laughter.

Illustration 8: [? Taylor Brothers], (left) 'The Hearty Laugh of the Gentler Sex', and (right) 'The Superlative Laugh, or Highest Degree of Laughter': in George Vasey, *The Philosophy of Laughter and Smiling.* (1875).

What then does Vasey make of the responsive reader of a humorous book? 'The reading [...] of the details of any incongruous, absurd, or grotesque transaction, or the recounting of nonsensical, outrageous, or obscene incidents or anecdotes, will tickle the intellect of those whose intellects are effeminate, stunted, or warped, or have not been properly trained; and the result will be cachinnations of a more or less stentorian character, according to the degree of piquancy in the description or anecdote'. To make his points more vividly, Vasey includes a number of portraits of examples of humanity whom laughter has partly bestialized. No wonder Murry in his childhood feared his laughter was a symptom of regression.

The antidote to Vasey's grim misogelasty would be Carlyle's Teufelsdröckh, in *Sartor Resartus* (1833–34): 'the man who cannot laugh is not only fit for treasons, stratagems, and spoils; but his whole life is already a treason and a stratagem'. Here is how Teufelsdröckh laughs, with unashamed robustness:

Gradually a light kindled in our Professor's eyes and face, a beaming, mantling, loveliest light; through those murky features, a radiant, ever-young Apollo looked; and he burst forth like the neighing of all Tattersall's,—tears streaming down his cheeks, pipe held aloft, foot clutched into the air,—loud, long-continuing, incontrollable; a laugh not of the face and diaphragm only, but of the whole man from head to heel.

There are several Dickensian qualities to this show of laughter. It sheds extraordinary radiance; just as Pickwick, the source of so much laughter, burst forth at the start of his adventures 'like another sun', so Carlyle's laugher is an Apollo. This Apollo is ever-young; Dickensian laughter is a great rejuvenator. And when the best folk in Dickens laugh, the *whole* of them laughs. That model employer and husband, Mr Fezziwig in *Christmas Carol* (Stave 2), 'laughed all over himself, from his shoes to his organ of benevolence'.

In his crusade to lighten up Victorian culture, Dickens encouraged audible public laughter. Prefacing his public readings performances, he would sometimes explicitly urge those present to overcome any reserve: '[If] any of his audience should feel disposed to give vent to any feeling of emotion, he would request them to do so in the most natural manner, without the slightest apprehension of disturbing him'. This is far from being a lofty permission; it is a positive encouragement. Dickens, like any stand-up comedian, fed hungrily off the sounds of laughter. He knew also that he was taking risks in some of the material aimed at provoking laughter; the reading of Mrs Gamp is one example, as is clear from a private letter from a woman attending his reading in Leeds in 1858 when she was in company with three friends: 'I must say we screamed with laughter almost the whole time; "Mrs Gamp" was irresistibly far beyond anything I had any idea of, though Mrs John Gote & Mrs McCarthy & Miss Betts thought it very shocking and improper indeed! It was quite a treat to be made to laugh so'. It was a treat for the audience as well as for the performer. Dickens's delight in making people laugh is evident in his exotic simile when he described the comic success of one of his amateur productions: 'It is one of the most ridiculous things ever done, and I have seen the people hang over their boxes with laughter, like over-ripe fruit'.

Outward and Inward Laughter

In Dickens's mind laughter, and particularly the release of audible, unreserved laughter, was usually the cause and sign of good moral health in individuals and communities. This contention about what might be termed the politics of emotion is in line with the thinking in a number of recent studies (for example, by Juliet John and Valerie Purton) which explore the significance in Victorian culture of the emphatic externalizing of emotional impulses. What I have been suggesting here in the cultural attitudes to laughter and in Dickens's own policy is associated with these critiques.

There are two inspiriting examples of small family-based communities in Dickens where laughter is buoyantly symptomatic of happiness and solidarity. The first, in *Pickwick Papers*, is at Dingley Dell, that idyllic, old-fashioned rural refuge from the modern world of nineteenth-century London with its noise, smoke and crowds, its crooked lawyers and squalid prisons (and where, as we will see, laughter can be a meanly deformed, internal commotion that 'bodes no good to other people'). Squire Wardle presides patriarchally over his extended family of daughters, sister, poor relations, friends and servants, in an idealized quasi-feudal community of devoted loyalties. In Chapter 6 the Pickwickians join them for an evening of cards and conviviality:

> Old Mr. Wardle was in the very height of his jollity; and he was so funny in his management of the board, and the old ladies were so sharp after their winnings, that the whole table was in a perpetual roar of merriment and laughter. There was one old lady who always had about half-a-dozen cards to pay for, at which everybody laughed, regularly every round; and when the old lady looked cross at having to pay, they laughed louder than ever; on which the old lady's face gradually brightened up, till at last she laughed louder than any of them. Then, when the spinster aunt got 'matrimony,' the young ladies laughed afresh, and the spinster aunt seemed disposed to be pettish; till, feeling Mr. Tupman squeezing her hand under the table, she brightened up too, and looked rather knowing, as if matrimony in reality were not quite so far off as some people thought for; whereupon everybody laughed again, and especially old Mr. Wardle, who enjoyed a joke as much as the youngest. As to Mr. Snodgrass, he did nothing but whisper poetical sentiments into his partner's ear, which made one old

gentleman facetiously sly, about partnerships at cards and partnerships for life, and caused the aforesaid old gentleman to make some remarks thereupon, accompanied with divers winks and chuckles, which made the company very merry and the old gentleman's wife especially so. And Mr. Winkle came out with jokes which are very well known in town, but are not at all known in the country: and as everybody laughed at them very heartily, and said they were very capital, Mr. Winkle was in a state of great honour and glory. And the benevolent clergyman looked pleasantly on; for the happy faces which surrounded the table made the good old man feel happy too; and though the merriment was rather boisterous, still it came from the heart and not from the lips: and this is the right sort of merriment, after all.

The laughter count here hits the ceiling. The euphoria is at a manic level, and it comes from good-humoured companionship that crosses all the boundaries of age and sex. The construction of the paragraph enacts the sense of merry community; the conjunctions are frequent and insistent, dragging every single person into the same festive mode, so that it feels like one long breathless sentence, punctuated by roars of laughter. Laughter here is the powerful fusing agent and as such is very important in Dickens's world, where so much of his creative energy was devoted to mending broken communities and bridging social and generational divisions. The laughter here is heartfelt—the 'right sort of merriment'; 'town' jokes may tickle the ribs of provincials, but in this context they also become triggers to release the more deep-seated laughter of the company. Laughter is the natural medium in which the Dingley Dell party exists and flourishes.

The other example of benign community laughter is on a smaller family scale, and comes late in *David Copperfield*. David returns to England after spending three years abroad, and tries to find his old school-friend Traddles, who has become a lawyer. In Chapter 59 David tracks him down in Gray's Inn, and has to climb to his set of chambers at the top of a grim old building:

A crazy old staircase I found it to be, feebly lighted on each landing by a club-headed little oil wick, dying away in a little dungeon of dirty glass.

In the course of my stumbling up-stairs, I fancied I heard a pleasant sound of laughter; and not the laughter of an attorney or barrister, or attorney's clerk, but of two or three merry girls.

David is greeted by a delighted Traddles, as crumpled as ever, 'and, both laughing, and both wiping our eyes, we both sat down, and shook hands across the hearth'. David is then introduced to his wife, Sophy, 'laughing and blushing', who is asked to fetch her sisters from the next room:

> Sophy tripped away, and we heard her received in the adjoining room with a peal of laughter.
> 'Really musical, isn't it, my dear Copperfield?' said Traddles. 'It's very agreeable to hear. It quite lights up these old rooms.'

(Charley Neckett in *Bleak House* (Chapter 36) has a laugh that similarly radiates joy and harmony: '[she] would stand still and laugh with such enjoyment, that her laughter was like music').

When David leaves Traddles he carries away with him a strong sense of the contrasts afforded by the presence of those laughing, playful girls:

> If I had beheld a thousand roses blowing in a top set of chambers, in that withered Gray's Inn, they could not have brightened it half so much. The idea of those Devonshire girls, among the dry law-station-ers and the attorneys' offices; and of the tea and toast, and children's songs, in that grim atmosphere of pounce and parchment, red-tape, dusty wafers, ink-jars, brief and draft paper, law reports, writs, decla-rations, and bills of costs, seemed almost as pleasantly fanciful as if I had dreamed that the Sultan's famous family had been admitted on the roll of attorneys, and had brought the talking bird, the singing tree, and the golden water into Gray's Inn Hall.

It is a characteristic Dickensian fancy, to summon up the world of the Arabian Nights in such a setting. But that is just how the contrasts have been developed in this episode. The England to which David has returned seems a gloomy old dungeon, epitomized by Gray's Inn and by the chief waiter at the Gray's Inn Coffee-house where he spends the night, an environment that 'had such a pre-scriptive, stiff-necked, long-established, solemn, elderly air'. Where in *Pickwick* the Dingley Dell laughter had sounded out only locally, through the benign old Manor Farm, remote from the modern world in the metropolis, here the laughter of the Devonshire girls and the good-natured Traddles resonates with David's broader sense of the condition of England, in which such playful high spirits and energy seem incongruous. The improbability of laughter is a critique of national culture. No wonder Dickens remarked (as mentioned earlier), on the eve of publishing the first number of *David Copperfield*, 'The world would not take another Pickwick from me, now; but we can be cheerful and merry I hope, notwithstanding, and with a little more purpose in us'.

The antithesis to these companionable boisterous laughers are those characters in Dickens who withhold their laughter in one way or another. They are a sinister collection. Take the example of the barrister's clerk in *Pickwick Papers* (Chapter 31) who is coaxed into a laugh: 'not a noisy boisterous laugh, but a silent, internal chuckle, which Mr Pickwick disliked to hear. When a man bleeds inwardly, it is a dangerous thing for himself; but when he laughs inwardly, it bodes no good to other people'. The clerk is exercising a professional reserve, in the service of his haughty superior Serjeant Snubbin; and that reserve has become so ingrained that it is now part of his personality. His interest is in fleecing rather than serving his clientele, and thus his laughter is hoarded within him rather than openly expressed and shared. The one thing that might release boisterous laughter in such cynical legal professionals is the triumph of their case or its futile exhaustion, as happens at the end of *Bleak House* (Chapter 65), when attorneys, solicitors, clerks and all the Chancery hangers-on pour out of Westminster Hall to announce the end of Jarndyce and Jarndyce, not because of resolution but because the whole Jarndyce estate has been absorbed in the legal costs:

> [They] put their hands in their pockets, and quite doubled themselves up with laughter, and went stamping about the pavement of the hall […] they were all exceedingly amused, and were more like people coming out from a Farce or a Juggler than from a court of Justice.

This is grimly apocalyptic laughter. The Chancery case has indeed been a Farce, but incidentally a lethal Farce, and is very soon to claim one more fatality.

The *Pickwick* clerk's miserly laughter also marks out Job Trotter in the same novel (Chapter 25). He has a 'low, noiseless chuckle, which seemed to intimate that he enjoyed his laugh too much, to let any of it escape'. Dickens so relished this idea of hoarding laughter that he repeated it in *David Copperfield* with Uriah Heep, whose 'light, noiseless chuckle [...] seemed to intimate that he enjoyed his laugh too much to let any of it escape in sound'. In all these cases sinister characters have sinister laughter. These are people who, for very good reasons, won't or can't share their laughter. Their moral deformity (their 'curvature of the soul', as Bergson picturesquely expresses it) issues in deformed laughter.

These are chuckles rather more than full laughter. When such characters laugh more violently and yet still try to contain the laughter the results are quite grotesque. In Chapter 42 of *David Copperfield* Heep, to David's embarrassment, has become aware of the dangerous flirtation between Annie Strong and Jack Maldon, and with prurient delight he catches sight of Maldon arriving at her house:

> [he] put his hands between his great knobs of knees, and doubled himself up with laughter. With perfectly silent laughter. Not a sound escaped from him. I was so repelled by his odious behaviour, particularly by this concluding instance, that I turned away without any ceremony; and left him doubled up in the middle of the garden, like a scarecrow in want of support.

The scarecrow simile is such a characteristic touch. David's fastidious disgust is suddenly lightened and distanced by this comical vision. Laughter in Uriah Heep only enhances his deformity.

The sour Benjamin Britain, Dr Jeddler's manservant in *The Battle of Life*, has a similarly grotesque manner of stifling his laughter (Part the First):

> [he] seemed suddenly to decide in favour of the same preference [laughter rather than crying], if a deep sepulchral sound that escaped him might be construed into a demonstration of risibility. His face, however, was so perfectly unaffected by it, both before and afterwards, that although one or two of the breakfast party looked round as being startled by a mysterious noise, nobody connected the offender with it.

Likewise Mrs Guppy in *Bleak House* (Chapter 38) 'made no sound of laughter; but she rolled her head, and shook it, and put her handkerchief to her mouth, and appealed to Caddy with her elbow, and her hand, and her shoulder, and was so unspeakably entertained altogether that it was with some difficulty she could marshal Caddy through the little folding-door'. The diabolical Major Bagstock in *Dombey and Son* undergoes terrible physical transformations in privately venting his huge delight and amusement in plotting Dombey's courtship with Edith (Chapter 25): 'The Major, under cover of the dimness, swelled, and swelled, and rolled his purple face about, and winked his lobster eye, until he fell into a fit of wheezing, which obliged him to rise and take a turn or two about the room'. It is as if he has ingested some toxic substance and is in danger of swelling and exploding as it works its course through his system. In Chapter 10, 'His whole form, but especially his face and head, dilated beyond all former experience; and presented [...] nothing but a heavy mass of indigo'.

Those who laugh internally only, often at some risk of rupturing their physical constitutions, are usually the villains, and these include a range of sadistic fiends who have no inhibitions about laughing at the torment of others, such as the goblins with the wretched sexton or the madman in the *Pickwick* tales, or Quilp. One exception is old Tony Weller, who dilates dangerously as he describes to Sam (Chapter 45) how he took his *bête noire*, the red-nosed man, for a hectic coach-ride, 'accidentally' running into posts and taking very sharp, jolting corners:

> The old gentleman shook his head from side to side, and was seized with a hoarse internal rumbling, accompanied with a violent swelling of the countenance, and a sudden increase in the breadth of all his features; symptoms which alarmed his son not a little.
>
> 'Don't be frightened, Sammy, don't be frightened,' said the old gentleman, when, by dint of much struggling, and various convulsive stamps upon the ground, he had recovered his voice. 'It's only a kind o' quiet laugh as I'm a tryin' to come, Sammy.'
>
> 'Well, if that's wot it is,' said Sam, 'you'd better not try to come it agin. You'll find it rayther a dangerous inwention.'
>
> 'Don't you like it, Sammy?' inquired the old gentleman.
>
> 'Not at all,' replied Sam.
>
> 'Well,' said Mr. Weller, with the tears still running down his cheeks, 'it 'ud ha' been a wery great accommodation to me if I could ha' done it, and 'ud ha' saved a good many vords atween your mother-in-law and me, sometimes; but I am afeerd you're right, Sammy: it's too much in the appleplexy line—a deal too much, Samivel.'

Such performances give an alarmingly literal meaning to 'expansive' laughter. This demonstration of internal seismic laughter (and the reader is meant to feel the ground trembling here) should endear us to old Weller in his covert skirmishes with the red-nosed man, but it strikes Sam as a dangerous invention. It is dangerous because it is held within, as a 'quiet laugh'. Laughter shouldn't be quiet. Laughter is meant to spread around; that is its social function. It has a yeasty power to increase its own volume, which is why it can be dangerous to lock it up tight. Imprisoned laughter can cause apoplectic injury to the laugher. More than that, it can injure others and one's relation to other people.

Ringing laughter is an act of defiance to those, like the red-nosed man, whose puritanical or genteel habits have suppressed open enjoyment. For Dickens these evangelizing figures spread a life-denying gospel, and it is very often women who fall under their noxious spell: Mrs Weller and the red-nosed man; Mrs Nubbles and the Little Bethel preacher; Mrs Snagsby and Chadband. Laughter is an anarchic force, physiologically as well as culturally, and its battles with the forces of repression (old Weller vs the red-nosed man) take place both in the broader cultural arena as well as sometimes within a single person. Morally healthy laughers, as Carlyle and Dickens both emphasize, laugh with their whole body and voice, not just one or two parts.

A robust challenge to the puritanical inhibitions about laughter is expressed by Kit Nubbles in *The Old Curiosity Shop* when, in Chapter 22, he rallies his mother for her undue deference to the gloomy, repressive ethos of Little Bethel, the dissenting chapel she attends so piously.

> 'Can you suppose there's any harm in looking as cheerful and being as cheerful as our poor circumstances will permit? Do I see anything in the way I'm made, which calls upon me to be a snivelling, solemn, whispering chap, sneaking about as if I couldn't help it, and expressing myself in a most unpleasant snuffle? On the contrairy, don't I see every reason why I shouldn't? Just hear this! Ha, ha, ha! An't that as nat'ral as walking, and as good for the health? Ha, ha, ha! An't that as nat'ral as a sheep's bleating, or a pig's grunting, or horse's neighing, or a bird's singing? Ha, ha, ha! Isn't it, mother?'

One can hear Kit's author putting a little extra pressure behind the boy's special pleading for a cause to which Dickens was himself strongly committed—combating the grim seriousness that Puritan-Evangelicalism and the creed of moral earnestness was impressing on early Victorian culture. Moral earnestness, to which Dickens came to subscribe, was not, or need not have been, incompatible with Kit's version of natural, healthy laughter. Some of the most extravagant laughers in early Dickens are salt-of-the-earth characters who combine a generous thoughtfulness with a capacity for high enjoyment—Kit, Scrooge's nephew, John Browdie in *Nicholas Nickleby* (Chapter 42), who 'chuckled, roared, half suffocated himself by laughing large pieces of beef into his windpipe'. Their laughter can also overcome the inhibitions of others.

> There was something contagious in Kit's laugh, for his mother, who had looked grave before, first subsided into a smile, and then fell to joining in it heartily. [...] laughing together in a pretty loud key, [they] woke the baby, who, finding that there was something very jovial and agreeable in progress, was no sooner in its mother's arms than it began to kick and laugh, most vigorously.

Laughter of this kind thaws reserve and, as mentioned earlier, generates the impulse for companionship. This is the 'social glue' theory of laughter's purpose. Those unable or unwilling to laugh out loud are also those lacking in true gregariousness. Mr Murdstone despite spending a day in the company of his jovial friends Passnidge and Quinion, who joke and laugh throughout, doesn't laugh at all (except briefly at his own 'Brooks of Sheffield' joke). Murdstone shares some of Little Bethel's morbid distaste for laughter, as David reflects (Chapter 4): 'the gloomy theology of the Murdstones made all children out to be a swarm of little vipers [...] and held that they contaminated one another'. This fear of contagion is symptomatic of one who is wary of any human bonding that doesn't have an ulterior motive in serving his own mean interests.

Murdstone is a dark, chill presence, incapable of lighting up with genial laughter. This is a reminder of how laughter can raise the temperature. One person ablaze with laughter heats up those around to combustion point, and soon there's a laughing wildfire. In Dickens's world it promotes moral, social and *physical* health.

'An't that as natural as walking, and as good for the health?' demanded Kit Nubbles between his guffaws. It is indeed a tonic for the body, as Laughter Clinics today recognize. It takes ten minutes on a rowing machine to reach the heart rate produced by just one minute of laughter. Laughter is marketed as 'jogging for the insides', a 'callisthenic' for body and soul. As it relaxes the body it can also strengthen the immune system, and there is clinical evidence for its health benefits. This therapeutic effect seems to have been common knowledge centuries ago. Jonathan Swift observed in *A Tale of a Tub* (1704) that laughter 'clears the breast and the lungs, is sovereign against the spleen, and the most innocent of all diuretics'. Henry Fielding in his Preface to *Joseph Andrews* (1742) speculated on its psychosomatic benefits: 'mirth and laughter [...] are probably more wholesome physic for the mind, and conduce better to purge away spleen, melancholy, and ill affections, than is generally imagined'. This makes laughter seem as powerfully therapeutic as Aristotle's contention about the cathartic effect of tragedy.

Scrooge and the Father of all Laughs

Laughter as therapy and as a raiser of temperatures is underlined in *A Christmas Carol*, where this essay opened. It is associated with that embodiment of the Christmas spirit, Scrooge's nephew Fred. Scrooge and his nephew are distilled to their principal attributes: Scrooge is all misanthropic frostiness, and nephew, benevolent warmth: 'he was all in a glow [...] his eyes sparkled, and his breath smoked'. Scrooge is the refrigerator, emitting his own chill and icing his own office; his nephew is the radiator, heating up the company around him. This he does most effectively by laughter.

> 'Ha, ha!' laughed Scrooge's nephew. 'Ha, ha, ha!'
>   If you should happen, by any unlikely chance, to know a man more blest in a laugh than Scrooge's nephew, all I can say is, I should like to know him too. Introduce him to me, and I'll cultivate his acquaintance.

This jolly challenge by the narrator in Stave 3 ushers in a paean to laughter: 'It is a fair, even-handed, noble adjustment of things, that while there is infection in disease and sorrow, there is nothing in the world so irresistibly contagious as laughter and good-humour'.

When Scrooge's nephew laughs, we see him 'holding his sides, rolling his head, and twisting his face into the most extravagant contortions'. A little later he laughs again, 'and as it was impossible to keep the infection off; though the plump sister tried hard to do it with aromatic vinegar; his example was unanimously followed'. The nephew is giving a demonstration of how to laugh—openly and extravagantly. Accordingly, Scrooge's change of heart in the last Stave is signalled by his discovery of his capacity to laugh. Though he had cracked a few sour jokes in the earlier part of the *Carol*, he never laughed at any of them, however much he might have relished their wit.

Michael Slater has shown in illuminating detail how Scrooge's passage to conversion is also a passage 'from the "caustic" wit of his earlier self to sympathetic humour [...]. He can now laugh and in the right way, neither derisively nor frivolously but out of pure love for life and humanity'. Scrooge's first laugh on Christmas morning, 'for a man who had been out of practice for so many years [...] was a splendid laugh, a most illustrious laugh. The father of a long, long line of brilliant laughs'. It's as though laughter bestows a fruitful paternity on the desiccated Scrooge. It certainly helps to immunize him from the laughing sneers of others: for that kind of derisive laughter is not the truly contagious kind. It is the same sort of laughter as the unreformed Scrooge might have indulged in when he found it so contemptibly stupid in Stave 1 that his nephew should have married for *love*: ' "Because you fell in love!" growled Scrooge, as if that were the only thing in the world more ridiculous than a merry Christmas'. So when at the end people laughed cynically to see the change in Scrooge, he had by then become 'wise enough to know that nothing ever happened on this globe, for good, at which people did not have their fill of laughter in the outset'; and so he let them laugh and wasn't bothered. 'His own heart laughed: and that was quite enough for him'. That is literally 'hearty' laughter. In Carlylean terms (in *Sartor Resartus*), it is the final guarantee of the man's conversion; 'no man who has once heartily and wholly laughed can be altogether irreclaimably bad'.

Scrooge's euphoria in these final scenes reaches high levels of intoxication. His decades of misanthropy have engendered an immunity from the normal contagiousness of laughter; but now that his immune system has failed, he suffers a redemptive breakdown. He laughs and cries in the same breath, is 'light as a feather', 'giddy as a drunken man'. The manically high euphoria here and in the scenes of laughing contagion with the nephew oddly resembles the effects of nitrous oxide (laughing gas) on early experimental subjects. 'It made me laugh and tingle in every toe and finger-tip', reported one such subject in 1799; 'It makes one strong and happy! So gloriously happy!' Another subject 'burst into a violent fit of laughter, and [like Scrooge] capered about the room without having the power of restraining [him]self'. It is unlikely that Dickens would have witnessed the use of laughing gas, though he would have known of its effects, which had become proverbial since its discovery by Humphry Davy in the 1790s. Rowlandson in 1820 had depicted Dr Syntax and his wife abandoning

DOCTOR SYNTAX
AND HIS WIFE MAKING AN EXPERIMENT IN PNEUMATICS

Illustration 9: Thomas Rowlandson, 'Doctor Syntax and his Wife Making an Experiment in Pneumatics': in [William Combe] *Doctor Syntax in Paris or a Tour in Search of the Grotesque*. (1820). British Cartoon Archive, University of Kent.

Laughing Gas.

Illustration 10: George Cruikshank, 'Laughing Gas': Frontispiece to [John Scoffern], *Chemistry No Mystery*. (1839)

themselves to the delights of this recreational drug, and George Cruikshank had drawn a Laughing Gas lecture in 1839.

Dickens's friend Daniel Maclise, in a letter to Dickens, alluded mischievously to the 'laughing gas lighted eyes' of a young woman of their acquaintance. A reviewer of *Pickwick* in 1836 drew on the analogy with laughing gas: 'Even where the deviations into farce and coarseness are somewhat too broad, our grins cannot refrain from broadness too. The atmosphere in which the Pickwickians meet is laughing gas, and Boz, when breathing it, may be excused from some extravagances'. The 'atmosphere' in which Scrooge discovers his reprieve is also metaphorically 'laughing gas'. Here, as in the scenes with the laughing nephew, Dickens tries to synthesize an atmosphere in which the contagiousness of the laughter lifts off the page and invades the reader, and many readers have testified to the eruption of laughter and tears in these exhilarating final pages of the *Carol*. And why not? That is just how its creator behaved in composing these scenes, as Dickens confessed to a friend:

> Charles Dickens wept, and laughed, and wept again, and excited himself in a most extraordinary manner, in the composition; and thinking whereof, he walked about the black streets of London, fifteen and twenty miles, many a night when all the sober folks had gone to bed.

Writing Laughter

'Ha, ha!' laughed Scrooge's nephew. 'Ha, ha, ha!'

How is that for a speech? Scrooge's nephew has a whole line to himself consisting of nothing but 'ha' sounds. 'Ha!' on its own doesn't signify much of anything (except perhaps indignation or a solution to a problem). Add another 'Ha!' and the sounds convey something else. Visitors to a grand garden might suddenly find their tree-lined walk terminating in a sheer drop to a carefully designed ditch, and are conventionally supposed to have gasped 'Ha-*ha*!', thereby naming one of the great innovations in garden design, the sunken fence. The double 'Ha!' registers shock. Add one more 'Ha!' to that and it becomes laughter, another kind of shock perhaps, producing three gasps barked out to the accompaniment of exclamation marks. Language seems impoverished when it comes to recording verbally the sounds of one of life's richest pleasures.

Laughter comes in so many different forms, as the various expressions for describing the types indicate: we can 'chortle, chuckle, giggle, guffaw, howl, roar, scream, shriek, snigger, snort, or titter'. But how do you write the *sound* of laughter to make it actually interesting, to make it as person-specific as the sounds and meanings of all the other utterances in a particular character's speaking voice? For all his ingenuity in phonetic reproductions of distinctive speech styles and other vocal idiosyncrasies, for all his acute observation of different laughers caught in seismic action, when it comes to the actual voicing of laughter Dickens is stuck with the conventional 'Ha! Ha! Ha!' The variations on this are equally dull and bathetic: for instance the standard hearty 'Ho! Ho! Ho!' and the somewhat sinister 'Heh! Heh!' How dull is that—just at the point in a speech where a character's distinctive energy and colour might be at their most intense, just as hilarity and high spirits overflow, the actual eruption of joyous laughter on the page issues in the flat 'Ha! Ha! Ha!' Leigh Hunt, in his 'Illustrative Essay' on wit and humour (1846), cites Dr William King's lines about the poverty of written laughter:

> Nature a thousand ways complains,
> A thousand words express her pains;
> But for her laughter has but three,
> And very small ones, Ha, ha, he!

Perhaps, though, this toppling of speech into grunting and gasping inarticulacy is the appropriate verbal representation of a process that becomes inexpressible in language? Laughter is, after all, the point where, though language fails, voicing continues. It also thereby becomes comprehensible to everyone, an international language. The *OED* soberly defines the sequence of 'Ha' sounds as 'a natural utterance occurring in most languages'. Translators of Dickens's stories into other languages must breathe a sigh of relief when they come to laughter; it can stay as 'Ha! Ha! Ha!' in pretty well any Latin-alphabet language (Japanese distinguishes between male and female laughter: the latter is 'Ohoho!' or 'Uhuhu!'). Like music, the sound of laughter generally rises above language barriers.

What does a non-linguistic denotation of laughter look like? Spectrographic recordings of laughter show it on the monitor screen 'as a series of short vowel-like notes (syllables), each about 75 ms long, that are repeated at regular intervals about 210 ms apart.' Laughter 'syllables' are repetitive: 'laughs may sound like "ha-ha-ha" or "ho-ho-ho" but not "ha-ho-ha-ho", and they have a strong harmonic structure, a multiple of a low (fundamental) frequency'. The expression of laughter, though it may have some musical elements, is below language, signalling that the body is taking over from the mind. It is like breaking wind. Laughter is a gut reaction, as vividly described by Michael Holland in an article on 'Belly Laughs'. The belly laugh causes a wholesale loss of control over our bodily functions: 'The belly laugh does not just come *from* the belly: it results in an escape of bodily fluids that rapidly extends *to* the belly, as we cry with laughing, wet ourselves, and eventually even lose control of our bowels'.

Dickens was comically aware of some of the stage conventions for expressing laughter. One of his histrionically most sophisticated characters is Dick Swiveller in *The Old Curiosity Shop*, prone to soliloquize in self-consciously theatrical manner. Jilted by his love Sophy Wackles, and finding himself alone in Brass's office (Chapter 56), he laments his loss in florid language: ' "in remembrance of her with whom I shall never again thread the windings of the mazy; whom I shall never more pledge in the rosy; who, during the short remainder of my existence, will murder the balmy. Ha, ha, ha!" '

> It may be necessary to observe [...] that Mr. Swiveller did not wind up with a cheerful hilarious laugh, which would have been undoubtedly at variance with his solemn reflections, but that, being in a theatrical mood, he merely achieved that performance which is designated in melo-dramas 'laughing like a fiend'—for it seems that your fiends always laugh in syllables, and always in three syllables, never more nor less.

Pantomime or melodrama fiends deliver scripted 'Ha, ha, ha!'s, where the last syllable is drawn out with sadistic relish. Dickens resorted to this convention on several occasions in his letters. For instance, in writing to Phiz to thank him for portraits of characters from *Dombey and Son* and reminding him to add some watercolour to one featuring Little Paul Dombey, he shifts the last part of his letter into high pantomime style, marked in large lettering:

> ...for if ever I had a boy of my own, that boy is
> MINE!
> And, as the Demon says at the Surrey [theatre]
> I claim my Victim.
> Ha! IIa! Ha!
>
> At which you will imagine me going down into a
> sulphurous trap, with the boy in my grasp...

The fiend's laughter of maliciousness is a self-congratulatory laughter at the satisfaction of power. It does not have the contagiousness of hearty benign laughter, nor does it have the same magical ability to transform its social environment. Benign laughter has a beauty of its own in Dickens. It can overcome the forces of darkness, of English puritanical constraints and institutional grimness; and it can animate even the most forbidding physical environments. Fountain Court, in the heart of London's gloomy legal-land, is the improbable trysting place for Ruth Pinch and John Westlock in *Martin Chuzzlewit* (Chapter 45). Ruth's presence alone vivifies the dullest of sites until it breaks out in laughter that is as captivating as any instance elsewhere in Dickens's work:

> Merrily the fountain leaped and danced, and merrily the smiling dimples twinkled and expanded more and more, until they broke into a laugh against the basin's rim, and vanished.

7

What Made Dickens Laugh?

'Merrily the smiling dimples twinkled and expanded more and more, until they broke into a laugh'. That animistic description of Temple Fountain from *Martin Chuzzlewit*, with which I closed the last essay, has a curious similarity with Dickens's own changing expressions of mirth. He had an enormous capacity for laughter. To elaborate the water metaphor, he often gave the impression of a man with a huge inner reservoir of laughter and with too few occasions for letting the dam open, or the fountain jet skywards. 'Kindling mirth' (to change the metaphor!) was the expression that would have struck most casual acquaintances in meeting him, according to Thomas Trollope. Metaphors abound when trying to describe his love of the comical. When Dickens sniffed comic prey his nose wrinkled up and his eyes glittered with anticipation. That spectacle of 'kindling' laughter and the keen appetite for the ludicrous was confirmed by his friend Percy Fitzgerald:

> when there was anything droll suggested, a delightful sparkle of lurking humour began to kindle and spread to his mouth, so that, even before he uttered anything, you felt that something irresistibly droll was at hand. No one ever told a story so drolly, and, what is not so common, relished another man's story so heartily.

With some small variations, Fitzgerald would repeat this description of Dickens warming up to a comic story:

> He called up the scene, his eyes became charged with humour, the wrinkles at the corners of his mouth quivered with enjoyment, his voice and richly unctuous laugh contributed, with his strangely grotesque glances, and so he told the tale.

As a schoolboy (13 or 14 years old) Dickens was 'given to laugh immoderately without any apparent sufficient reason'. When the world failed to supply enough occasions for laughter he made up his own: 'Often, while writing, his face would be convulsed with laughter at his own fun'. This self-generated fun is confirmed by his son, Henry, who recalled being taught shorthand by Dickens. Dickens would deliver absurd speeches for Henry to record in shorthand, Henry would collapse in laughter, and so would Dickens: 'he himself, tickled by the ridiculous nature of his own fancies, gave way to fits of laughter only equalled by wild bursts on my part'. His laugh was contagious. Another friend described it as 'most hearty and sonorous, quite infectious to the hearer'. Fitzgerald heard the sound of Dickens's laughter as 'richly unctuous'. In middle age he laughed 'with a wheezing gasp' which gradually struggled into 'a hearty ring', according to his artist friend Marcus Stone. 'Hearty' is a cliché adjective for laughter, but when witnesses apply it to Dickens it seems to carry more force. 'His own heart laughed', Dickens wrote of the euphorically reformed Scrooge, and that seems to describe Dickens's laughter. 'He laughed all over', according to his American friend James Fields. And Arthur Helps in his obituary notice of Dickens described his laughter as of 'the largest and heartiest kind, irradiating his whole countenance, and compelling you to participate in his immense enjoyment of it'.

Laughter seemed to be Dickens's natural element. This certainly was the opinion of many who watched him in his public readings. Here is the *New-York Daily Tribune*:

> Mr. Dickens was happiest in his humorous embodiments. The moment he enters the realm of humor he is a monarch, and a merry one. His clear eyes twinkle, his face is expressive of bubbling mirth that is almost forcibly restrained, his voice grows richer with jollity, his whole being seems aroused.

'His laugh was brimful of enjoyment', recalled Thomas Trollope. 'There was a peculiar humorous protest in it when recounting or hearing anything specially absurd, as who should say "'Pon my soul this is *too* ridiculous! This passes all bounds!" and bursting out afresh as though the sense of the ridiculous overwhelmed him like a tide, which carried all hearers away with it'. Hearers were submerged in the flood of his laughter or caught it as a contagion; either way they were irresistibly drawn into it. So, what were the kinds of things that provoked this magnificent laughter?

Ridiculous Solemnities

Dickens evidently loved extravagantly comical moments, and much of his own humour, as we have seen, characteristically intensifies such experiences until they become almost '*too* ridiculous'. It would be interesting to know more about his responses to the humorous writing of his contemporaries; but one suspects that while he might have enjoyed their irony and burlesque they would not have satisfied his appetite for the grotesquely absurd. Besides, it was more often the random comedy of life rather than art that so appealed to him, times when he discovered the ridiculous in what others might have seen as solemn (we will come on to funerals in a minute).

There was one occasion, however, when he confessed to being quite overwhelmed with laughter at a piece of comic writing and acting: 'I don't think I ever saw anything meant to be funny, that struck me as so extraordinarily droll'. This happened during a visit to the theatre in March 1856. He had gone with three friends to see a production of Tom Taylor's *Still Waters Run Deep* at the Olympic Theatre, where the manager had seated them in a conspicuous private box, so that when he had an uncontrollable fit of laughter he became the object of the auditorium's attention. What triggered that laughter was a scene near the end of the play, when the character Mr Potter (an amiable, old-fashioned gentleman, with no small talk at all) is receiving guests for a dinner party. Potter was played by Samuel Emery, a veteran comic actor. Here is the exchange that set Dickens off:

> [Potter is alone on stage, dressed for dinner. A servant announces the arrival of a guest, Mr Langford, who enters]
>
> POTTER. Ah, Langford, my dear fellow, delighted to see you. Mrs Sternhold will be down directly. Well, (rubbing his hands.) any news to-day?
>
> LANG. Nothing particular. Uncommonly seasonable weather.

POTTER. Uncommonly seasonable weather—uncommonly seasonable—uncommonly—(bell heard.) I shouldn't wonder if that's Markham.
   [servant announces Markham, who enters]

POTTER. Ah! It is Markham! How are you all at home?—that's right! You know Langford, I think. (LANGFORD *and* MARKHAM *bow*.) Well, anything new?

MARKHAM. No—nothing stirring but stagnation! Infernally disagreeable weather—

POTTER. Infernally disagreeable—infernally—very disagreeable weather! (aside) I wish Jane would come! She has such a flow of conversation.

Reporting on the evening to Georgina Hogarth, Dickens wrote: 'I laughed (in a conspicuous corner) to that extent at Emery when he received the dinner-company, that the people were more amused by me than by the Piece. I don't think I ever saw anything meant to be funny, that struck me as so extraordinarily droll. I couldn't get over it at all'. The exchange between Potter and the guests is a gift for a skilful actor: the Potter character can milk the embarrassment with excruciating pauses as he ransacks his mind for conversational fillers, and ends up lamely endorsing utterly contradictory sentiments on the weather. Timing in these speeches would be everything. Presumably Sam Emery had a mastery of this, otherwise Dickens would not have subsided into helpless laughter. His remarks about what was 'meant to be funny' suggest a category of deliberately scripted ludicrousness that he wasn't particularly responsive to, or at least not as responsive as he was to life's accidental comic moments.

I mentioned funerals a little earlier. Dickens is well known to have deplored the extravagant mourning formalities of Victorian funerals, and to have directed in his will that his own be conducted 'in as inexpensive, unostentatious, and strictly private manner'; furthermore that 'those who attend my funeral wear no scarf, cloak, black bow, long hat-band, or other such revolting absurdity'. It is as though Dickens, who can never keep his hands off any part of a show in which he is involved, is giving his cast instructions for this posthumous performance, down to the smallest details of costume. That phrase 'revolting absurdity' encapsulates the mix of the grotesque and the ridiculous that often characterizes Dickens's fictional funerals. One fine example is Mrs Joe's funeral in *Great Expectations* (Chapter 35). Pip arrives back at the Forge to discover that the undertaker, Mr Trabb, has taken full charge of the proceedings, and he recognizes in the undertaker's staff several notorious locals, one of the solemn black-garbed attendants being a carpenter who had once eaten two geese for a bet. Another pious employee is a boy sacked from the local inn for 'turning a young couple into a sawpit on their bridal morning, in consequence of intoxication rendering it necessary for him to ride his horse clasped round the neck with both arms'. A procession of mourners is formed to follow the coffin. ' "Pocket-handkerchiefs out, all!" cried Mr Trabb at this point, in a depressed business-like voice [...]. So we all put our pocket-handkerchiefs to our faces, as if our noses were bleeding'. The procession moved off, the coffin travelling on the shoulders of six bearers, blanketed under a large black drape: 'the whole looked like a blind monster with twelve human legs, shuffling and blundering along'. At every point, the narrator sees through the pompous mummery to its sordid human constituents, refuses to view the ritual through the spectacles of convention. It is a good example of the comic mechanism of 'descending incongruity'.

Pip the narrator may cause the reader to laugh at his grotesque analogies but he is not laughing himself because he is too emotionally involved with his dead sister and the forlorn Joe. A real-life experience of a similar kind happened to Dickens when he attended the funeral in 1843 of William Hone, the radical writer and bookseller. He described it as a 'scene of mingled comicality and seriousness', and was still laughing at the memory of it five months later. He and George Cruikshank had attended the funeral as mourners. The day was foggy, cold and very wet.

Now, George has enormous whiskers which straggle all down his throat in such weather, and stick out in front of him, like a partially unravelled bird's-nest; so that he looks queer enough at the best, but when he is very wet, and in a state between jollity [...] and the deepest gravity (going to a funeral, you know) it is utterly impossible to resist him: especially as he makes the strangest remarks the mind of man can conceive, without any intention of being funny, but rather meaning to be philosophical. I really cried with an irresistible sense of his comicality, all the way, but when he was drest out in a black

cloak and a very long black hatband by an undertaker, who (as he
whispered me with tears in his eyes—for he had known Hone many
years—was 'a character, and he would like to sketch him') I thought
I should have been obliged to go away.

What seems to be so irresistibly funny here for Dickens is his sense
of compounded incongruities: Cruikshank's dishevelled appearance
at a ceremonial occasion, his incontrollable sodden whiskers at odds
with his formal mourning wear, his bizarrely misjudged conversation, his professional enthusiasm (to sketch the undertaker) bursting
through his grief. All these could be funny enough, but in addition
Cruikshank seems wholly unaware of his eccentric remarks and
behaviour and the bizarre figure he cuts. It looks like a perfect
example of Bergson's conviction that a character is comical in proportion to his ignorance of himself; for 'a defect that is ridiculous, as
soon as it feels itself to be so, endeavours to modify itself'. Here,

Illustration 11: Portrait of George Cruikshank, after a photograph. Print
(?1870s).

Dickens is laughing on his own and presumably trying hard to conceal it from Cruikshank as well as from the assembled mourners; but, as we all know, the effort to suppress a fit of laughter seems perversely to be an extra stimulus to laughter. In telling his story Dickens adds one very characteristic touch, likening Cruikshank's whiskers to a 'partially unravelled bird's-nest'. It makes the spectacle suddenly very vivid in detail at the same time as it sharply strikes the key-note of the whole scene, the threatened comical 'unravelling' of a tightly formal, dignified occasion.

The strain between how one ought to be feeling on such occasions and how one actually feels makes one particularly susceptible to the relief of laughter, and embarrassingly so on formal occasions of this kind. Dickens knew the problem well. In April 1839 his friend the great actor Macready announced his retirement from managing Covent Garden theatre (which had proved financially disastrous). Dickens wrote both to commiserate with his personal loss and to lament the more general loss to the theatre-going public. 'If I may jest with my misfortunes', he went on to say, he would quote Mr Curdle's grandiloquent tribute in *Nicholas Nickleby* to the passing of the great age of drama, about 'human intellectuality gilding with a refulgent light our dreamy moments', and concluding with 'the drama is gone—perfectly gone'. Dickens realizes this is an odd note to strike in a letter of commiseration, and his partial apology to Macready illuminates his behaviour at Hone's funeral: 'With the same perverse and unaccountable feeling which causes a heartbroken man at a dear friend's funeral to see something irresistibly comical in a red-nosed or one-eyed undertaker, I receive your communication with ghastly facetiousness'. It is as though Dickens seizes on an opportunity for laughter's relief. It is a way of detaching himself, albeit temporarily, from distressing experience. He explicitly invoked this remedy on one occasion when confronting the painful reality of his mother's dementia:

> My mother, who was also left to me when my father died (I never had anything left to me but relations), is in the strangest state of mind from senile decay: and the impossibility of getting her to understand what is the matter, combined with her desire to be got up in sables like a female Hamlet, illumines the dreary scene with a ghastly absurdity that is the chief relief I can find in it.

'Ghastly absurdity' is much the same partial oxymoron as his confessed 'ghastly facetiousness', part of the vocabulary of Dickens's black humour.

This kind of black humour is self-defensive. Freud thought it heroic. He regarded such humour (as opposed to wit, the 'outlet for aggressive tendencies') as 'the ego's victorious assertion of its own invulnerability. It refuses to be hurt by the arrows of reality or to be compelled to suffer [...]. Humour is not resigned; it is rebellious'. Humour hoists us into superiority over our misfortunes.

The problem of how one is supposed to adjust one's demeanour on solemn occasions—the appropriate mask to take out of one's wardrobe—is one that fascinated Dickens and was a staple of his humour: for instance, the pompous funerals of Mrs Joe and Anthony Chuzzlewit, the chilling christening of little Paul Dombey. Births, marriages and deaths conventionally require formal celebrations, but the degrees of formality exercised by Victorian middle-class families on all such occasions could be formidable; and the strain this must have imposed on all involved would have made the relief of irreverent laughter even more intense. How, for example, should one comport oneself at a wedding ceremony? Here is Dickens's account of the day his daughter Katey was married, in the little country church at Higham. Though he had tried to keep the wedding quiet, the whole village got to know of it and wanted to contribute to the festivities. The blacksmith somehow acquired two small cannon and kept firing them off during the night before, with the Dickens family 'not having the slightest idea what they meant'. On the day itself:

> One very funny thing was, the entrance into church of the few friends whom I had caused to be brought down straight from town by Special Train. They didn't know whether they were to look melancholy, beaming, or maudlin; and their uncertainty struck me as so uncommonly droll, that I was obliged to hide my reverend parental countenance in my hand on the altar Railing.

The same kind of tension between conventional solemnity and comical accident happened again to Dickens when he was being shown the ingenious astronomical clock in Lyons cathedral where mechanical figures enacted a Bible scene during the ringing out of

the hour. The episode was reported in *Pictures from Italy*. The cathedral sacristan accompanied Dickens as he watched this:

> It was set in motion, and thereupon a host of little figures staggered
> out of [a host of little doors], and jerked themselves back again,
> with that special unsteadiness of purpose, and hitching in the gait,
> which usually attaches to figures that are moved by clockwork. [...]
> There was a centre puppet of the Virgin Mary; and close to her, a
> small pigeon-hole, out of which another and a very ill-looking pup-
> pet made one of the most sudden plunges I ever saw accomplished:
> instantly flopping back again at sight of her, and banging his little
> door violently after him. Taking this to be emblematic of the vic-
> tory over Sin and Death, and not at all unwilling to show that
> I perfectly understood the subject, in anticipation of the showman,
> I rashly said, 'Aha! The Evil Spirit. To be sure. He is very soon
> disposed of.' 'Pardon Monsieur,' said the Sacristan, with a polite
> motion of his hand towards the little door, as if introducing some-
> body—'The Angel Gabriel!'

What Dickens represents as a kind of Punch-and-Judy show was a
clockwork enactment of the Annunciation. But the solemnity of
the Biblical scene was difficult to sustain with this clumsy pup-
petry. This, by the way, is of a piece with Dickens's general
response to Catholic ceremonials in Europe in *Pictures*: they are
often approximated to puppet shows in his descriptions—proces-
sions with comically lurching effigies, and so on. 'Laughter degrades
and materialises': Bakhtin's comment precisely catches Dickens's
rendering of this Lyons Annunciation. The holy personages were
all too material as they staggered and jerked, plunged and flopped,
and banged doors. Characteristically Dickens winds up his language
to a level of intensity exceeding the dynamic of the clockwork
antics, so that the action takes on the farcical violence of traditional
pantomime.

Dickens gave a lively and rather more irreverent version of this
episode in a private letter to a friend describing 'the Virgin Mary—
with a very blunt nose, like the hangman in Punch's show'. In that
letter he remarked of the episode, 'I made a good mistake there, at
which I used to laugh afterwards; before I had lost the strength of
mind which laughing requires'. I'm not clear what Dickens meant
by that last statement—laughing requires 'strength of mind'? Isn't

laughing more usually associated with mental relaxation, if not indeed collapse? I asked some fellow Dickens enthusiasts what they thought it meant. One of them, Robert Patten, suggested Dickens really believed that humour could be an intelligent mode of thinking. That is an attractive proposition. My guess is that the strength of mind refers to the capacity to see his own mistakes objectively, and to laugh at himself. That in itself might be seen as an 'intelligent mode of thinking'.

In the funeral scene with Cruikshank and in the Annunciation performance, Dickens is relishing both the eccentricities of the actors (human and mechanical) and their (unwitting) threat to the starchy dignity of the occasion. The two, of course, are co-dependent; the pious solemnity of the background throws into even sharper relief the ludicrous antics of the actors. It is that subversive edge in comical events that so appealed to him. Pantomime for him was a stronghold of that kind of subversiveness: 'it really was a comfortable thing', he wrote after watching one pantomime, 'to see all conventional dignity so outrageously set at naught'.

But sometimes even pantomime could falter, and then the gap between *that* stage illusion and mundane reality offered more opportunities for laughter. An example of this (briefly mentioned earlier in this book) happened when Dickens was in the audience at Covent Garden theatre for a Christmas pantomime:

> suddenly and without a moment's warning, every scene on that immense stage fell over on its face and disclosed Chaos by Gaslight, behind! There never was such a business—about sixty people who were on the stage, being extinguished in the most remarkable manner. Not a soul was hurt. In the uproar, some moon-calf rescued a porter pot, six feet high (out of which the clown had been drinking when the accident happened), and stood it on the cushion of the lowest Proscenium Box P. S. [Prompt Side] beside a lady and gentleman who were dreadfully ashamed of it. The moment the House knew that nobody was injured, they directed their whole attention to this gigantic porter pot in its genteel position (the lady and gentleman trying to hide behind it), and roared with laughter. When a modest footman came from behind the Curtain to clear it, and took it up in his arms, like a Brobdingnagian Baby, we all laughed more than we had ever laughed in our lives. I don't know why.

Once again, the laughter comes from sudden undignified disruptions to a ceremonial event. After the initial calamity it becomes focused on the porter pot, which has migrated from the make-believe world into the real world. From belonging to the pantomime clown it now seems to belong to the respectable couple in the box, to their consternation. But why the intensified laughter ('more than we had ever laughed in our lives') when the pot was removed? Dickens didn't know. Was it just the final turn in the mounting absurdity and confusion between what and who belonged to which world in this Chaos by Gaslight?

This interpenetration of imaginary and real worlds is very much Dickens's favourite kind of drollery. He habitually tries to interfuse the two as part of his programme as a writer, just as in his social life he casts his friends as characters with parts to play. His more extravagant conceits reach across the conventional divide to pull into sudden relationship the fanciful and the mundane, and so often his laughter is triggered by the abrupt confrontation between them. As we have already heard him confess, 'I have such an inexpressible enjoyment of what I see in a droll light that I dare say I pet it as if it were a spoilt child'.

Here he is again, responding to another calamity—not quite Chaos by Gaslight but (apparently) Chaos by Gaslight Failure. It seems his *Household Words* sub-editor, W. H. Wills, had an accident with the gas system, probably at the magazine's offices, and possibly disrupting local supplies more widely (one can't be sure of this). Dickens writes to Wilkie Collins:

> I have seen nothing of Wills since he disarranged the whole metropolitan supply of Gas. I have a general idea that he must have been upside-down ever since, in some corner,—like the Groom to whom the Sultan's daughter was to have been sacrificed [...]. I went about the streets all next day, laughing like a Pantomime Mask. I never did see anything so ridiculous.

It is frustrating not to know more about this event; what did Dickens actually *see*? His response in narrating it is very characteristic in its embellishments. He refers to the *Arabian Nights* tale of the humpback stable-groom who was seized by a genie and kept upside-down through a whole night. Dickens weaves this fantastic analogy into the

gas-supply scenario and makes the whole episode sumptuously ludicrous for himself, enough to set him off laughing for a whole day.

What he sees 'in a droll light' he does indeed pet as if it were a
spoilt child (and even that statement humorously inflates and adorns
an otherwise bald confession). Comical and (literally) fabulous
aggrandisement of mundane accidents is his stock-in-trade, an
instinctive burlesquing of daily life. 'It was the way he told it', as a
comedian might say admiringly of a fellow pro; and it seems that
Dickens did have a distinctive form of comic delivery, as one witness
observed of him in 1840: 'His humorous remarks were generally
delivered in an exaggerated, stilted style, and sometimes with a complete perversion of facts, quite astounding to matter-of-fact minds,
and were accompanied by a twinkle in the eyes, and a comic lifting
of one eyebrow'. We can't see Dickens's face, but as he unfolds his
written narratives with comical exaggeration, we as readers become
aware of a heightened and hyperbolic manner of delivery creeping
into his style: it's not hard to infer his facial expression, eyes twink-
ling and eye-brow arching, as he composes these scenes.

When Dickens famously observed in his preface to *Bleak House*
that he 'purposely dwelt upon the romantic side of familiar things',
he was not referring to his comedy; but, as may be clear from
the discussion and examples above of his extravagant associations
of the mundane and the exotic, that is just what characterizes much
of his humour. He felt there was a therapeutic value in forging such
links, as he made clear in his 'Preliminary Word' to *Household
Words*:

> In the bosoms of the young and old, of the well-to-do and of the
> poor, we would tenderly cherish that light of Fancy which is inherent
> in the human breast [...] in all familiar things, even in those which
> are repellant [sic] on the surface, there is Romance enough, if we will
> find it out.

Later on in this manifesto statement he illustrates his point by suggesting analogies between the scenes of industrialization in modern
England, the 'towering chimneys [...] spirting out fire and smoke
upon the prospect', and the 'Slaves of the Lamp of Knowledge
[who] have their thousand and one tales, no less than the Genii of
the East'. In similar vein, his sense of humour in responding to poor

Wills's accident improbably brought together London Gas supplies and the *Arabian Nights*. There is romance in all familiar things, 'if we will find it out': Dickens made it his mission, in his journalism and fiction, to educate his readership in how to 'find it out'. As I suggested in the discussion of incongruity, Dickens's fusing of fancy with the dullest of familiar things is at the heart of his humour as much as it is at the heart of his broader programme as a writer.

A fine example of Dickens's seeing humour in the ungainly union between the mundane and the romantic occurred during his first trip to America. Once again, as he reported in a letter, he had to try to smother his laughter. He and Catherine were staying overnight in Hartford, Connecticut, exhausted by the sequence of daily levees. They had gone to bed when suddenly they became aware of being serenaded by a couple of singers just outside their bedroom door:

> when they began, in the dead of the night, in a long, musical, echoing passage outside our chamber door; singing, in low voices to guitars, about home and absent friends and other topics that they knew would interest us; we were more moved than I can tell you. In the midst of my sentimentality though, a thought occurred to me which made me laugh so immoderately that I was obliged to cover my face with the bedclothes. 'Good Heavens!' I said to Kate, 'what a monstrously ridiculous and commonplace appearance my boots must have, outside the door!' I never *was* so impressed with a sense of the absurdity of boots, in all my life.

Dickens was imagining his boots, bereft of their usual occupant, being the only visible addressees for the singers' serenade: melodic sentimental plaints to a pair of impassive boots.

The bathos of boots in that episode follows the curve from the sentimental sublime to the ridiculous. Equally funny for Dickens was the reverse, the extravagant burlesque elevation of the mundane (it was the launching joke of *Pickwick Papers*, after all). For one of his Tavistock House amateur theatricals he cast his children in various roles, including his youngest, the 2-year-old Edward, who, so the playbill trumpeted, '*has been kept out of bed at a vast expense*'. Again, one can imagine him hugging this Crummlesian hyperbole, and chuckling over it.

Dickens Laughs at Dickens

Let us turn now to what made Dickens laugh in his own writings.
I mentioned at the start of this essay that if Dickens felt the world
didn't supply enough material for laughter he made up his own.
That was meant to draw a distinction between his enjoyment of
life's humorous accidents and his crafting of comical scenes in his
fiction. But when one reflects on the various episodes he reports
above, it's clear that he often manipulates the character of the real-
life event so that its humorous potential is realized to the full; in
effect, he is already working creatively on it.

We have just left him (in imagination) chuckling to himself at his
playbill joke. His study must often have echoed to his laughter as
he steered his characters into comical situations or coaxed them
into their idiosyncratic speeches. All those portraits and capriccios
representing Dickens at his desk or in his study, sometimes with a
crowd of his own characters, show him earnestly concentrating or
in a sombre creative daydream. None, so far as I know, shows him
laughing as he conjures into being eccentric characters, preposterous speeches, outrageous analogies, farcical antics. Yet he often told
friends how much he had laughed as he brought them all alive.
'Laughed'?—he had 'always roared in the most unblushing manner' when he re-read one of his own scenes (which we will come
to soon).

Here for example is one creation he was very enthusiastic about.
It is the comically contorted style he contrived for Christopher the
Waiter, his framework narrator for the collection of Christmas
stories for *All The Year Round* (1862), 'Somebody's Luggage'. In the
concluding story, 'His Wonderful End', Christopher describes his
state of anxiety:

> I too soon discovered that peace of mind had fled from a brow
> which, up to that time, Time had merely took the hair off, leaving
> an unruffled expanse within [...] It were superfluous to veil it,—the
> brow to which I allude is my own.
>
>   Yes, over that brow uneasiness gathered like the sable wing of the
> fabled bird, as—as no doubt will be easily identified by all right-
> minded individuals. If not, I am unable, on the spur of the moment,
> to enter into particulars of him. The reflection that the writings must

now inevitably get into print, and that He might yet live and meet
with them, sat like the Hag of Night upon my jaded form. The elasticity of my spirits departed. Fruitless was the Bottle, whether Wine
or Medicine. I had recourse to both, and the effect of both upon my
system was witheringly lowering.

Dickens exploits the same kind of deformed syntax and eccentric
punctuation as he contrived for another comical narrator in the
Christmas stories, Mrs Lirriper. He told Forster that he felt the result
to be 'exceedingly droll', a phrase he used for the same purposes in
a letter to Wills and 'very droll' to Wilkie Collins. Christopher's
speech style strains for dignity and poise but in the effort contorts
itself into the strangest shapes. The discrepancy between aspiration
and realisation is at the heart of the comedy—an amiable kind of
affectation.

This raises a question about the appropriateness of laughter when
the object of that laughter is a form of disability, physical or mental.
It has certainly made some critics queasy, to think that Dickens
laughs at the ungainliness of speech in under-educated people. It is
like laughing at physical deformity. His defence might be along the
lines of Fielding's argument, in his Preface to *Joseph Andrews*, about
affectation as a source of the ridiculous. Here is the point Fielding
makes about the dangers of laughing at others' misfortunes:

> Surely he hath a very ill-framed mind, who can look on ugliness,
> infirmity, or poverty, as ridiculous in themselves: nor do I believe any
> man living who meets a dirty fellow riding through the streets in a
> cart, is struck with an idea of the Ridiculous from it; but if he should
> see the same figure descend from his coach and six, or bolt from his
> chair with his hat under his arm, he would then begin to laugh, and
> with justice. In the same manner, were we to enter a poor house and
> behold a wretched family shivering with cold and languishing with
> hunger, it would not incline us to laughter, (at least we must have very
> diabolical natures, if it would): but should we discover there a grate,
> instead of coals, adorned with flowers, empty plate or china dishes on
> the side-board, or any other affectation of riches and finery either on
> their persons or in their furniture; we might then indeed be excused,
> for ridiculing so fantastical an appearance. Much less are natural
> imperfections the object of derision: but when ugliness aims at the
> applause of beauty, or lameness endeavours to display agility; it is

> then that these unfortunate circumstances, which at first moved our
> compassion, tend only to raise our mirth.

It is only under those last conditions—when ugliness aims at the
applause of beauty and lameness (though we are not actually
laughing at the defect *per se*) tries to display agility—that we have
permission to laugh at ugliness or lameness, or, as in the case of
Christopher, at his ungainly speech. That is the theory. In practice
it is often harder to be so morally discriminating. Dickens found
himself in precisely this kind of difficulty on one occasion, and he
was candid about the complex and contradictory responses he was
experiencing. He had received a letter from a man called Job Joynes,
possibly the father of one of the girls at Urania House:

> [The letter] is so very affecting that I am angry with myself for hav-
> ing laughed until I cried, at it. The most comical circumstance about
> it seems to be that poor Joynes plumes himself immensely on his
> composition—and there is something, I am ashamed to say, quite
> irresistible in that idea, and in his extraordinary use of the 'unworthy'
> adjective, and the wonderful means he resorts to for spelling some of
> his words. But really it is very touching for all that.

How might one apply Fielding's prescription here? Without having
Joynes's letter it's impossible to tell, but Dickens does suggest that
the writer, like Christopher the Waiter, is aiming to impress and
adopts a dignified style and tone that he cannot sustain. So Dickens
is partly laughing at the transparently unsuccessful affectation, and
at the same time touched by the writer's efforts. It is a little like the
superb scene in *Great Expectations* (Chapter 27) when Joe visits Pip in
his London lodgings. Joe's clothes—his Sunday best and 'state
boots'—and his tortuously formal speech are both monstrously ill-
fitting. He becomes a kind of clown during the meeting and the
whole episode is both hilarious and moving. It is moving partly
because we know Joe is presenting himself like this only because he's
been bullied into it by his wife and thinks it will please Pip; it is far
from his natural manner (and dress), as he acknowledges when saying farewell. But this has also been Pip's responsibility, as his older
self makes clear: 'I had neither the good sense nor the good feeling
to know that this was all my fault, and that if I had been easier
[i.e. more at ease] with Joe, Joe would have been easier with me'.

Dickens must have realized that Job Joynes wrote his letter in the way he did because he knew he was addressing an Important Man— and a great writer.

Joe's visit to London would have been written to raise laughter. The relationship between Pip and Joe, though it deepened after Pip's change of heart later in the novel, was in Dickens's original conception of the novel designed to restore high comedy to his fiction. 'You will not have to complain of the want of humour as in *The Tale of Two Cities*', he wrote to Forster. In the opening chapters at the Forge he put 'a child and a good-natured foolish man, in relations that seem to me very funny'. This was a deliberate effort by Dickens to revive his characteristic humour, to please not only Forster but most of his readers who had regretted its relative absence from the novels of the 1850s. Pip's festive oppression by the gruesome collection of adults gathered for the Christmas lunch—all out to badger him on any pretext that came to hand— revives some of the humour of Little Paul Dombey's bullying by the ogress Mrs Pipchin. Joe, who is in effect an overgrown oppressed child in such company, silently spoons compensatory gravy into Pip's plate. 'Exceedingly droll', Dickens hoped it would prove. He himself certainly found it so and encouraged friends to read the opening numbers for that reason: 'Pray read Great Expectations. I think it is very droll. It is a very great success, and seems universally liked—I suppose because it opens funnily and with an interest too.'

'Droll', 'funny', 'humour': Dickens uses each of these words within a couple of sentences in emphasizing this element to Forster. In several letters he uses 'droll' to describe what he felt he had achieved with Christopher the Waiter. To what extent is he meaning exactly the same thing each time? By and large, in combing through several mentions of 'droll' in his letters, one senses the term is more than just a synonym for 'funny'. It seems to denote a particular kind of humour. For instance, in a letter to Frank Stone about his (Frank's) role in a planned farce (which never came to anything) Dickens uses 'droll' to mean something odd and inconsequentially whimsical:

> I have got a capital part for you in the Farce—not a difficult one to
> learn, as you never say anything but 'Yes' and 'No'. You are called,

in the Dramatis Personae, an able bodied British Seaman, and you are never seen by mortal eye to do anything (except inopportunely producing a Mop), but stand about the Deck of the boat in Everybody's way, with your hair immensely touzled, one brace on, your hands in your pockets, and the bottoms of your trousers tucked up. Yet you are inextricably connected with the plot, and are the man whom everybody is enquiring after. I think it is a very whimsical idea and extremely droll. It made me laugh heartily when I jotted it all down yesterday.

This, I think, goes to the heart of what Dickens found particularly funny. Although he uses 'droll' in a variety of different contexts, more often than not it means for him a particular kind of quirkiness of character or incident and some whimsical incongruities: the solemn grotesqueries of Christopher the Waiter's language, the odd and touching relationship between child Pip and the big but slow-witted Joe, and the dishevelled 'British Seaman' who hardly speaks, gets in everybody's way, and yet is the focus of attention. These are instances of eccentric behaviour that has become ingrained as someone's normality.

There are even riper examples of this particular species of drollery. During his stay in Italy in 1845 Dickens described to Forster the antics of two English travellers who had temporarily occupied part of the Palazzo Peschiere in Genoa, where the Dickens family were staying. Forster's account quotes a letter from Dickens:

They had with them a meek English footman who immediately confided to Dickens's servants, among other grievances, the fact that he was made to do everything, even cooking, in crimson breeches; which in a hot climate, he protested, was 'a grinding of him down.' 'He is a poor soft country fellow; and his master locks him up at night, in a basement room with iron bars to the window. Between which our servants poke wine in, at midnight. His master and mistress buy old boxes at the curiosity shops, and pass their lives in lining 'em with bits of parti-coloured velvet. A droll existence, is it not?'

What, one wonders, was the full truth behind this sketch? Dickens is no doubt revelling in the oddity of this behaviour, which he has come to know at *third* hand, and for which there may be more rational (and grimmer) explanations which would reduce its scope for laughter. But the fragmentary glimpses are all he needs in order to construct his droll scenarios of striking whimsicality. The conjunction of formality and routine with spectacularly odd behaviour gives this kind of humour of eccentricity an extra edge. The same concoction features briefly in a scene Dickens witnessed while dining with the old actor Macready: 'An old waiter whom I have seen there before, was in attendance; and the way in which Macready and he were at cross purposes about the decanters and wine glasses was dismally droll'. The two old men became over-heated about trivial formalities, and the juxtaposition tickled Dickens.

Dickensian laughter, by which I mean both Dickens's laughter and our own laughing recognition of his signature humour, is stirred by situations such as these: when eccentricity becomes conventionalized, or when there is a breakdown of conventional behaviour patterns and yet some of the conventions persist among the ruins, or when anarchy is seething at the edge of formal occasions. One such scene, where barely suppressed rage and violence foment just below the surface of a polite exchange, comes in one of Dickens's Mrs Lirriper pieces, written for the 1864 Christmas number of *All The Year Round*. It is particularly interesting because Dickens was so enthusiastic about its humour. In a letter to Forster he reports as follows:

> I have finished the job I set myself, and [...] it has in it something— to me at all events—so extraordinarily droll, that though I have been reading it some hundred times in the course of the working, I have never been able to look at it with the least composure, but have always roared in the most unblushing manner. I leave you to find out what it was.

Forster identifies it as the encounter between the Major and Mr Buffle the Tax Collector, in 'Mrs Lirriper Relates How She Went On, and Went Over'. One cannot be entirely sure where in the Major's encounters with the Tax Collector Dickens found such extraordinary humour, but it is most likely to have been the following scene. The Tax Collector, Mr Buffle, is a harmless bureaucrat with an unfortunate habit of seeming to snoop at the property when he makes his official visit to households, and he also inadvertently causes offence by neglecting to remove his hat indoors. Mrs Lirriper's

fiercely loyal lodger, the irascible Major, is mightily offended by
these traits, which he regards as an insult to his landlady's dignity.
Mrs Lirriper relates:

> So at last [...] the Major lay in wait for Mr. Buffle, and it worrited
> me a good deal. Mr. Buffle gives his rap of two sharp knocks one
> day and the Major bounces to the door. 'Collector has called for two
> quarters' Assessed Taxes' says Mr. Buffle. 'They are ready for him'
> says the Major and brings him in here. But on the way Mr. Buffle
> looks about him in his usual suspicious manner and the Major fires
> and asks him 'Do you see a Ghost sir?' 'No sir' says Mr. Buffle.
> 'Because I have before noticed you' says the Major 'apparently look-
> ing for a spectre very hard beneath the roof of my respected friend.
> When you find that supernatural agent, be so good as to point him
> out sir.' Mr. Buffle stares at the Major and then nods at me. 'Mrs.
> Lirriper sir' says the Major going off into a perfect steam and intro-
> ducing me with his hand. 'Pleasure of knowing her' says Mr. Buffle.
> 'A—hum!—Jemmy Jackman sir!' says the Major introducing him-
> self. 'Honour of knowing you by sight' says Mr. Buffle. 'Jemmy
> Jackman sir' says the Major wagging his head sideways in a sort of
> obstinate fury 'presents to you his esteemed friend that lady Mrs.
> Emma Lirriper of Eighty-one Norfolk Street Strand London in the
> County of Middlesex in the United Kingdom of Great Britain and
> Ireland. Upon which occasion sir,' says the Major, 'Jemmy Jackman
> takes your hat off.' Mr. Buffle looks at his hat where the Major
> drops it on the floor, and he picks it up and puts it on again. 'Sir'
> says the Major very red and looking him full in the face 'there are
> two quarters of the Gallantry Taxes due and the Collector has
> called.' Upon which if you can believe my words my dear the Major
> drops Mr. Buffle's hat off again. 'This—' Mr. Buffle begins very
> angry with his pen in his mouth, when the Major steaming more
> and more says 'Take your bit out sir! Or by the whole infernal sys-
> tem of Taxation of this country and every individual figure in the
> National Debt, I'll get upon your back and ride you like a horse!'
> which it's my belief he would have done and even actually jerking
> his neat little legs ready for a spring as it was. 'This,' says Mr. Buffle
> without his pen 'is an assault and I'll have the law of you.' 'Sir'
> replies the Major 'if you are a man of honour, your Collector of
> whatever may be due on the Honourable Assessment by applying to
> Major Jackman at the Parlours Mrs. Lirriper's Lodgings, may obtain
> what he wants in full at any moment.'

Forster introduces this example of Dickens's roaring with laughter at his own work in the context of his general observation that Dickens, by his own confession, had a 'readiness in all forms [...] thus to enjoy his own pleasantry'. But I wonder whether Dickens found this particular episode funnier than we are likely to do? I suspect that while we might smile or chuckle at the encounter here, it's unlikely to provoke roars, whereas Dickens, so he says, read it to himself 'some hundred times' and each time it seems to have thrown him into fits of laughter. What do we draw from this? If we find it only *quite* funny, perhaps we have an underdeveloped sense of humour? Or, a second possibility, Dickens's is overdeveloped? When, in confronting charges of habitual exaggeration, he addressed the question of different degrees of responsiveness to his writings, he framed it as follows (in a preface written late in life):

> What is exaggeration to one class of minds and perceptions, is plain truth to another. [...] I sometimes ask myself [...] whether it is *always* the writer who colours highly, or whether it is now and then the reader whose eye for colour is a little dull?

Likewise with dulled or heightened senses of humour, it is simply a matter of varying subjectivities. A third possibility is that in this instance the comic potency of the scene imagined by the author hasn't translated into description. Each reading of it for Dickens very likely triggered the imaginary re-enactment of the scene as he had first conceived it before describing it. So, is he laughing at what he has written on the page, or at the 'original' as it came to him in imagination (and possibly as partly acted and voiced by him in composition, as was often his practice)?

In suggesting this distinction between the 'original' comical event as imagined by Dickens (and which sets him off roaring with laughter) and its description in the story, and in speculating that it might have lost something in the transition, I am taking account of the fact that the scene is not given to us in Dickens's own voice. By his own voice I mean the voice we hear, for example, in his letters as he builds a humorous anecdote with a mixture of his characteristic exotic hyperbole and heavy irony. In this instance, the comical encounter between the Major and the Tax Collector is narrated by Mrs Lirriper who, although she does have a distinctive style of discourse and quirky turns of phrase, is not given the descriptive resources we are used to in Dickens. She reproduces for us the heated dialogue, with very little commentary. Were Dickens to have given it in his own words, in his own anecdotal style, the impact would be quite different, colouring up those eccentric details of behaviour that he found especially funny in order to galvanize his reader into laughter. Mrs Lirriper is an involved party, whereas Dickens the anecdotalist would not have been; he would have developed a detachment and thereby liberated himself to exploit the humour which is somewhat masked by Mrs Lirriper's style of narration.

What exactly is the comic kernel in this scene? Why did it cause Dickens to laugh so much? I suspect that what made it so extraordinarily droll for him was the Major's fury seething beneath the formality. The Tax Collector seems unaware that he has wandered on to an active volcano as he is politely conducted into the Lirriper lodgings. The Major has become an embodiment of barely suppressed rage; he 'bounces' to answer the rap on the front door, then 'fires' at the first sign of the Collector's snooping manner, then goes off into a 'perfect steam', wags his head in 'an obstinate fury', and continues 'steaming more and more'. All this time the obtuse official plods on prosaically with his business. The friction between the manically overwrought, hyperactive Major and the dully officious functionary generates great comic energy. We saw something of the same mix in Dickens's report of that ill-assorted couple, Mr and Mrs Davis, visiting the sights of Italy. The nearest modern popular equivalent I can think of is John Cleese's frantic Basil Fawlty, foaming with rage beneath a veneer of fawning politeness, fire curling round the edges of each gushing courtesy.

Dickens produces some of his funniest (most 'droll'?) scenes with this formula, or variations on it. In *Little Dorrit* the courteous and harmless Arthur Clennam becomes the unwitting focus of Mr F's Aunt's ferocious conversation-stoppers, as on the occasion (Book I, Chapter 23) when she and Flora visit him in Bleeding Heart Yard and Arthur is subjected to his old fiancée's sentimental monologues. There is an interruption:

A diversion was occasioned here, by Mr F.'s Aunt making the following inexorable and awful statement:

'There's mile-stones on the Dover road!'

With such mortal hostility towards the human race did she discharge this missile, that Clennam was quite at a loss how to defend himself; the rather as he had been already perplexed in his mind by the honour of a visit from this venerable lady, when it was plain she held him in the utmost abhorrence. He could not but look at her with disconcertment, as she sat breathing bitterness and scorn, and staring leagues away. Flora, however, received the remark as if it had been of a most apposite and agreeable nature; approvingly observing aloud that Mr F.'s Aunt had a great deal of spirit. Stimulated either by this compliment, or by her burning indignation, that illustrious woman then added, 'Let him meet it if he can!' And, with a rigid movement of her stony reticule (an appendage of great size and of a fossil appearance), indicated that Clennam was the unfortunate person at whom the challenge was hurled.

This is another scene of comically polarized and antagonistic moods and energies, with Flora's anodyne gentility and self-centredness oblivious to the abrupt savagery of Mr F's Aunt's behaviour, and poor Clennam unable to retire from or retaliate against this hostility. It has much the same kind of combustible social chemistry as Dickens had enjoyed in the Lirriper scene. He revelled in these scenes, greatly enjoying Mr F's Aunt (according to Forster, with whom he worked on the proofs) and Flora herself: 'There are some things in Flora in number seven [Chapters 23–5] that seem to me to be extraordinarily droll'. None more so than the climax to one of Flora's chaotic monologues later in that same number (Chapter 24), where she is relating for Arthur's benefit the final days of her husband's life:

'I will draw a veil over that dreamy life, Mr F. was in good spirits his appetite was good he liked the cookery he considered the wine weak but palatable and all was well, we returned to the immediate neighbourhood of Number Thirty Little Gosling Street London Docks and settled down, ere we had yet fully detected the housemaid in selling the feathers out of the spare bed Gout flying upwards soared with Mr F. to another sphere.'

This mesmerizing equivalence of detail and the unpunctuated rush come to a sudden end with Mr F's death. 'Flying gout' was the term used to describe the sudden spread of gout from the feet through the nervous system and eventually to the brain. Both Mr F and his gout seem in Flora's description to enjoy an apotheosis. 'Nothing in Flora,' wrote Dickens, 'made me laugh so much as the confusion of ideas between gout flying upwards and its soaring with Mr. F—to another sphere'.

Was this comic masterstroke Dickens's own invention or drawn from something he might have heard? I wonder about this because he describes his enjoyment of it almost as though it were something happening 'out there', something he was watching and listening to, rather than something he is congratulating himself on having created. Dickens, according to his public readings manager Dolby, had an odd habit 'of regarding his own books as the productions of some one else, and would almost refer to them as such.' That 'some one else' may be related to the 'beneficent power' once gratefully acknowledged by Dickens as being the agent who showed him his fictional world: 'I don't invent it—really do not—*but see it*, and write it down'. Did the soaring duo of gout and Mr. F arrive by that route?

I put the question here in conclusion, because at the outset of this essay I made a tentative distinction between Dickens's laughter at life's accidental comical moments and his laughter at his own created comedy. Perhaps that distinction has by now become too indistinct to be worth maintaining. For, as we have seen earlier in this book, Dickens's accounts in his letters or other forms of anecdote creatively embellish real-life incidents to fit his sense of humour; and conversely, the comical moments in his fiction may often have had a spontaneity of production of the kind he suggested was his practice. Colliding incongruities, whimsical drolleries, extravagant affectations, conventional dignity 'outrageously set at nought', sudden impolite rasps on the smooth surfaces of life: some such cluster of humorous stimulants could always kindle Dickens's laughter. That laughter irradiated his whole countenance, his whole person, 'compelling you to participate in his immense enjoyment.' Long may it continue to compel us all.

Afterword

Dickensian Laughter in a Popular Dark Age

Dickens once referred to the middle decades of the nineteenth century as 'a kind of popular dark age' in which literature had a tendency to be 'frightfully literal and catalogue-like'. He combated this tendency by resolutely maintaining in his own writing the 'fanciful treatment' for which he was so often pilloried: his choice was purposely (as he wrote in the Preface to *Bleak House*) to dwell on the romantic side of familiar things. Throughout this book on Dickens's humour we have seen that fanciful treatment at work in the distinctive nature of Dickensian laughter—the extravagant incongruities, the pantomimic transformations of scenes from ordinary life, the revelling in human eccentricities of speech and behaviour—all designed to counteract what he saw as the prevailingly grey spirit of the times. To set people laughing by such means was to give them relief from the strain of maintaining the tone of mid-Victorian culture in that 'popular dark age'. And there is an edge to such laughter. George Orwell closed his landmark essay on Dickens with this imagined glimpse of his subject, 'a face that is not quite the face of the photographs, though it resembles it' (not surprisingly, since no photograph ever caught him laughing): 'It is the face of a man of about forty, with a small beard and a high colour. He is laughing, with a touch of anger in his laughter, but no triumph, no malignity'. It's hard to improve on that snapshot.

This book has concentrated on Dickens's techniques for provoking laughter, since that is where my interests particularly lie. But in this brief Afterword I would like to finish with just a few thoughts on the broader cultural implications of Dickensian laughter.

We have seen something of the prejudices of the age towards laughter. Lord Chesterfield's legacy and the writings of Carlyle and George Vasey represented a range of views about the value of laughter in its social context. Vasey, in pursuing his arguments, also committed what to Dickens would have seemed a sacrilege: he attacked children's stories and nursery rhymes:

> Can we wonder at the immense number of silly, frivolous, giddy, giggling, full-grown fools, who, in the present reign of Queen Victoria, infest all ranks of society, when we reflect that their nascent minds were perverted, and distorted, and shrivelled in their infancy and childhood by such surpassing nonsense and trashy garbage as the nursery rhymes and juvenile literature we have just described, and which are not only permitted, but universally encouraged?

Vasey's fierce book cast a further shadow over an age darkened by the brooding presence of Dombeyism, Murdstonism (the disciplined repression of feeling), Gradgrindism, the Tite Barnacles, and the blighting creed of Mrs Clennam. As we have seen, Dickens crusaded to lighten this popular dark age: 'Brighten it!' he would editorially urge on contributions to *Household Words*, and he encouraged public laughter at his readings in an effort to break the fast-congealing mode of respectable solemnity that was becoming the approved demeanour. As Dickens observed, laughing requires 'strength of mind'.

For Vasey laughter was as pernicious and pathologically threatening as the fanciful literature on which the nation's children had been reared. His project, as I mentioned in the essay on 'Laughers', belonged with a number of later nineteenth-century expressions of anxiety about symptoms of degeneration in the English race. It also capitalized on the cultural elevation of a type of reserved firmness: it helped in the construction of respectability, and thereby its antithesis, vulgarity. In this age of disconcerting social mobility, vulgarity was a condition associated with where you might have come from, in terms of social class. Respectability was what you were hoping to attain. 'Everybody thinks it is his *duty* to try to be a "gentleman"', wrote Ruskin in 1851.

A respectable person is, literally, a person simply worthy of respect. But that term slid from being a simple description of an abstract moral attribute to denoting a certain type of conservative, conventional outward appearance, an attitude, even a dress-style. The result of arguments like Vasey's is the production of respectability as a kind of uniform. Vasey quoted approvingly a *Daily Telegraph* eulogy of Lord Grey: 'Lord Grey was always dignified, decorous, and incapable of a joke; and in such men a popular confidence is placed which is seldom or never given to men of wit and humour about town'. Dickens's term for this type is the buttoned-up man whom we met earlier, in the essay on 'Falling Apart Laughing', and who is perfectly represented by Tite Barnacle in *Little Dorrit* (Book II, Chapter 12):

> Mr. Tite Barnacle was a buttoned-up man, and consequently a weighty one. All buttoned-up men are weighty. All buttoned-up men are believed in. Whether or no the reserved and never-exercised power of unbuttoning, fascinates mankind; whether or no wisdom is supposed to condense and augment when buttoned up, and to evaporate when unbuttoned; it is certain that the man to whom importance is accorded is the buttoned-up man.

Tite Barnacle's associates, as blighting figures of strict respectability, have already been named: Dombey, Murdstone, Gradgrind, Mrs Clennam, exclusive, humourless, and rigid in mind and body, presiding over this popular dark age in their individual spheres—in, respectively, politics, commerce, family, education and religion. These are reflections of a pervasive rigidity of mind, where that mind is too narrowly and intensively focused, a cultural characteristic perhaps especially marked in the 1840s and 1850s. By the late 1860s, one commentator, Henry Sidgwick, reflected that compared with those earlier decades 'we suspend our judgment much more than our predecessors, and much more contentedly [...]. We are gaining in impartiality and comprehensiveness of sympathy'.

I have often invoked Bergson's famous argument that rigidity, inelasticity, was the prime source of laughter. 'The laughable element', he writes, 'consists of a certain *mechanical inelasticity*, just where one would expect to find the wide-awake adaptability and the living pliableness of a human being'. Dickens, I think, had a near pathological horror of this kind of rigidity which resulted from congealed respectability. It may explain his loathing of public statues, which were the ultimate materialization of human rigidity. (Many of these buttoned-up characters give the impression of posing for their statues: Tite Barnacle 'seemed to have been sitting for his portrait to Thomas Lawrence all the days of his life'.) Dickens also thought the English people, especially perhaps the more phlegmatic of the middle-classes (whether 'respectable' or not), needed stirring into greater vitality; or, perhaps one might say, they needed something to disinhibit those natural energies which the culture of reserve and conventionality had suppressed. The House of Commons needed 'the occasional application of sharp stimulants' to keep it properly alive and effective; the people of England, under the influence of 'too much Ministerial narcotic', needed to be 'hustled and pinched in a friendly way'. In the field of the arts and entertainment more should be done to rouse and energize people. Dickens provided this incentive to revitalize people's constitutional immobility in his books, his journalism and his public readings, and where he saw it lacking in national culture he pointed it out. Viewing an art exhibition in Paris in 1855, in which a number of his own countrymen—indeed his own friends—were exhibiting paintings, he complained of the staidness of their work: 'a horrid respectability about most of the best of them', compared with the French paintings and 'the passion and action in them!' (notice especially the call to 'action'). Two years later, at the Manchester Exhibition of paintings, while admiring much of the work himself, he felt 'the common people' wanted something more: they 'want more amusement, and particularly (as it strikes me) *something in motion*, though it were only a twisting fountain. The thing is too still...'

'*Something in motion*' is Dickens's emphasis. This is Dickens's prime target, the undermining of this blighting rigidity now constituted as 'horrid respectability' in his society, whether applied to persons or public institutions: 'the thing is too still'. In looking back at the writings quoted in this book, how often has the target for his humour been this kind of starched complacent dignity? Dickensian laughter is a solvent. It is designed to degrade that conventional respectability and correspondingly to elevate conventional vulgarity; to restore a more relaxed sense of proportion in the social value system. I have already cited Alexander Bain's definition of ridiculousness, in *The Emotions and the Will* (1859), but it is worth repeating here: 'It is the *coerced* form of seriousness and solemnity, without the reality [i.e. without sincere respect and earnestness], that gives us that stiff position, from which a contact with triviality or vulgarity relieves us to our uproarious delight'. And this is often Dickens's method, the humorous application of mischievous vulgarity. Dickens's project is in line with Bergson's ideas about laughter's social function as a corrective: by ridiculing inelasticity of character, our laughter (Bergson insists) 'pursues a utilitarian aim of general improvement'. That utilitarian corrective aim of laughter is a part of Dickens's agenda; and so too is the social bonding agency of laughter.

I close with a short comical scene from Dickens, illustrative, I hope, of some of the points I've been developing, particularly, in this case, the disruption of conventional rigidity adopted for formal, respectable occasions. It comes from a letter of 29 January 1868. Dickens is reporting an episode during his Atlantic crossing to America in the winter of 1867, when a church service was to be held on board during a very rough sea. It was, he said, 'one of the most comical spectacles I have ever seen in my life'.

> The officiating minister, an extremely modest young man, was brought in between two stewards exactly as if he were coming up to the scratch in a prize fight. The ship was rolling and pitching so, that the two big stewards had to stop and watch their opportunity of making a dart at the reading desk with their reverend charge, during which pause he held on, now by one steward and now by the other, with the feeblest expression of countenance and no legs whatever. At length they made a dart at the wrong moment, and one steward was immediately beheld alone in the extreme perspective! while the other and the reverend gentleman held on to the mast in the middle of the saloon—which the latter embraced with both arms as if it were his wife. All this time the congregation were breaking up into sects and sliding away [...]. And when at last the reverend gentleman had been tumbled into his place, the desk (a loose one, put upon the dining table) deviated from the church bodily, and

went over to the Purser. The scene was so extraordinarily ridiculous, and was made so much more so by the exemplary gravity of all concerned in it, that I was obliged to leave before the service began.

'*Something in motion*' is precipitated by the mischievous ocean. Dickens doesn't have to do much to raise laughter except focus details on the scene as it happened. But look at the characteristic activity of his two similes: the curate being supported by two burly stewards as if he were parading in for a prize fight; and the embrace of the mast as if he were passionately cuddling his wife. Both introduce a low-comedy touch to what is meant to be a solemn, stately occasion: 'the contact with triviality or vulgarity relieves us to our uproarious delight'.

This scene, one of the most comical Dickens ever saw, epitomizes much of what I have highlighted in this book about the distinctive nature of his humour: the pantomimic and the farcical breaking through the polished surface; the hilarious incongruity of exemplary gravity riding the bucking anarchy; the comical falling apart of solemn ceremony—sliding furniture and the congregation breaking up into sects. Dickensian laughter and the Atlantic Ocean—those dissident, turbulent and elemental forces of nature—are mighty levellers.

Abbreviations

The place of publication is London, unless indicated otherwise.

Bergson, *Laughter* Henri Bergson, *Laughter: An Essay on the Meaning of the Comic*, translated C. Brereton and F. Rothwell (this 'Authorised Translation' was originally published in 1911: references are to the recent edition published by Arc Manor, Rockville, Maryland, 2008).

Collins, *Heritage* Philip Collins (ed.), *Charles Dickens: The Critical Heritage* (1971).

Collins, *Interviews* Philip Collins (ed.), *Dickens: Interviews and Recollections* (2 vols., Houndmills, 1981).

Forster John Forster, *The Life of Charles Dickens*, ed. J. W. T. Ley (1928).

Letters *The Letters of Charles Dickens*, ed. Madeline House, Graham Storey et al. (12 vols., Oxford, 1965–2002).

Notes

The place of publication is London, unless indicated otherwise.

1. Opening a Fresh Vein of Humour

p. 1   **'Every author...'.** William Wordsworth, 'Essay, Supplementary to the Preface' (1815): *The Poetical Works of William Wordsworth*, ed. E. de Selincourt, Volume Two (2nd edn, Oxford 1952), 426.

p. 1   **'The wit of the writer...'.** *The Atlas*, 3 April 1836: repr. in *The Dickensian* 32 (1936), 216.

p. 2   **Hood and Poole as *Pickwick* candidates.** Arthur Waugh, 'The Birth of "Pickwick"', *The Dickensian* 32 (December 1935), 8.

p. 2   **'Only a new strain...'.** In a letter to Dickens, cited in George Ford, *Dickens and His Readers: Aspects of Novel-Criticism since 1836* (Norton, NY, 1955), 12.

p. 2   **'Whims and oddities...'.** *The News and Sunday Herald*, 10 April 1836: *The Dickensian* 32 (1936), 216.

p. 2   **'The idea of the work...'.** *The Court Journal*, 30 April 1836: ibid., 217.

p. 2   **'The *Pickwick Papers*...'.** *The Athenaeum*, 3 December 1836: in Collins, *Heritage*, 32.

p. 2   **'Truth to nature...'.** [Charles Buller], 'The Works of Dickens', *London and Westminster Review*, July 1837, xxix: in Collins, *Heritage*, 53.

p. 2   **'A sort of rollicking...'.** Percy Fitzgerald, *The History of Pickwick* (1891), 222.

p. 3   **'Boz should be compared...'.** [G. H. Lewes attrib], *National Magazine and Monthly Critic*, December 1837: in Michael Hollington ed., *Charles Dickens: Critical Assessments* (Helm Information, 1995) I, 246.

p. 3   **'The style is that...'.** *Sunday Times*, 12 June 1836.

p. 3   **'NIMROD CLUB...'.** Dickens, 'Preface' to the Charles Dickens Edition (1867) of *Pickwick Papers*.

p. 4   **'I believed I had...'.** Letter to Forster [?30–31 December 1844 and 1 January 1845]: *Letters* 4, 244.

p. 4   **'Being from my earliest...'.** [Arthur Locker?], 'Charles Dickens', *Graphic*, 18 June 1870, 687: Collins, *Heritage*, 41.

p. 4   **Dickens's fondness for Poole's humour.** Years ago Kathleen Tillotson remarked that Dickens's 'early stories as a whole are more like Poole's than any of his other predecessors', and points to some specific parallels or near-parallels between some of Dickens's Sketches and tales from Poole's *Sketches and Recollections* (1835): *Dickensian* 52 (1956), 69–70. For Poole's possible influence on Dickens's first published sketch, see Robert Douglas-Fairhurst, *Becoming Dickens: The Invention of a Novelist* (2011), 119–20.

p. 5   **'I had visited...'.** [John Poole], 'Personal Narrative of a Journey to Little Pedlington', *New Monthly Magazine & Literary Journal*, 1835, Part 2, 337.

p. 5   **'A wretched attempt...'.** *News and Sunday Herald*, April 1836: see Walter Dexter, 'How Press and Public received "The Pickwick Papers"', *Nineteenth Century* 119 (1936), 321.

p. 5   **'The Universal Deluge...'.** John Poole, op. cit., 338.

p. 6   **'Full of sly...'.** *Bath Chronicle* review of *Pickwick* Number 2: in W. Dexter, op. cit., 324.

p. 6   **'Genuine humour...but of nature'.** *Metropolitan Magazine*, May and August 1836: in Collins, *Heritage*, 30–31.

p. 6   **'The humour and talent...very humorously'.** *Literary Gazette*, 9 July 1836, 442, and 10 September 1836, 584.

p. 7   **'A fresh vein...but the first'.** Anon, review of *Pickwick*, Nos. I–XVII, and *Sketches by Boz*, *Quarterly Review* 59 (October 1837): in Collins, *Heritage*, 57.

p. 7   **'Our readers cannot...'.** Anon, 'Some Thoughts on Arch-Waggery, and in especial, on the Genius of "Boz"', *Court Magazine*, April 1837, 184: in Collins, *Heritage*, 33–4.

p. 8   **'Before *Pickwick*...most kindly way'.** Anon, 'Remonstrance with Dickens', *Blackwood's Magazine* 81 (January–June 1857).

p. 9   **'Laughter always...'.** Bergson, *Laughter*, 11.

p. 9   **Editorial and inclusive 'we'.** Robert Douglas-Fairhurst, op. cit., see esp. pp. 153–5.

p. 9   **'Boz is really...'.** *The Satirist*, 30 April 1836: repr. in *Dickensian* 32 (1936), 217.

p. 9   **'So you have never...'.** Mary Russell Mitford, from a letter 30 June 1837: in Collins, *Heritage*, 35.

p. 9   **'It is conceivable...'.** Mowbray Morris, 'Charles Dickens', *Fortnightly Review* 32 (1 December 1882): in Collins, *Heritage*, 601.

p. 10   **'In less than six months...'.** Anon, review of *Pickwick*, Nos. I–XVII and *Sketches by Boz*, *Quarterly Review* 59 (October 1837): in Collins, *Heritage*, 57.

p. 10   **'From the peer...'.** [G.H. Lewes attr] *National Magazine and Monthly Critic*, December 1837: Hollington, op. cit., I, 245–6.

p. 10   **'Verisimilitude...full impression'.** Anon, 'Some Thoughts on Arch-Waggery, and in especial, on the Genius of "Boz"', *Court Magazine*, April 1837, 184: in Collins, *Heritage*, 33–4.

p. 11   **'He has much comic power...'.** *Chambers's Edinburgh Journal*, 9 April 1836: quoted in *The Dickensian* 32 (December 1935), 50.

p. 11   **'There is a peculiar...'.** Anonymous article in *National Review*, 13 (July 1861): in Collins, *Heritage*, 193.

p. 11   **'His language...'.** [G. H. Lewes attr] *National Magazine and Monthly Critic*, December 1837: in Hollington, op cit., I, 248.

p. 11 **'It is in the intermixture…'.** *Court Magazine*, April 1837: in Collins, *Heritage*, 35.

p. 12 **'The leading idiosyncrasy…'.** Edgar Allan Poe, *Graham's Magazine*, 19 (February 1842): in Collins, *Heritage*, 111.

p. 12 **'A little point…'.** Anonymous article in *National Review*, 13 (July 1861): in Collins, *Heritage*, 194.

p. 12 **'Treating as a moral agent…'.** Walter Bagehot, 'Charles Dickens', *National Review* 7 (October 1858): in Hollington, op. cit, I, 180.

p. 13 **'The *situation*…'.** George Ford, *Dickens and His Readers* (Princeton, New Jersey, 1965), 16–17.

p. 13 **Syntax and Pickwick:** For a fuller examination of correspondences between *Pickwick* and the Dr Syntax satires, see B. C. Saywood, 'Dr Syntax: A Pickwickian Prototype?' *The Dickensian* 66 (1970), 24–9.

p. 14 **'Rejects all that is predatory…'.** James Kincaid, *Dickens and the Rhetoric of Laughter* (Oxford, 1971), 23.

p. 15 **'Throughout this book…'.** Preface to the First Edition of *Pickwick Papers* (1837).

p. 16 **'If our sisters wanted…'.** W. M. Thackeray, 'John Leech's *Pictures of Life and Character*', *Quarterly Review* 191 (December 1854).

p. 16 **'There used to be…'.** W. M. Thackeray, 'On the Genius of George Cruikshank', *Westminster Review*, August 1840: excerpted in *The Comic Cruikshank*, ed. M. Bryant (1992), 54.

p. 17 **'Big round Satyr's…'.** George Meredith, 'On the Idea of Comedy and the Uses of the Comic Spirit' (1877); in D. J. Palmer ed., *Comedy: Developments in Criticism* (Houndmills, 1984), 61.

p. 18 **'If we turn back…'.** Dickens, Review: *The Rising Generation* […], *The Examiner*, 30 December 1848: in M. Slater ed., *Dickens' Journalism* (1996), II, 144.

p. 19 **'Within a very short time…'.** Fitzgerald, op. cit, 162.

p. 19 **'He was both witty…'.** Sir Arthur Helps, 'In Memoriam', *Macmillan's Magazine* 22 (July 1870).

p. 19 **'Humour is the growth…'.** William Hazlitt, 'On Wit and Humour', *Lectures on the English Comic Writers* (1819), 22.

p. 19 **'Wit is more…'.** [Gerald Massey], 'American Humour', *North British Review* 33 (November 1860), 462–3.

p. 19 **'Furnish a constant…'.** R. H. Horne, 'Charles Dickens', in *A New Spirit of the Age* (1844): in Hollington, op. cit., I, 98.

p. 20 **'The favourite employment…'.** William Hazlitt, op. cit., 24.

p. 20 **'He will make…'.** Anon, 'Two English Novelists: Dickens and Thackeray', *Dublin Review* NS 16 (April 1871): in Collins, *Heritage*, 552.

p. 21 **'May be ashamed…'.** G. H. Lewes, reviewing the first volume of Forster's *Life*, *Fortnightly Review* 17 (February 1872): in Collins, *Heritage*, 570–1.

p. 21 **'One might easily suppose...'.** [G. H. Lewes attr] *National Magazine and Monthly Critic*, December 1837: in Hollington, op. cit., I, 248.

p. 22 **'We ourselves...'.** [Obituary] *British Medical Journal*, 18 June 1870: in Collins, *Heritage*, 514.

p. 22 **'True humour...so ethereal'.** Thomas Carlyle, 'Jean Paul Friedrich Richter', *Edinburgh Review*, 1827: repr. in Thomas Carlyle, *Critical and Miscellaneous Essays* (Boston, 1838), I, 1–27.

p. 23 **'The world never saw...'.** *Metropolitan Magazine*, January 1837, xviii, 6: in Collins, *Heritage*, 31.

p. 23 **Dickens and *Don Quixote*.** Forster, 5.

p. 23 **'The modern Quixote...'.** [T. H. Lister] *Edinburgh Review*, October 1838, lxviii: in Collins, *Heritage*, 75.

p. 23 **'Old Pickwick...'.** Irving Letter of 26 May 1841: *Letters* 2, 269, fn. 1.

p. 23 **'The world...'.** Letter to Dudley Costello, 25 April 1849: *Letters* 5, 527.

2. Staging Comic Anecdotes

p. 25 **'The President got up...'.** Letter to Albany Fonblanque, 12 [and? 21] March 1842: *Letters* 3, 117.

p. 26 **'Remarkably unaffected...'.** *American Notes and Pictures from Italy: Notes*, ed. F. S. Schwarzbach (1997), 133.

p. 26 **'He looked...in both'.** Sir Arthur Helps, 'In Memoriam', *Macmillan's Magazine* 22 (July 1870).

p. 27 **'Circle of stage fire'.** John Ruskin, *Unto This Last*, ed. P. M. Yarker (1970), 33.

p. 27 **'It is necessary...'.** Letter to Mrs Young, 16 February 1854: *Letters* 7, 277–8.

p. 27 **'To say that...'.** Letter to Basil Hall, 16 March 1841: *Letters* 2, 235.

p. 27 **'One of the stories...'.** Mary Cowden Clarke, 'Peeps at Dickens', *The Dickensian* 32 (Winter 1935–36), 55.

p. 29 **'INIMITABLE...Dat was me!'** Letter to Georgina Hogarth, 25 August 1858: *Letters* 8, 638–9.

p. 31 **'What he desired...'.** Forster, 381.

p. 31 **'There was one Mrs Davis...'.** Letter to Countess of Blessington, 9 May 1845: *Letters* 4, 303–4.

p. 33 **'It was impossible...'.** *Pictures from Italy*, ed. L. Ormond (Everyman Dickens, 1997), 408.

p. 34 **'There are two men...'.** Letter to Thomas Beard, 21 October 1846: *Letters* 4, 639–40.

p. 39 **Pantomime model for Dickens's work.** See e.g. J. Hillis Miller,
'The Genres of *A Christmas Carol*', *The Dickensian* 89 (1993), 198; and
Edwin Eigner, *The Dickens Pantomime* (1989), *passim*.

p. 39 **'The king of pantaloons'.** *Shaw on Dickens*, eds D. H. Laurence
and M. Quinn (New York, 1985), 23–4.

p. 39 **Paul Schlicke.** Paul Schlicke, *Dickens and Popular Entertainment* (1985).

p. 39 **'If we think…'.** Eigner, op. cit., 7.

p. 41 **J. Hillis Miller.** J. Hillis Miller, 'The Genres of *A Christmas Carol*'.
The Dickensian 89 (Winter 1993), 193–206.

p. 41 **'The distinguishing mark…'.** Charles Baudelaire, 'The Essence
of Laughter', translated by Gerard Hopkins; in *The Essence of Laughter
and Other Essays, Journals, and Letters*, ed. Peter Quennell (New York,
1956), 124–7.

p. 41 **'That wild abandonment…'.** Letter to Forster, 23 March 1851:
Letters 6, 329.

p. 42 **'He would insist…'.** Mamie Dickens, *My Father as I Recall Him*
(1897), 31.

p. 42 **'The absolute comic…pantomime actor'.** Baudelaire, op. cit.,
156–7 and 189.

p. 44 **'It is impossible…'.** Letter to Forster ?5 and 6 July 1856: *Letters*
8, 154–5.

p. 44 **'Behind a venetian blind…or suffering'.** Letter to Miss
M. E. Tayler, 6 November 1849: *Letters* 5, 640 and fn.

p. 45 **'The moment…'.** Letter to Mary Boyle, 28 December 1860:
Letters 9, 354.

p. 46 **'Having released…'.** James Kincaid, *Dickens and the Rhetoric of
Laughter* (Oxford 1971), 16.

p. 46 **'*We laugh*…'.** Bergson, *Laughter*, 33. The italics are Bergson's.

p. 47 **'Entertainment and moral conviction…'.** Paul Schlicke,
op. cit., 35.

p. 49 **'I have also done…'.** Letter to Forster [?late August 1861]: *Letters*
9, 450.

p. 49 **'One scarcely knows…'.** *The Courant* (Edinburgh), 19 April
1866.

p. 49 **'Impresses us…'.** Kate Field, *Pen Photographs of Charles Dickens's
Readings: Taken from Life* (1868: New York, 1998), 34.

3. Comic Timing

p. 50 **'The secret…detonate laughter'.** Oliver Double, *Getting the
Joke: The Inner Workings of Stand-up Comedy* (2005), 200–1.

p. 51 **'Light the fuse…'.** Franklyn Ajaye, *Comic Insights: The Art of
Stand-up Comedy* (California, Silman James Press, 2002), 20: cited in
S. Attardo and L. Pickering, 'Timing in the Performance of Jokes',
Humor: International Journal of Humor Research 24 (2011), 233–50.

p. 51 **'Timing...Jokes'.** Ibid.

p. 51 **'Reifying timing...'.** N. R. Norrick, 'On the Conversational Performance of Narrative Jokes: Toward an Account of Timing', *Humor* 14 (2001), 255–74: 256.

p. 51 **'Comic timing...audience'.** Greg Dean, *Step by Step to Standup Comedy* (Portsmouth, NH, Heineman, 2000), 127.

p. 54 **'Listeners expect...'.** Norrick, op. cit., 264.

p. 55 **'I have such...'.** Letter to Sir Edward Bulwer Lytton, ?28 November 1865: *Letters* 11, 113.

p. 63 **'The classic version...'.** Double, op. cit., 207.

p. 64 **'Every word uttered...'.** Forster, *Life*, 720.

p. 65 **'Take a comb...'.** Kate Field, *Pen Photographs of Charles Dickens's Readings* (1868): ed. C. Moss (New York, 1998), 81–4.

p. 66 **Micawber's discourse.** M. Andrews, 'Performing Character': *Palgrave Advances in Charles Dickens Studies*, eds J. Bowen and R. L. Patten (Houndmills, 2006), 74.

p. 66 **Micawber's tipping forward.** Kate Field, op. cit., 26.

p. 70 **'These things...quite right'.** Edgar Rosenberg, 'Writing *Great Expectations*', Norton Critical Edition of *Great Expectations*, ed. Edgar Rosenberg (New York, 1999), 434–5.

p. 71 **'*Don't...a-gain!*'** Kate Field, op. cit., 62.

p. 76 **'Speaking the dialogue...'.** Wilkie Collins in a letter of 16 September 1852: Catherine Peters, *The King of Inventors: A Life of Wilkie Collins* (1991), 113.

4. Laughter and Incongruity

p. 77 **'I think it is my infirmity...'.** Letter to Sir Edward Bulwer Lytton, ?28 November 1865: *Letters* 11, 113.

p. 77 **'Sir, I would like to ask...bodily context'.** Arthur Koestler, *Janus: A Summing Up* (1978), 122, 112–14.

p. 78 **'Once our attention...'.** Bergson, *Laughter*, 57.

p. 78 **'[Ridicule's] object...'.** Alexander Gerard, *An Essay on Taste...with Three Dissertations on the Same Subject...* (London and Edinburgh, 1759), 66.

p. 78 **'The discriminating cause...'.** Sydney Smith, *Elementary Sketches of Moral Philosophy* (1864), 132.

p. 79 **'Humour is a sense...'.** P. J. Jagger ed., *Mr Gladstone: Founder's Day Lectures, St. Deiniol's Library, 1931–1955* (Hawarden: Monad Press, 2001), 121.

p. 79 **'Wit is the clash...'.** Leigh Hunt, *Wit and Humour, Selected from the English Poets* (1846), 9.

p. 79 **'What emerges...'.** M. Gervais and D. S. Wilson, 'The Evolution and Function of Laughter and Humor: A Synthetic Approach', *The Quarterly Review of Biology* 80, 4 (December 2005), 395–430.

p. 79 **'Frame-shifting'.** See e.g. S. Coulson et al., 'Looking Back: Joke Comprehension and the Space structuring Model', *Humor* 19(3) (2006), 229–50. See also Tony Veale, 'Incongruity in Humor: Root Cause or Epiphenomenon?' *Humor* 17 (2004), 419–25.

p. 79 **'More subtle aspect…incongruity'.** T. R. Shultz, 'A Cognitive-developmental Analysis of Humour', *Humour and Laughter: Theory, Research and Application*, eds A. J. Chapman and H. C. Foot (1976), 12–13.

p. 79 **'Both humor and sublimity…'.** John Bowen, 'Dickens and the Force of Writing', *Palgrave Advances in Charles Dickens Studies*, eds J. Bowen and R. L. Patten (Houndmills, 2006), 262.

p. 80 **'If the process…'.** Alan Partington, *The Linguistics of Laughter: A Corpus-assisted Study of Laughter-talk* (2006), 25.

p. 80 **'Journalistic vulgarization'.** Salvatore Attardo, 'Cognitive Linguistics and Humor', *Humor* (19)3, 341–62.

p. 80 **'Humor begins…'.** Steven Pinker, *How the Mind Works* (New York, 1997), 549.

p. 81 **Herbert Spencer,** 'The Physiology of Laughter', *Macmillan's Magazine* (March 1860): repr. in Herbert Spencer, *Essays: Scientific, Political, and Speculative* (1868) I, 194–209.

p. 82 **'The sigh of relief…laughter'.** John Dewey, 'The Theory of Emotion', *The Early Works, 1882–1898*, vol.4 (Southern Illinois, 1971), 158.

p. 82 **'*Laughter is an affection…*'.** Immanuel Kant, *Critique of Judgement*, translated by J. H. Bernard (1914), 223: Kant's italics.

p. 86 **Bodenheimer.** Rosemary Bodenheimer, *Knowing Dickens* (Ithaca, 2007), ch.2, esp. 32–9.

p. 86 **'You will be greatly shocked…notwithstanding'.** Letter to Daniel Maclise, 12 March 1841: *Letters* 2, 230–1.

p. 88 **'So far recovered…severely'.** Letter to Basil Hall, 16 March 1841: *Letters* 2, 237.

p. 89 **'He did it…'.** Letter to Thomas Latimer, 13 March 1841: *Letters* 2, 234.

p. 89 **'To express…'.** Bergson, *Laughter*, 62.

p. 90 **'Hearty literalism'.** John Carey, 'Dickens' Humour', *The Violent Effigy* (1973), 54–79, 57.

p. 93 **'A comic character…'.** Bergson, *Laughter*, 15.

p. 94 **'I was in my heart…'.** Charles Dickens, *David Copperfield*, ed. Nina Burgis (Oxford, 1981), 415, fn. 7.

p. 95 **'The passion of Laughter…'.** Thomas Hobbes, *The Treatise on Human Nature* (1650: 1812), ch. 9, sect. 13, 65.

p. 95 **'The comic demands…'.** Bergson, *Laughter*, 11.

p. 97 **'To perceive relations…'.** Forster, 721.

p. 98 **'An original…together'.** Anon, 'Wit and Humour', *British Quarterly Review* 56 (July 1872), 43–9.

5. Falling Apart Laughing

p. 100 **'A drama...inner castle'.** Lacan's paper was originally read to the International Psychoanalytic Congress in Zurich in July 1949. It was printed in Jacques Lacan, *Ecrits* (Paris, 1966). The English translation used here appeared in *New Left Review* 51 (September–October 1969), and is reprinted in C. Harrison and P. Wood eds, *Art in Theory, 1900–1990* (Oxford, 1992), 609–13.

p. 100 **'It is the *coerced*...'.** Alexander Bain, *The Emotions and the Will* (1859: Bristol, 1998), 283.

p. 101 **'The comic temperament...'.** Ibid., 284.

p. 101 **'It is presented...'.** Mikhail Bakhtin, *Rabelais and His World*, translated by H. Islowsky (Indiana, 1984), 19.

p. 107 **Bakhtinian *Pickwick* illustrations.** I have discussed these images at greater length in 'Illustrations', D. Paroissien ed., *A Companion to Charles Dickens* (Oxford, 2008), 112–13.

6. Laughter and Laughers in Dickens

p. 124 **Canned laughter experiment.** Antony J. Chapman, 'Funniness of Jokes, Canned Laughter and Recall Performance', *Sociometry* 36(4) (December 1973), 569–78.

p. 125 **'Laughter always...'.** Bergson, *Laughter*, 11.

p. 125 **'[Kissinger] inspired banter...'.** R. Valeriani, *Travels with Henry* (Boston, 1979), 9 and 166.

p. 125 **'We also find...in a group'.** Sophie Scott, 'The Neuro-Science of Laughter; A Mini-Lecture' http://www.youtube.com/watch?v=M7lE2cl2zFo (accessed 4 January 2012); and cited in 'Study Finds Laughter Truly Contagious', *Washington Post*, 14 December 2006.

p. 126 **'Listen to it...'.** Bergson, *Laughter*, 11.

p. 126 **'The audience...'.** Letter to Georgina Hogarth, 7 November 1861: *Letters* 9, 500.

p. 127 **'Spontaneous impulse...'.** William Hazlitt, op. cit., 11.

p. 128 **Charles Douglas's 'sweetening machine'.** Adam Bernstein, 'Charles Douglas, 93: Gave TV Its Laugh Track', *Washington Post*, 24 April 2003.

p. 129 **'I was persuaded...'.** John Middleton Murry, *Pencillings* (1923), 37.

p. 129 **'Browne laughed...'.** Letter to Catherine Dickens, 1 November 1838: *Letters* 1, 448.

p. 129 **'In my mind...'.** Lord Chesterfield, *Letter to his Son*, 9 March 1748: *The Letters of the Earl of Chesterfield to His Son*, vol. 1, no. 144, ed. Charles Strachey (New York and London, 1901).

p. 129 **'Observe it...'.** *Lord Chesterfield's Letters to His Godson*, no. 135, 12 December 1765: ed. Earl of Carnarvon (1889).

p. 130 **'Always roared...'.** Letter to Forster, [?8 October 1864]; *Letters* 10, 435.

p. 130 **'The laughing propensity...incessant'.** George Vasey, *The Philosophy of Laughter and Smiling* (1875), 165.

p. 130 **'Morally annoying...prone to laughter'.** Ibid., 116 and 98.

p. 130 **'Free from...vocal organs'.** Ibid., 107.

p. 130 **Degeneration fears.** See e.g. J. E. Chamberlin and S. L. Gilman eds, *Degeneration: The Dark Side of Progress* (New York, 1985).

p. 131 **'The reading...or anecdote'.** Vasey, op. cit., 146–7.

p. 131 **'The man who cannot laugh...to heel'.** Thomas Carlyle, *Sartor Resartus the Works of Thomas Carlyle* (Centenary Edition, 1896), 26.

p. 132 **'[If] any of his audience...'.** *The Speeches of Charles Dickens* ed. K. J. Fielding (Hemel Hempstead, 1988), 246.

p. 132 **'I must say...'.** Private letter, 2 November 1858: *The Dickensian* 108 (2012), 280.

p. 132 **'It is one...'.** Letter to Mrs Watson, 24 September 1850: *Letters* 6, 179.

p. 133 **Externalizing emotional impulses.** See for instance Juliet John, *Dickens's Villains: Melodrama, Character, Popular Culture* (Oxford, 2001), Gesa Stedman, *Stemming the Torrent: Expression and Control in the Victorian Discourses on Emotion, 1830–1872* (Ashgate, 2004), and Valerie Purton, *Dickens and the Sentimental Tradition* (2012).

p. 136 **'The world...'.** Letter to Dudley Costello, 25 April 1849: *Letters* 5, 528.

p. 141 **Laughter Clinics.** See e.g. http://www.laughternetwork.co.uk/ (accessed 21 October 2009).

p. 141 **Rowing machine.** Robert Provine, *Laughter: A Scientific Investigation* (2000), 190.

p. 141 **Clinical evidence....** See F. Rosner, 'Therapeutic Efficacy of Laughter in Medicine', *Cancer Investigation* 20 (2002), 434–6.

p. 141 **'Clears the breast...'.** Jonathan Swift, *Tale of a Tub* (1704): *The Works of the Rev. Jonathan Swift* (New York, 1812), III, 164.

p. 141 **'Mirth and laughter...'.** Henry Fielding, Preface to *Joseph Andrews* (1742: 1962), xix.

p. 142 **'From the "caustic"...'.** Michael Slater, 'The Triumph of Humour: The *Carol* Revisited', *The Dickensian* 89 (1993), 184–92.

p. 142 **'No man...'.** Thomas Carlyle, op. cit., I, 26.

p. 143 **'It made me...restraining [him]self'.** The volunteer subjects, in 1799 experiments, were Robert Southey and Lovell Edgeworth: see Richard Holmes, *The Age of Wonder: How the Romantic Generation Discovered the Beauty and Terror of Science* (2009), 264–5.

p. 145 **'Laughing gas lighted eyes'.** See *Letters* 2, 22, fn. 3.

p. 145 **'Even where...'.** *The Satirist*, 11 December 1836, reviewing *Pickwick* No 9: *The Dickensian* 32 (1936), 282.

p. 145 **'Charles Dickens...'.** Letter to Felton, 2 January 1844: *Letters* 4, 2.

p. 146 **'We can...titter'.** S. Kipper and D. Todt, 'The Sound of Laughter: Recent Concepts and Findings in Research into Laughter Vocalizations', *The Anatomy of Laughter*, eds T. Garfitt, E. McMorran and J. Taylor (Legenda MHRA and Maney Publishing, 2005), 27.

p. 146 **'Nature a thousand...'.** 'Dr King', quoted in Leigh Hunt, *Wit and Humour, Selected from the English Poets* (2nd edn, 1848), 1.

p. 147 **'As a series...frequency'.** J. M. S. Pearce, 'Some Neurological Aspects of Laughter', *European Neurology* 52 (2004), Pt 3.

p. 147 **'The belly laugh...'.** Michael Holland, 'Belly Laughs': *The Anatomy of Laughter*, eds T. Garfitt, E. McMorran and J. Taylor (Legenda– MHRA and Maney Publishing, 2005), 43.

p. 148 **'For if ever I...'.** Letter to H. K. Browne, 13 June 1848: *Letters* 5, 334.

7. What Made Dickens Laugh?

p. 149 **'Kindling mirth'.** Thomas Adolphus Trollope, *What I Remember* (1887), II, 117.

p. 149 **'When there was anything droll...'.** Percy Fitzgerald, *Recreations of a Literary Man* (1883), 60–1.

p. 149 **'He called up...'.** Percy Fitzgerald, *Life of Dickens* (1905), I, 207.

p. 150 **'Given to laugh...'.** Anon., 'A School-fellow and Friend', 'Recollections of Charles Dickens', *The Dickensian* 7 (1911), 229.

p. 150 **'Often, while writing...'.** George Washington Putnam, 'Four Months with Charles Dickens, during his First Visit to America', *Atlantic Monthly* 26 (1870); in Collins, *Interviews* I, 59.

p. 150 **'He himself, tickled...'.** Henry Fielding Dickens, *Recollections of Sir Henry Dickens, Q.C.* (1934), 42: in Collins, *Interviews* I, 164.

p. 150 **'Most hearty...'.** Francesco Berger, *97* (1931), 19–22: in Collins, *Interviews* II, 240.

p. 150 **'With a wheezing...'.** Marcus Stone, Unpublished Reminiscences, *c.* 1911, Charles Dickens Museum: in Collins, *Interviews* II, 184.

p. 150 **'He laughed all over'.** James Fields, *Yesterdays with Authors* (Boston, 1872), 127–9: in Collins, *Interviews* II, 305.

p. 150 **'The largest...'.** Arthur Helps, 'In Memoriam', *Macmillan's Magazine*, 22 (1870), 236–40.

p. 150 **'Mr. Dickens...'.** *New-York Daily Tribune*, 11 December 1867, 4.

p. 150 **'His laugh...away with it'.** Thomas Adolphus Trollope, *What I Remember* (1887), II, 114.

p. 152 **'POTTER...'.** Tom Taylor, 'Still Waters Run Deep' ('Lacy's Acting Edition', Thomas Lacy, ?1855), 51–2.

p. 152 **'I laughed...'.** Letter to Georgina Hogarth, 14 March 1856: *Letters* 8, 70–1.

p. 152 **'Those who attend...'.** Forster, 859.

190 *Notes*

p. 153 **'Scene of mingled…go away'.** Letter to C. C. Felton, 2 March 1843: *Letters* 3, 453.

p. 154 **'A defect…'.** Bergson, *Laughter*, 15.

p. 155 **'If I may jest…facetiousness'.** Letter to W. C. Macready, ?7 April 1839: *Letters* I, 539.

p. 155 **My mother…'.** Letter to Frances Dickinson, 19 August 1860: *Letters* 9, 287.

p. 156 **'The ego's victorious…'.** Sigmund Freud, 'Humour', *The International Journal of Psycho-Analysis* 9 (January 1928), Pt 1, 1–6.

p. 156 **'One very funny…'.** Letter to Frances Dickinson, 19 August 1860: *Letters* 9, 288. For the cannon firing see p. 273 and fn. 2.

p. 157 **'It was set…'.** *Pictures from Italy* (1846), 19.

p. 157 **'I made a good…'.** Letter to Count D'Orsay, 7 August 1844: *Letters* 4, 170.

p. 158 **'It really was…'.** Letter to Wilkie Collins, 4 April 1855: *Letters* 7, 585.

p. 158 **'Suddenly and without…'.** Letter to Mary Boyle, 28 December 1860: *Letters* 9, 354.

p. 159 **'I have such…'.** Letter to Sir Edward Bulwer Lytton, ?28 November 1865: *Letters* 11, 113.

p. 159 **'I have seen nothing…'.** Letter to Wilkie Collins, 11 May 1855: *Letters* 7, 616.

p. 160 **'His humorous remarks…'.** Eleanor Christian, 'Reminiscences of Charles Dickens: From a Young Lady's Diary', *Englishwoman's Domestic Magazine* 10 (1871), 336–44: in Collins, *Interviews*, I, 34.

p. 160 **'In the bosoms…Genii of the East'.** 'A Preliminary Word', *Household Words* 1 (1850), 1.

p. 161 **'When they began…'.** Letter to Forster, 17 February 1842: *Letters* 3, 69.

p. 161 **Tavistock House playbill.** The Playbill is reproduced as the frontispiece to *Letters* 7.

p. 163 **'Exceedingly droll'.** Letter to Forster, [?mid September 1862]: *Letters* 10, 126. See also his letters to Wills, 14 September, and to Wilkie Collins, 20 September 1862.

p. 163 **'Surely he hath…'.** 'Author's Preface': Henry Fielding, *Joseph Andrews* (1742: 1962), xxi.

p. 164 **'[The letter] is so…'.** Letter to Miss Burdett Coutts, 8 June 1849: *Letters* 5, 552.

p. 165 **'You will not have…'.** Letter to John Forster, [early October 1860]: *Letters* 9, 325.

p. 165 **'Pray read…'.** Letter to Mary Boyle, 28 December 1860: *Letters* 9, 354.

p. 165 **'I have got…'.** Letter to Frank Stone, 9 July 1856: *Letters* 8, 158.

p. 166 **'They had with them…'.** Forster, 374.

p. 167 **'An old waiter...'.** Letter to Georgina Hogarth, 24 January 1869: *Letters* 12, 282.

p. 167 **'I have finished...'.** Letter to Forster, [?8 October 1864]: *Letters* 10, 435.

p. 167 **Major and Mr Buffle.** Forster, 726.

p. 169 **'What is exaggeration...'.** Preface to the 'Charles Dickens Edition' of *Martin Chuzzlewit* (1867).

p. 171 **'There are some things...'.** Letter to Forster, [7 April 1856]: *Letters* 8, 82.

p. 172 **'Of regarding...'.** G. Dolby, *Charles Dickens As I Knew Him* (1885), 19.

p. 172 **'I don't invent...'.** Letter to Forster, [? October 1841]: *Letters* 2, 411.

p. 172 **'Outrageously set...'.** Letter to Wilkie Collins, 4 April 1855: *Letters* 7, 585.

Afterword

p. 173 **'A kind of popular...'.** Forster, 728.

p. 173 **'A face that is...'.** George Orwell, 'Charles Dickens', *Inside the Whale and other Essays* (1940).

p. 174 **'Can we wonder...'.** George Vasey, op. cit., 85.

p. 175 **'Everybody thinks...'.** John Ruskin, *Pre-Raphaelitism, Lectures on Architecture & Painting: Etc* (1906), 8.

p. 175 **'Lord Grey...'.** Vasey, op. cit., 70.

p. 175 **'We suspend our judgment...'.** Henry Sidgwick, *Miscellaneous Essays and Addresses* (1904), 60. On the issue of the rigid early- and mid-Victorian mind and the growing emphasis on flexibility, see Walter Houghton, *The Victorian Frame of Mind* (New Haven, 1957), 173–80.

p. 175 **'The laughable element...'.** Bergson, *Laughter*, 13.

p. 176 **'The occasional application...friendly way'.** *The Speeches of Charles Dickens*, ed. K. J. Fielding (Hemel Hempstead, 1988), 202–3.

p. 176 **'A horrid respectability...'** Letter to Forster, [?11–12 November 1855]: *Letters* 7, 743.

p. 176 **'The common people...'.** Letter to Macready, 3 August 1857: *Letters* 8, 399.

p. 177 **'It is the *coerced*...'.** Alexander Bain, *The Emotions and the Will* (1859: Bristol, 1998), 283.

p. 177 **'Pursues a utilitarian...'.** Bergson, *Laughter*, 17.

p. 17 **'The officiating minister...'.** Letter to Samuel Cartwright, 29 January 1868: *Letters* 12, 25.

Index